OPENING SKINNER'S BOX

OPENING SKINNER'S BOX

Great Psychological Experiments
of the 20th Century

Lauren Slater

BLOOMSBURY

LONDON · NEW DELHI · NEW YORK · SYDNEY

First published in Great Britain 2004
This paperback edition published 2005

Copyright © by Lauren Slater 2004

Many names in this book have been changed to protect the privacy of certain
individuals

The moral right of the author has been asserted

Bloomsbury Publishing Plc, 50 Bedford Square, London WC1B 3DP

Bloomsbury Publishing, London, New Delhi, New York and Sydney

A CIP catalogue record for this book is available from the British Library

ISBN 978 0 7475 6860 5

13

Printed in Great Britain by CPI Group (UK) Ltd, Croydon CR0 4YY

www.bloomsbury.com

MIX
Paper from
responsible sources
FSC
www.fsc.org
FSC® C020471

IN MEMORY OF PSYCHOLOGIST AND PROFESSOR SIGMUND KOCH
MENTOR, FRIEND

Contents

Acknowledgments

My editor, Angela von der Lippe, has been a source of humor, support, ideas, and inspiration throughout the process of writing this book. Kim Witherspoon loved the project from the beginning, and that gave me confidence. Tina Polhman, formerly of Vintage, originally proposed the idea to me, so thanks go to her for the actual etiology of this volume. There were many people along the way who graciously and generously offered me their time: special thanks to Thomas Blass, Lee Ross, David Karp, Alexandra Milgram, James Harlow, Jack Rosenhan, Florence Keller, the Santo family, Julie Vargas, Alan Elms, Eric Kandel, and Elizabeth Loftus; Charlie Newitz and his wife Sasha, both pseudonyms to protect their privacy, and Joshua Chaffin and Jacob Plumfield, also both pseudonyms, gave me information that was invaluable and brave in the sharing. The staff at the various hospitals who tended to my pseudosymptoms were generally caring, if not outstanding, and gave me a faith in the compassion that fuels many of today's psychiatrists. Harold Sackheim agreed to a long, long interview with me in which he illuminated some of the future's promising treatments for disease and distress; I am grateful for his time. Ian Parker was instrumental in my thinking and writing about Stanley Milgram; his piece in *Granta* and his conversation with me helped clarify some of my own thinking about the complex issues involved in this particular experiment. Elliot Valenstein's excellent book, *Great and Desperate Cures: The Rise and Decline of Psychosurgery and Other Radical Treatments for Mental Illness*, is a must-read for anyone interested in the bizarre and ethically complicated history of somatic treatments for the mentally ill. My last chapter, "Chipped: This Century's Most Radical Mind Cures," owes almost everything to his impeccable research, from which I drew. Finally, Bruce Alexander took enormous amounts of time not only to explicate his own experiment and the evolution of his thinking since then, but also to read and comment on other chapters in this book; his grasp of the history of psychology is impressive. Nate Greenslit of MIT and George Alder of Simon Frasier University were excellent fact-checkers.

My husband, Benjamin Alexander, spent countless hours helping me formulate my thoughts, interpret the data, and in some cases, evaluate the methodology regarding the range of these experiments. My daughter, Clara Alexander, helped mitigate the inevitable downturns in the writing process with her insistence on digging in dirt, *The Cat in the Hat*, and somersaults; Pagan Kennedy, Priscilla Sneff, Karen Propp, Susan Mahler, and Tehilia Lieberman listened and commented on many drafts, as did my colleague and close friend Jennifer Coon, Psy.D., who gave me a much-needed clinical perspective on experimental psychology. Lisa Schiffman listened to each and every one of these chapters on the phone, long distance; she was always my initial, most immediate audience, and her comments, not to mention patience and literary acumen, are reflected in the best parts of this book. As always, Audrey Schulman and Elizabeth Graver are, and have been, for over twenty years now, companions in writing, cross-pollinators, critics, friends.

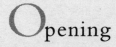

Opening

Skinner's

Box

Introduction

I did my first psychological experiment when I was fourteen years old. There were raccoons living in the walls of our old Maine vacation house, and one day I stuck my hand in the crumbling plaster and pulled out a squalling baby, still milk-smeared, its eyes closed and its tiny paws pedaling in the air. Days later the sealed eye slits opened, and because I'd heard of Konrad Lorenz and his imprinted ducklings, I made sure the mammal saw me first, its streaming field of vision taking in my form—hands and feet and face. It worked. Immediately the raccoon—I called her Amelia Earheart—began to follow me everywhere, wreathing around my ankles, scrambling up my calves when she was afraid. She followed me to the town bookstore, to school, down busy streets, into bed, but in truth, I began to take on more of her behaviors than she mine. Even though I was the imprinter, with Amelia at my side I learned to fish in a pond with my human paws; I learned to latch on to the soft scree at the base of a rotting tree and climb; I learned the pleasures of nocturnity, the silver-wet grass, black rings beneath my tired eyes. The results: "Imprinting," I wrote in my science notebook, "happens to the mother too." Who, I wondered, influenced whom in this symbiotic pairing? Could species shift from their specific shapes and become, through exposure, something altogether other? Was there really a boy raised by wolves, a chimpanzee who signed with words? The questions fascinated me then, and still do today. More fascinating to me became, over time, as I grew older, the means by which one explored these questions: the hypothesis, the experimental design, the detailed qualitative description, the breathless or boring wait for results. I was first hooked on Amelia and later hooked on the pure plot that structures almost all psychological experiments, intentional or not.

While it would be reductive to say a raccoon rests at the bottom of this book, Amelia is certainly the image that comes to mind when I think of its etiology. Beyond that, I have for a long time felt that psychological experiments are fascinating, because at their best they are compressed experience, life distilled to its potentially elegant essence, the metaphorical test tube parsing the normally blended parts so you might see love, or fear, or conformity, or cowardice play its role in particular circumscribed contexts. Great psychological experiments amplify a domain of behavior or being usually buried in the pell-mell of our fast and frantic lives. Peering through this lens is to see something of ourselves.

When I studied psychology in graduate school, I again had the chance to perform experiments and observations on all sorts of animals. I saw the embryo of an angel fish grow from a few single cells to a fully finned thing in forty-eight hours flat—life putting together its puzzle pieces right before my eyes. I saw stroke victims deny the right sides of their faces and blindsight patients mysteriously read letters despite their dead eyes. I observed people waiting for elevators and had this as my salient question: Why is it that people continuously press the button when they're waiting in the lobby, even though they know, if interviewed, that it won't make the elevator come any faster? What does "elevator behavior" say about human beings? I also, of course, read the classic psychological experiments where they had been housed—in academic journals, mostly, replete with quantified data and black-bar graphs—and it seemed somewhat sad to me. It seemed sad that these insightful and dramatic stories were reduced to the flatness that characterizes most scientific reports, and had therefore utterly failed to capture what only real narrative can—theme, desire, plot, history—this is what we are. The experiments described in this book, and many others, deserve to be not only reported on as research, but also celebrated as story, which is what I have here tried to do.

Our lives, after all, are not data points and means and modes; they are stories—absorbed, reconfigured, rewritten. We most fully integrate that which is told as tale. My hope is that some of these experiments will be more fully taken in by readers now that they have been translated into narrative form.

Psychology and its allied professions represent a huge disparate field that funnels down to the single synapse while simultaneously radiating outward to describe whole groups of human beings. This book does not contain, by any means, all the experiments that represent the reach of that arc; it would take volumes to do that. I have chosen ten experiments based on the input of my colleagues and my own narrative tastes, experiments that for me and others seem to raise the boldest questions in some of the boldest ways. Who are we? What makes us human? Are we truly the authors of our own lives? What does it mean to be moral? What does it mean to be free? In telling the stories of these experiments, I revisit them from my contemporary point of view, asking what relevance they have for us now, in this new world. Does Skinner's behaviorism have meaning for current-day neurophysiologists who can probe the neural correlates of his habit-driven rats? Does Rosenhan's horrifying and comedic experiment on mental illness, its perception and diagnoses, still hold true today, when we supposedly abide by more objective diagnostic criteria in the naming of "disease"? Can we even define as disease syndromes that have no clear-cut physiological etiology or pathophysiology? Is psychology, which deals half in metaphor, half in statistics, really a science at all? Isn't science itself a form of metaphor? A long time ago, in the late 1800s, Wilhelm Wundt, long considered psychology's founding father, opened one of the first instrument-based psychology labs in the world, a lab dedicated to measurement, and so a science of psychology was born. But as these experiments demonstrate, it was born breech, born badly, a chimerical organism with ambiguous limbs. Now, over one hundred years later, the beast has grown up. What is it? This book doesn't answer this question, but it does address it in the context of Stanley Milgram's shock machine, Bruce Alexander's addicted rats, Darley and Latané's smoke-filled rooms, Moniz's lobotomy, and other experiments as well.

In this book we see how psychology is inevitably, ineluctably, moving toward a deeper and deeper mining of biological frontiers. We see how the clumsy cuts of Moniz transformed, or transmogrified, depending on your point of view, into the sterile bloodless surgery called cingulotomy. We hear about the inner workings of a neuron, and how genes encode proteins that build those blue eyes, that memory, right there. And yet, while we can explain something of the process and mechanisms that inform behavior and even thought, we are far from explaining why we have the thoughts, why we gravitate toward this or that, why we hold some memories and discard others, what those memories mean to us, and how they shape a life. Kandel, or Skinner, or Pavlov, or Watson can demonstrate a conditioned response, or operant, and the means by which it gets encoded in the brain, but what we do with that information once it's there depends on circumstances outside the realm of science entirely. In other words, we may be able to define the physiological substrates of memory, but in the end we are still the ones who weave, or not, still the ones who work the raw material into its final form and meaning.

Writing about these experiments has been, therefore, an exercise in writing about both science and art. It has provided me with a chance to learn about outcomes while studying the personalities of the players who chose to investigate, for all sorts of reasons, the set of events that led them to their final data. And then to observe how that data fueled their futures and their pasts, how they used it, or failed to do so. This book, above all, has been a chance for me to go back in history, and to think forward as well. What comes next, in this twenty-first century? I have an inkling. In the meantime, Pavlov's bell is ringing. Surgeons are, this very moment, mining our crenulated brains. We are conditioned, revealed, freed, and accountable. Someone shouts an order. We do or do not obey. Now, turn the page.

Opening Skinner's Box

B. F. SKINNER'S RAT RACE

B. F. Skinner, America's leading neo-behaviorist, was born in 1904 and died in 1990. He is known in the field of psychology for his famous animal experiments in which he demonstrated the power of rewards and reinforcements to shape behavior. Using food, levers, and other environmental cues, Skinner demonstrated that what appear to be autonomous responses are really cued, and in doing so he threw into question the long-cherished notion of free will. Skinner spent much of his scientific career studying and honing what he came to call operant conditioning, the means by which humans can train humans and other animals to perform a whole range of tasks and skills through positive reinforcement.

Skinner claimed that the mind, or what was then called mentalism, was irrelevant, even nonexistent, and that psychology should only focus on concrete measurable behaviors. His vision was to build a worldwide community where the government would consist of behavioral psychologists who could condition, or train, its citizens into phalanxes of benevolent robots. Of all the twentieth century's psychologists, his experiments and the conclusions he drew about the mechanistic nature of men and women may be the most reviled, yet continuously relevant to our increasingly technological age.

So this, perhaps, is the story. There's a man called Skinner, which is an ugly name by any account, a name with a knife in it, an image of a skinned fish, flopping on a dock, it's heart barely visible in its mantel of muscle, Ka-boom. Say the name Skinner to twenty college-educated people and most will respond with an adjective like "evil". This I know to be true, as I've done it as an experiment. And yet in 1971, *Time* magazine named him the most influential living psychologist. And a 1975 survey identified him as the best-known scientist in the United States. Still today, everywhere, his experiments are held in the highest esteem.

So why this infamy? Here's why. In the 1960s, Skinner gave an interview to biographer Richard I. Evans in which he openly admitted that his efforts at social engineering had implications for fascism and might be used for totalitarian ends. The story goes that Skinner desired nothing more than to shape—and shape is the operative word here—the behaviour of people subjected to gears and boxes and buttons, whatever humanity he touched turning to bone. The legend says he built a baby box in which he kept his daughter Deborah for two full years in order to train her, tracking her progress on a grid. The legend also says that when she was 31 she sued him for abuse in a genuine court of law, lost the case, and shot herself in a bowling alley in Billings, Montana. None of this is true, and yet the myths persist. Why? What is it about Skinner that so scares us?

Type "B. F. Skinner" into your search engine and you will get thousands of hits, among them the website of an outraged father who damned the man for murdering an innocent child; a website with a skull, and Ayn Rant writing, "Skinner is so obsessed with the hatred of man's mind and virtue, so intense and consuming a hatred that it consumes itself and in the end what we have are only grey ashes and a few stinking coals"; a memorial of sorts for Deborah, who had supposedly died in the 1980s: "Deborah, our hearts go out to you." And then a tiny red link that reads, "for Deborah Skinner herself, click here." I did. A picture of a brown-haired middle-aged woman scrolled down. The caption said that here was Deborah Skinner herself, that her suicide was a myth, that she was alive and well.

Legends. Myths. Stories. Tall tales. What is Skinner's true legacy? Perhaps the challenge of understanding Skinner's experiment will be primarily discriminatory, separating content from controversy, a sifting through. Writes psychologist and historian John A. Mills, "[Skinner] was a mystery wrapped in a riddle wrapped in an enigma."

I decide to wade in, slowly.

HE WAS BORN in 1904. This much is for sure. Beyond that, though, what I find is a tangle of contradictions. He was one of America's premier behaviorists, a man of real rigidity who slept in a bright yellow cubicle from Japan called a *beddoe*, but at the same time he could not work unless his desk was cluttered, and he said of his own course, "It is amazing the number of trivial accidents which have made a difference. . . . I don't believe my life was planned at any point." But then he often wrote he felt like god and "a sort of savior to humanity."

When Skinner was a fellow at Harvard, he met and fell in love with a woman named Yvonne, who would later become his wife. I see them on Friday nights, driving to Monhegan's Gull Pond with the black convertible top folded back and some kind of moody jazz playing on the radio. Once at the pond, they take off their clothes and skinny-dip, the brackish waters on their bodies, the cool night air, the moon a snipped hole in the sky. I read in a dusty text in the basement of a library that after training sessions, he used to take his caged pigeons out and hold them in his huge hand, stroking their downy heads with his first finger.

I was very surprised to learn that before he went to Harvard to study psychology in 1928, Skinner's aspiration was to be a novelist, and he had spent eighteen prior months holed up in his mother's attic writing lyric prose. How he went from lyric prose to timed rates of reinforcement is not all clear to me—how a man can make such a sharp swerve. He writes that when he was around twenty-three, he came across an article by H. G. Wells in the *New York Times Magazine* in which Wells stated that given the chance between saving the life of Ivan Pavlov or George Bernard Shaw, Wells would choose Pavlov, because science is more redemptive than art.

And indeed, the world needed redemption. The Great War had ended one decade ago. Shell-shocked soldiers suffered from flashbacks and depressions; asylums were packed; there was an urgent need for some kind of treatment scheme. When Skinner went to Harvard, in 1928, as a graduate student, the scheme was largely psychoanalytic. Everyone everywhere was lying down on leather couches and fishing ephemeral tidbits from their pasts. Freud ruled, along with the venerable William James, who had written *The Varieties of Religious Experience*, a text about introspective soul states, with not one equation in it. That, in fact, was the state of psychology when Skinner entered; it was a numberless field sharing more with philosophy than physiology. A typical leading question in the field might be, "What is it within us that sees, feels and thinks every moment when we are awake, vanishes temporarily when we sleep and disappears permanently or instantly when we die?"

Introspection. Mentalism. These were the tropes into which Skinner stepped, a lean young man with a stiff helmet of hair flipped up at the top in greased pompadour. His eyes were fierce blue, like chips of a china plate. He wanted, he writes, to make a real difference, to feel things palpable in his hands and in his heart. Poised between the first world war and a future one soon to come, Skinner may have sensed—although he would reject such a flimsy word—the need for action, for interventions and results that could be bronzed, each one, like bullets.

He therefore avoided anything "soft." He started off in Hudson Hoagland's physiology course studying frog reflexes. He pricked the taut skin of a frog's thigh and measured the animal's jerk, and then its jump. His hands smelled swampy, and he was full of vigor.

One day, early in his Harvard career, Skinner came across the Harvard Psychology Workshop in Emerson Hall. Skinner saw an array of instruments, pieces of red tin, chisels, nails, and nuts in Salisbury cigarette tins. I imagine his hands itched then. He wanted to do something great, and he had always been dexterous, wielding scissors and saws with precision. So there, in that tiny shop, Skinner started to build his famous boxes out of cast-off wires and rusty nails and blackened bits he found.

Did he know what he was building, and the huge effects it would have on American psychology? Was he pursuing a prepackaged vision, or just following the lyric push and pull of a tin-and-wire poem, so in the end what he saw surprised even him: a box operated by compressed air, a silent releasing mechanism, all gadgets and gears, the box an ordinary object that, like ladders and mirrors and black cats, immediately acquired a kind of dense glow.

Of this time Skinner writes, "[I] began to become unbearably excited. Everything I touched suggested new and promising things to do."

Late at night now, in his rented rooms, Skinner was reading Pavlov, to whom he owes an enormous debt, and Watson, to whom he owes a lesser but still significant debt. Pavlov, the great Russian scientist, had practically lived in his lab, such was his dedication. He had spent years studying the salivary glands of his beloved canines. Pavlov discovered that the salivary gland could be conditioned to leak at the sound of a bell. Skinner liked that idea, but he wanted to go beyond a small mucous membrane, he wanted the whole entire organism; where was the poetry in saliva?

Pavlov discovered what is called classical conditioning. This simply means that a person can take a preexisting animal reflex, like blinking or being startled or salivating, and condition it so it occurs in response to a new stimulus. Thus, the famous bell—a stimulus—that Pavlov's dogs learned to associate with food and salivated at the sound of. Now, this might not seem like a great discovery to you or me, but back then this was huge. This was as hot as the spliced atom or the singular position of the sun. Never, ever before in all of human history had people understood how *physiological* were our supposed mental associations. Never before had people understood the sheer malleability of the immutable animal form. Pavlov's dogs drooled and the world tipped over twice.

Skinner wondered. He was up there in his rooms, and he had made some of his not-yet-famous, or infamous, boxes, which were still empty, and there were always squirrels just below in Harvard Yard. He watched the squirrels and wondered if it would be possible to, say, condition the whole shebang, not just a simple silly gland. In other words, could a person shape a behavior—what Skinner came to call an operant—that was not a reflex? Conditioned or not, salivation is and was and always will be a reflex, a fully formed action that occurs on its own in addition to being brought on by a bell. However, when you jump in the air, or sing "Howdy Doodie," or press a lever in the hopes of finding food, you are not acting reflexively. You are just behaving. You are operating on your environment. If one can condition a reflex, would it not be too much to try to go one step further and condition cartwheels, or other supposedly free-form movements? Would it be possible to take a completely random movement, like turning one's head to the right, and reward it consistently, so pretty soon the person keeps looking to the right, the operant inscribed? And if this was possible, how far could it go? What sorts of hoops might we learn to jump through, and with what sort of awful ease? Skinner wondered. He moved, I imagine, his hands this way and that. He leaned way out on the window ledge and smelled squirrel, a musky odor of night and scat, of fur and flowers.

In June of that year, Skinner was given rats by a departing graduate student. He brought the animals to a box. Then he started. After a long, long time, years in fact, he discovered that these rats, who have brains no bigger than a boiled bean, could quickly learn how to press a lever if they were rewarded with food. Thus, while Pavlov focused on an animal's behavior in response to a *prior stimulus*—the bell— Skinner focused on an animal's behavior in response to an after-the-fact *consequence*—the food. It was a subtle and not terribly exciting nuance to Pavlov's earlier work, and a frank extension of Thorndike's studies, which had already demonstrated that cats in slatted boxes that were rewarded for accidentally stepping on a treadle could learn to do so purposefully. But Skinner went further than these two men. After he demonstrated that his rodents could, by accident, step on the lever and release a pellet, and then turn the accident into intention based on prior reward, he played with removing or altering the rate at which the rewards occurred and by doing so, Skinner discovered replicable and universal laws of behavior that still hold true today.

For instance, after Skinner consistently rewarded the lever-pressing rat with food, he tried what he called a fixed-ratio schedule. In this scenario, if the animal pressed the lever three times, he'd get his goodie. Or five times. Or twenty times. Picture yourself as a rat. First, whenever you press a lever, you get food. Then, you press the lever once and you don't get food; you do it again, still no food. You do it again and down the silver spout comes a pellet. You eat the pellet and walk away. You come back for more. This time, you don't bother pressing once with your pink padded foot. You press three times. The reinforcement contingencies change the way in which the animal responds.

Skinner also played around with what he termed fixed-interval schedules and extinction. In the extinction version of the experiment Skinner removed the reinforcer all together. He discovered that if he ceased rewarding the rats with food, they would eventually cease pressing the lever even when they heard the pellets' raining sound. Using a cumulative recorder attached to his box, Skinner could pictorially plot just how long it takes to learn a response when it is regularly rewarded and how long it takes to extinguish a response when it is abruptly discontinued. His ability to precisely measure these rates under differing circumstances yielded quantifiable data on how organisms learn and on how we can predict and control the learning outcome. With the achievement of predictability and control, a true science of behavior was born, with bell curves and bar graphs and plot points and math, and Skinner was the first one to do it to such a nuanced and multileveled extent.

But Skinner didn't stop there. He then proceeded to what he called variable schedules of reinforcement, and it was here that he made his most significant discoveries. He tried intermittently rewarding the animals with food when they pressed the lever, so that most times the animals came away empty, but every once in a while, after, say, the fortieth bar press, or the sixtieth, they'd get a treat. Intuition tells us that random and far-flung rewards would lead to hopelessness and extinction of behavior; they didn't. Skinner discovered that by intermittently rewarding the rats with food, they would continue to press that lever like some sort of saw-toothed junkie, regardless of the outcome. He experimented with what happens when intermittent rewards are given at regular intervals (say, every fourth bar press) or at irregular intervals. He found that irregularly rewarded behavior was the hardest of all to eradicate. Ah ha! He stopped there. This was a discovery as big as dog drool. Suddenly, Skinner was able to systematically evoke and explain much of human folly, why we do dumb things even when we're not consistently rewarded, why your best friend hangs on the phone, waiting for that mean boyfriend with an occasional streak of kindness to call, just call. Oh please call! Why perfectly normal people empty their coffers in smoky casinos and wind up in terrible trouble. Why women love too much and men stock-trade on margin. It was all about this thing called intermittent reinforcement and he could show it, its mechanisms, the contingencies of compulsion. And compulsion is huge. It has, no pun intended, dogged us and drowned us since the first person entered Eden. It is huge.

However, Skinner didn't stop there. If he could train rats to press levers, why not train pigeons to, say, play ping-pong? To bowl? What were the limits, he wondered, to how man could shape another being's behavior? Skinner writes about trying to train a bird to peck a dish: "We first give the bird food when it turns its head slightly in the direction [of the dish] from any part of the cage. This increases the frequency of the behavior. . . .We continue by reinforcing positions successively closer to the spot, then by reinforcing only when the head is moved slightly forward, and finally only when the beak makes contact with the spot. In this way, we can build rare, complicated operants which would never appear in the repertoire of the organism otherwise."

Rare, indeed. Using his behavioural methods, Skinner's followers were able to teach a rabbit to pick up a coin in its mouth and drop it into a piggy bank. They also taught a pig to vacuum.

Based on these experiments, he refined his relentlessly reductive philosophy. He began, surrounded by his pecking pigeons, to abhor words like *sensed*, or *feel* or *fear*. There is no fear, just certain galvanic skin responses and involuntary muscle tremblings that emit 2.2 volts of energy. Why didn't we just dismiss him as a tilted radical? Not only because he discovered the first science of behavior. His vision was also boldly, perhaps patriotically optimistic. It denied Americans their coveted autonomy while simultaneously returning it to them all new and improved. Skinner's was a world of extreme freedom wrought through its opposite: conformity. In the Skinnerian scheme, if we only submit to mindless training, we will be rendered biologically boundless, able to learn skills far outside the "repertoire" of our species. If pigeons can play ping-pong, then perhaps humans could learn still more amazing feats. All it takes is the right training, and we step out, over the boundaries of our bodies and their limitations.

Skinner's fame slowly grew. He went on to devise teaching machines, to construct a theory of language acquisition as operant conditioning, to train pigeons as missile guiders in World War II. He wrote a book called *Walden Two* in which he outlined a proposal for a community based on "behavioral engineering," wherein the power of positive reinforcement was used for the scientific control of humans. In Skinner's view, this ideal community would be governed not by politicians, but by benevolent behaviorists armed with candy canes and blue ribbons. He wrote a book called *Beyond Freedom and Dignity*, about which a reviewer wrote, "It is about the taming of mankind through a system of dog obedience schools for all."

Before Skinner could bring to fruition the social implications of his great experiments, he died. He died of leukemia in 1990. Did he realize, at the very end, that the final act of life, which is death, cannot be learned or otherwise overcome?

HOW CAN WE locate Skinner? His experiments are disturbing in their implications. On the other hand, his discoveries are absolutely significant. They, in essence, illuminate human stupidity, and anything that illuminates stupidity is brilliant.

Jerome Kagan is a contemporary of Skinner's who carries many memories and opinions of his colleague. A professor of psychology at Harvard, Kagan has insights into what sense to make of this man and his place in the twentieth century. I go to see him.

Kagan's office building, William James Hall, is under construction when I arrive, so I have to dodge and wend my way through a concrete maze, above me banners flapping, "Warning. Hard Hat Area." I ride the elevator up. The entire building is in a reverential hush. Deep, deep beneath me, in the bowels of the basement where artifacts are stored, where supposedly some of Skinner's black boxes are encased, jackhammers gnaw through old concrete and I can hear a tiny voice yelling, "Presto."

I get off on floor fifteen. The elevator doors part and before me, as though in a dream, sits a tiny black dog, a toy breed, its mouth a red rent in its otherwise dark fur face. The dog stares and stares at me, some sort of sentry—I don't know. I love dogs, although toys are not my preference. I wonder why they're not my preference. As a child I had a toy dog and it bit me, so perhaps I've been conditioned against them, and I could be reconditioned with rewards so I come to champion the shitzu over the shepherd. In any case, I bend down to pat the little dog, and as though it senses my dislike, it flies into a frenzy, baring a set of impressive and very un-toy-like teeth and snarling as it leaps up to grab my exposed wrist.

"Gambit!" a woman shouts, running out from one of the offices.

"Gambit stop that! Oh my god, did he hurt you?"

"I'm fine," I say, but I'm not fine. I'm shaking. I have been negatively reinforced—no, I have been punished. I will never trust a toy again, and I don't WANT that to change. Skinner would say he could change it, but how changeable am I, are we?

PROFESSOR KAGAN SMOKES a pipe. His office smells like pipe, that semisweet rancid odor of burnt embers. He says with the kind of total assurance I associate with the Ivy League cast, "Let me tell you, your first chapter should not be Skinner. It was Pavlov in the early twentieth century and then Thorndike a decade later who did the first experiments showing the power of conditioning. Skinner elaborated on this work. But his findings can't explain thought, language, reasoning, metaphor, original ideas, or other cognitive phenomena. Nor will they explain guilt or shame."

"What about," I say, "Skinner's extrapolations from his experiments? That we have no free will. That we are ruled only by reinforcers. Do you believe that?"

"Do *you* believe that?" Kagan asks.

"Well," I say, "I don't absolutely rule out the possibility that we are always either controlled or controlling, that our free will is really just a response to some cues that—"

Before I can finish my sentence, Kagan dives under his desk. I mean that literally. He springs from his seat and goes head forward into nether regions beneath his desk so I cannot see him anymore.

"I'm under my desk," he shouts. "I've NEVER gotten under my desk before. Is this not an act of free will?"

I blink. Where Kagan was sitting is just space. Beneath his desk, I hear a rustle. I'm a little worried about him. I think he said to me, over the phone when I asked for the interview, that he had a bad back.

"Well," I say, and suddenly my hands feel cold with fear, "I guess it could be an act of free will or it could be that you've—"

Again, Kagan won't let me finish. He's still under the desk, he won't come up, he's conducting the interview in a duck-and-cover crouch. I can't even see him. His voice rises, disembodied.

"Lauren," he says, "Lauren, there is no way you can explain my being under this desk right now as anything but an act of free will. It's not a response to a reinforcer or a cue. I've NEVER gotten under my desk before."

"Okay," I say.

We sit there for a minute, he down there, I up here. I think I hear that damn dog in the hall, scratching. I'm afraid to go back out there, but I no longer want to be in here. I am caged by contingencies, and so I sit very still.

KAGAN, IT APPEARS to me, is somewhat dismissive of Skinner's contributions. But certainly there *are* ways in which Skinner's experiments—even if they are derivative—are both currently relevant and helpful in the construction of a better world. In the 1950s and 1960s Skinner's behavioral methods were taken to state asylums and applied to the severely psychotic. Using his principles of operant conditioning, hopelessly schizophrenic patients were able to learn to dress themselves, to feed themselves, each rise of the spoon rewarded with a coveted cigarette. Later in the century, clinicians began using techniques like systematic desensitization and flooding, drawn directly from Skinner's operant repertoire, to treat phobias and panic disorders, and these behavioral treatments are still widely employed and obviously efficacious today. Says Stephen Kosslyn, professor of psychology at Harvard, "Skinner will make a comeback, I predict it. I myself am a real Skinner fan. Scientists are just now making exciting new discoveries that point to the neural substrates of Skinner's findings." Kosslyn explains the evidence that there are two major learning systems in the brain: the basal ganglia, a collection of spidery synapses located deep in the paste of the ancient brain, where habits are grooved, and the frontal cortex, that big rumpled bulge that rose in tandem with our reason and ambition. The frontal cortex, neuro-scientists hypothesize, is where we learn how to think independently, to visualize the future and plan based on the past. It is where creativ-ity and all its surprising swerves originate, but, says Kosslyn, "Only a portion of our cognitions are mediated by this cortex." The rest of learning, says Kosslyn, "a significant amount, is habit driven, and Skinner's experiments have led us to search for the neural substrates of these habits." In essence, Kosslyn is saying, Skinner led scientists to the basal ganglia, he led them down, down into the basement of the brain, where they sifted through neural tangles to find the chemistry behind the pecks and presses and all those conditioned cartwheels we do on the green grass, in the summer.

Says Bryan Porter, an experimental psychologist who applies Skinnerian-based behaviorism to address traffic safety problems, "Of course behaviorism is neither bad nor dead. Skinner's behaviorism is responsible for so many beneficial social interventions. Using behav-ioral techniques we have been able to reduce dangerous driving, in terms of the number of red lights run, by ten to twelve percent. Also because of Skinner, we know that people respond better to rewards than punishment. Skinner's techniques have been instrumental in helping the huge population of anxiety-disordered people overcome, or extinguish, their phobias. Thanks to Skinner, backward autistics now know how to put on clean shirts and feed themselves. Thanks to Skinner, you know how to give your kid positive reinforcement. You know that rewards work far better in the establishment of behavior than punishment, because Skinner so stressed the power of positive reinforcement. This has huge implications politically, if our govern-ment could just absorb that. In fact," says Porter, "in a weird circuitous way, we have Skinner to thank for the very popular belief that it's best to be kind to people, to give them A's when maybe they deserve B's, to keep saying, 'Oh what a good job you're doing' even if they're not. Skinner," says Porter laughing, "although he might not have liked it, is practically new age."

MY CHILD CRIES in the night. She wakes soaked in sweat, eyeballs bulging, dreams melting as she comes to consciousness. "Shhhh. Shhhh." I hold her body against mine. Her bedclothes are soaked, her hair a dark mat of pressed curls. I stroke her head, where the fontanels have long since sealed. I stroke the slope of her forehead, where the frontal cortex daily sprouts its exuberant rootwork, and then move my hand down to her taut neck, where I imagine I feel the basal ganglia, its seaweed-like snarls. I hold my child in the night, and outside her bedroom window a dog howls, and when I look, the animal is soap-white in the moonlight.

At first my child cries because she's scared, a series of bad dreams I'm guessing. She's two and her world is expanding with fearful speed. But then, as the nights go by, she cries simply because she longs to be held. She has become habituated to these predawn embraces, to the rocking chair's rhythm while the sky outside is so generously salted with stars. My husband and I are exhausted.

"Maybe we should Skinnerize her," I say.

"We should what?" he says.

"Maybe we should employ Skinnerian principles to break her of her habit. Every time we go to her and pick her up, we're giving her what Skinner would call positive reinforcement. We have to extinguish the behavior by reducing and then eliminating our responses."

My husband and I are having this conversation in bed. I'm surprised by how nimbly my tongue takes in and swirls out the language of B. F. I practically sound like an expert. Speaking Skinnerian is almost fun. Chaos confined. Rest returned.

"So you're suggesting," he says, "that we just let her cry it out." He sounds weary. All parents know this debate.

"No," I say. "Listen. Not cry it out. Put her on a strict rate of reduced reinforcement. The first time she cries, we pick her up for only three minutes. The next time she cries, we only pick her up for two minutes.

We could even use a stopwatch." My voice grows excited, or is it anxious? "Then we gradually lengthen the amount of time we allow her to cry. Just very very gradually," I say. "Slowly, we'll extinguish the behavior if we extinguish our responses . . . the contingencies," I say, tracing my hand along the sheet's pattern, a series of green grids, what once looked like country checkerboard but now looks like lab paper.

My husband eyes me, warily I might add. He is not a psychologist, but if he were, he would be of the Carl Rogers school. He has a soft voice, a still softer touch.

"I don't know," he says. "What exactly do you think we'll teach her by doing this?"

"To sleep through the night alone," I say.

"Or," he says, "to realize that when she needs help, we won't respond, that when there's danger real or imagined, we're not there. That's not the worldview I wish to impart."

Nevertheless, I win the debate. We decide to Skinnerize our girl, if only because we need rest. It's brutal in the beginning, having to hear her scream, "Mama mama, papa!," having to put her down as she stretches out her scrumptious arms in the dark, but we do it, and here's what happens: It works like magic, or science. Within five days the child acts like a trained narcoleptic; as soon as she feels the crib's sheet on her cheek, she drops into a dead ten-hour stretch of sleep, and all our nights are quiet.

Here's the thing. And all our nights are quiet. But sometimes now, we cannot sleep, my husband and I. Have we remembered to turn the monitor on? Is the dial up high enough? Did the pacifier break off in her mouth, so she will smother as she is soothed? We stay up, and through the monitor we can sometimes hear the sound of her breathing, like a staticky wind, but not once does her voice break through—not a yelp, a giggle, a sweet sleep-talk. She has been eerily gagged.

She sleeps so still, in her white baby box.

———

SOME OF THE actual boxes that Skinner used have been archived at Harvard. I go to view them. They are in the basement of William James Hall, still under construction. I have to wear a hard hat, a heavy yellow shell on my head. I go down, down the stairs. There is a moist stink in the air, and black flies buzz like neurons, each one plump with purpose. The walls themselves are porous, and when you press them, a fine white powder comes off in your hands. I pass a worker in hip-high boots, smoking a cigarette, the bright tip sizzling like a cold sore at the corner of his lip. I imagine this cellar is full of rats; they careen around the boxes, their glass-pink eyes, their scaly tails flicking: what freedom!

Up ahead, I see a huge dark stain—or is it a shadow?—on a brick wall. "There they are," my guide, a buildings and grounds person, says and points.

I go forward. Ahead of me in the cellar's dimness, I can make out large glass display cases, and within them some sort of skeleton. Closer up, I see it is the preserved remains of a bird, its hollow, flight-friendly bones arranged to give it the appearance of mid-soar, its skull full of tiny pinprick holes. One of Skinner's pigeons, perhaps, the eye sockets deep, within them a tiny living gleam, and then it goes.

I move my gaze from bones to boxes. It is at this point that I feel surprised by what I see. The bones are in line with this man's ominous mystery, but the boxes, the famous boxes—*these* are the famous black boxes? They are, for starters, not black. They are an innocuous gray. Did I read the boxes were black, or did I just concoct that, in the intersection where fact and myth meet to make all manner of odd objects? No, these boxes are not black, and they are rather rickety looking, with an external spindle graphing device and tiny levers for training. The push pedals are so small, almost cute, but the feeding dishes are a cold institutional chrome. This is what I do: I put my head in. I lift the lid and put my head deep inside a Skinner box, where the smell is of scat, fear, food, feathers, things soft and hard, good and bad; how swiftly an object switches from benign to ominous. How difficult it is to box even a box.

Perhaps, I think, the most accurate way of understanding Skinner the man is to hold him as two, not one. There is Skinner the ideologue, the ghoulish man who dreamt of establishing communities of people trained like pets, and then there is Skinner the scientist, who made discrete discoveries that have forever changed how we view behavior. There is Skinner's data, irrefutable and brilliant, the power of intermittent reinforcement, the sheer range of behaviors that can be molded, enhanced, or extinguished, and then there is Skinner's philosophy, where, I imagine, he earned his dark reputation. These two things perhaps have been mixed up in the public's mind, in my mind certainly, as science and the ideas it spawned melded into a mythical mess. But then again, can you really separate the significance of data from its proposed social uses? Can we consider *just* splitting the atom, and not the bomb and the bones that followed? Is not science indelibly rooted in the soil of social construction, so that the value of what we discover is inextricably tied to the value of the uses we discover for the discovery? Round and round we go. It's a lexical, syntactical puzzle, not to mention a moral one, not to mention an intellectual one of grave import—the idea that science and its data are best evaluated in a box, apart from the human hands that will inevitably give it its shape.

Questions of application as a means of measuring data's worth aside, what are all the mechanisms, so to speak, that contributed to Skinner's infamy? How and why did the bizarre myth of the dead daughter (who is supposedly quite alive), the black boxes, and the robotic scientist take precedence over what I am coming to see should maybe be a more nuanced view of a man who hovered between lyric prose and number crunching, a man who skinny-dipped just after he ran his rats and birds, a man who hummed Wagner, that composer of pure sentiment, while he studied the single reflex of a green frog? How did all this complexity get lost? Surely Skinner himself is partly to blame. "He was greedy," says a source who wishes to remain anonymous. "He made one discovery and he tried to apply it to the whole world, and so he fell over a ledge."

And yet, there's much much more than greed that turns us off. Skinner, in developing new devices, raised questions that were an affront to the Western imagination, which prides itself on liberty while at the same time harboring huge doubts as to how solid our supposed freedoms really are. Our fears of reductionism, our suspicions that we really may be no more than a series of automated responses, did not, as so many of us like to think, come to prominence in the industrial age. They are way, way older than that. Ever since Oedipus raged at his carefully calibrated fate, or Gilgamesh struggled to set himself free from his god's predestined plans, humans have wondered and deeply worried about the degree to which we orchestrate our own agentic actions. Skinner's work was, among other things, the square container into which those worries, forever resurrected, were poured in the shadow of the twentieth century's new gleaming machines.

BEFORE I LEAVE the Skinner archives for good, I make one more stop, and that's to view the famous baby box in which Skinner's daughter slept for the first two and a half years of her life. The box itself, I learn, has been dismantled, but I see a picture of it, from *Ladies' Home Journal*, which ran an article about the invention in 1945. If you wish to raise your reputation as a scientist, *Ladies' Home Journal* is probably not the best choice of outlets. The fact that Skinner chose to publish his supposed scientific inventions in a second-tier women's magazine speaks of his very poor "PR" skills.

"BABY IN A BOX"

the heading to the article reads, and beneath that there is, indeed, a picture of a baby in a box, a cherubic-looking Deborah grinning, hands plastered on Plexiglas sides. But read further. The baby box, it turns out, was really no more than an upgraded playpen in which young Deborah spent a few hours a day. With a thermostatically controlled environment, it guaranteed against diaper rash and kept nasal passages clear. Because the temperature was so fine-tuned, there was no need for blankets, and so the danger of suffocation, every mother's nightmare, was eliminated. Skinner outfitted his baby box with padding made of special material that absorbed odors and wet-ness so a woman's washing time was reduced by half, and she was free to use her hands for other pursuits—this in an era before disposable diapers. It all seems humane, if not downright feminist. And then, read still further. By giving the child a truly benevolent environment, an environment with no punishing dangers (if the baby fell down, it wouldn't hurt because the corners were padded to eliminate hard knocks), an environment, in other words, that conditioned by provid-ing pure reward, Skinner hoped to raise a confident swashbuckler who believed she could master her surroundings and so would approach the world that way.

It all seems, without a doubt, good intentioned, if not downright noble, and sets Skinner firmly in humane waters. But then (and there is always a *but then* in this tale), I read the name that others have pro-posed for his invention: Heir Conditioner. This is either frightening or just plain foolish.

THERE ARE THOUSANDS upon thousands of "Deborah Skinners" listed on-line, but none of them pan out. I'd like to find her, confirm her status as living. I telephone a Deborah Skinner, author of a cook-book titled *Crab Cakes and Fireflies*, and a four-year-old Deborah, and several disconnected numbers. I call Deborahs in flower shops, Deborahs on treadmills, Deborahs selling real estate and hawking credit cards, but none can claim they know a B. F. Skinner.

No, I don't find Deborah Skinner anywhere in America, nor do I find records of a death in Billings, Montana. But what I do find, in the circuitous, associative way that the Internet works, is her sister, Julie Vargas, a professor of education at the University of West Virginia. I dial.

"I'm writing about your father," I say after I establish that she is an actual offspring. In the background, pots and pans clang. I hear what sounds like a knife—chop chop—and I imagine her, Skinner's other girl, the one who missed the myth, boiling the plainest of potatoes, slicing bright chips of carrots on an old cutting board somewhere where no one can see her.

"Oh," she says, "and what about him are you writing?" There is no doubt I hear suspicion in her voice, an obvious edge of defensiveness.

"I am writing," I say, "about great psychological experiments, and I want to include your father in the book."

"Oh," she says, and won't go further.

"So, I was wondering if you could tell me what he was like."

Chop chop. I hear, on her side, a screen door slam shut.

"I was wondering," I say, trying again, "if you could tell me what you think of—"

"My sister is alive and well," she says. I have not, of course, even asked her this, but it's clear many others have; it's clear the question tires her; it's clear she knows that every query about her family begins and ends at this place, bypassing entirely the work itself.

"I saw her picture on the Web," I say.

"She's an artist," Julie says. "She lives in England. She's happily married. She taught her cat to play the piano."

"Was she close to your father?" I say.

"Oh, we both were," Julie says, and then she pauses, and I can practically feel things pushing against the pause—memories, feelings, her father's hands on her head—"I miss him terribly," she says.

The knife is silent now; the screen door no longer slams, and in the space where those sounds were comes Julie Skinner Vargas's voice, a voice loaded with memory, a kind of nostalgic incontinence, it pours through; she cannot help herself. "He had a way with children," she says. "He loved them. Our mother, well, our mother was—" and she won't finish that sentence. "But our father," she says, "Dad used to make us kites, box kites which we flew on Monhegan, and he took us to the circus every year and our dog, Hunter, he was a beagle and Dad taught him to play hide and seek. He could teach anything anything, so our dog played hide and seek, it was a world," she says, ". . . those kites," she says, "we made them with string and sticks and flew them in the sky."

"So to you," I say, "he was a really great guy."

"Yes," she says. "He knew exactly what a child needed."

"What about," I ask, "How do you feel about all the criticism his work has engendered?"

Julie laughs. The laugh is more like a bark. "I compare it to Darwin," she says. "People denied Darwin's ideas because they were threatening. My father's ideas are threatening, but they are as great as Darwin's."

"Do you agree with all your father's ideas?" I say. "Do you agree with him that we are just automatons, that we have no free will, or do you think he took his experimental data too far?"

Julie sighs. "You know," she says, "if my father made one mistake, it was in the words he chose. People hear the word *control* and they think fascist. If my father had said people were *informed* by their environments, or *inspired* by their environments, no one would've had a problem. The truth about my father," she says, "is that he was a pacifist. He was also a child advocate. He did not believe in ANY punishment because he saw firsthand with the animals how it didn't work. My father," she said, "is responsible for the repeal of the corporal punishment ruling in California, but no one remembers him for that.

"No one remembers," she says, her voice rising—she's angry now—"how he always answered EVERY letter he got while those *humanists*," and she practically spits the word out, "those *supposed humanists*, the I'm okay you're okay school, they didn't even bother to answer their fan mail. They were too busy. My father was never too busy for people," she says.

"No, no, he wasn't," I say, and suddenly I'm a little frightened. She seems a little edgy, this Julie, a little too passionate about dear old dad.

"Let me ask you something," Julie says. I can tell from the tone of her voice that this question is going to be big, pointed; it's going to put me on the spot.

"Can I ask you something?" she says. "Tell me honestly."

"Yeah," I say.

"Have you actually even READ his works like *Beyond Freedom and Dignity*, or are you just another scholar of secondary sources?"

"Well," I say, stumbling, "I've read A LOT of your dad's work, believe me—"

"I believe you," she says, "but have you read *Freedom and Dignity*?"

"Well no," I say. "I was sticking to the purely scientific texts, not the philosophical treatises."

"You can't separate science from philosophy," she says, answering my earlier question. "So do your homework," and now she sounds like any old mother, or aunt, her voice calm, creased with warmth, chop chop, she is back to the carrots, the plain old potatoes. "Do your homework," she says, "and then we'll talk."

THAT NIGHT, I put the baby to bed. I take down the worn, dog-eared copy of *Beyond Freedom and Dignity*, the treatise I have associated with other totalitarian texts, the treatise that, like *Mein Kampf*, I have long owned but never really read, and now I begin.

"Things grow steadily worse and it is disheartening to find that technology itself is increasingly at fault. Sanitation and medicine have made the problems of population control more acute. War has acquired a new horror with the invention of nuclear weapons, and the affluent pursuit of happiness is largely responsible for pollution."

Although this was written in 1971, I might as well be reading a speech by Al Gore, or a Green Party mission statement from 2003. It is true that further into the text Skinner says some troubling things like, "By questioning the control exercised by autonomous man and demonstrating the control exercised by the environment, a science of behavior questions the concepts of dignity and worth."

But these sorts of statements are buried in a text immensely pragmatic. Skinner is clearly proposing a humane social policy rooted in his experimental findings. He is proposing that we appreciate the immense control (or influence) our surroundings have on us, and so sculpt those surroundings in such a way that they "reinforce positively," or in other words, engender adaptive and creative behavior in all citizens. Skinner is asking society to fashion cues that are most likely to draw on our best selves, as opposed to cues that clearly confound us, cues such as those that exist in prisons, in places of poverty. In other words, stop punishing. Stop humiliating. Who could argue with that? Set the rhetoric aside. Do not confuse content with controversy.

The content says, "Our age is not suffering from anxiety but from wars, crimes, and other dangerous things. The feelings are the byproducts of behavior." This statement is the sum total of Skinner's reviled antimentalism, his insistence that we focus not on mind but on behavior. Really it's no different than your mother's favorite saying: actions speak louder than words. According to Skinner—and New Age author Norman Cousins—when we act meanly, we feel meanly, and not vice versa. Whether you agree with this or not, it's hardly antihumanitarian. And later on in the book, when Skinner writes that man exists irrefutably in relationship to his environment and can never be free of it, is he talking about confining chains, as most have interpreted it, or simply the silvery web work that connects us to this and this and that? I saw Jerome Kagan jump under his desk, assuring me he had free will and could exist independently of his environment. Maybe he is acting out of a more problematic tradition, patriarchal and alone. In Skinner's view, we appear to be entwined and must take responsibility for the strings that bind us. Compare this to the current-day feminist Carol Gilligan, who writes that we live in an interdependent net and women realize and honor this. Gilligan, and all of the feminist psychotherapists who followed, claim we are relational as opposed to strictly separate, and that until we see our world that way, and build a morality predicated on this irrefutable fact, we will continue to crumble. From where did Gilligan and Jean Baker Miller and other feminist theorists draw their theories? Skinner's spirit hovers in their words; maybe he was the first feminist psychologist, or maybe feminist psychologists are secret Skinnerians. Either way, we have viewed the man too simply. It seems we boxed him before he could quite box us.

JULIE, WHO IS coming to Boston for business, invites me to visit B. F. Skinner's old house, at 11 Old Dee Road in Cambridge. It is a beautiful day when I drive there, gardens growing tall spires of purple. Julie is old, much older than I expected, her skin translucent and delicate, her eyes green. She lets me in. This is B. F. Skinner's house, where he went home after long lab days during which he discovered this incredibly pliant nature of mammalian life, our ties to our communities and all their various contingencies. *Operant conditioning*—a cold phrase for a concept that might really mean we are sculptors and sculpted, artists and artwork, responsible for the prompts we fashion.

The house has stayed in the family. Speaking of fashion, its current occupant is Skinner's granddaughter, Kristina, who, Julie informs me, is a buyer for Filene's. The kitchen table is covered with Victoria's Secret catalogues, pictures of black lace panties set side by side with old photos of Pavlov and his drooling dog.

Julie leads me downstairs, to the study Skinner was sitting in just before, nearly one decade ago, he was taken to the hospital to die. She opens the door. "I have preserved everything exactly as it was when he was taken away," Julie says, and I think I hear tears in her voice. The study is musty. There is against one wall that huge yellow box where he napped and listened to music. On the walls are pictures of Deborah, of Julie as a child, of Hunter the dog. A huge book is open to the precise page it was so many years ago. His glasses are folded on the desk. His vitamins are lined up, several bullet-shaped capsules he never got to swallow on that dim day when he was carted away, and not much later buried in his final box, the real black box, bones now.

I touch the vitamins. I lift a glass with some blue evaporated elixir in a residue around the rim. I think I smell him, B. F. Skinner, the smell of old age and oddity, stale sweat, dog drool, bird scat, sweetness. His files are open and I read the labels: "Pigeons Playing Ping Pong," "Air Crib Experiment," and then on a file in the very back, "Am I a Humanist?" There is something quite vulnerable about having a file that so openly asks such a question, perhaps the central question. "Can I read it?" I ask, and Julie says, "Sure." We are both whispering now, hushed in the past preserved. She pulls it out. His handwriting is cramped and messy, and only very little of it is legible. I read, "for the good of man" and then, several sentences later, "to preserve and survive we must," and toward the end of the old decaying page, what looks like, "I wonder if I am worthwhile."

I look at Julie. "Are you going to formally archive this material?" I ask, "Or are you just going to keep it here?" Her eyes are brilliant in the study's dimness, and that, along with the way she has obsessively enshrined her father's world, leads me to think that, for her, he is the one contingency she will never question, the one environmental cue she is truly enslaved to. Would B. F. Skinner have wanted such slavish devotion or would he have encouraged her to go forth, go wider in search of new reinforcers that would generate new responses that would give rise to new data and ideas while the pigeons peck and the rats keep running and running.

"You see this," says Julie, and she points to a small end table next to a reclining chair. "Here is the piece of chocolate my father was eating before he went to the hospital," and when I look down, it is there, a piece of dark chocolate on a china plate with a real B. F. bite mark fossilized in the chunk. "I want to save this chocolate forever," she says. I ask, "How old is it?" and she says, "It's over a decade old and still in good shape." I stare at her. A little later, after she leaves the room, I lift the gnawed square and study it closely. I see precisely where his mouth met the candy's edge, and then, pulled by some string I cannot see, a cue I never knew was coming, or perhaps a streak of utter freedom (for I do not know the answer after all this, I do not know the answer), I raise my arm—or my arm is raised—and I envision the chocolate in my mouth. It would be old chocolate, dusty chocolate, on my teeth the taste of something very strange and slightly sweet.

2

Obscura

STANLEY MILGRAM AND
OBEDIENCE TO AUTHORITY

In 1961, a twenty-seven-year-old Yale assistant professor of psychology, Stanley Milgram, wanted to study obedience to authority. In a post-Holocaust world, people were struggling to understand how scores of SS officers had shot, gassed, noosed, and otherwise tortured twelve million people to death, supposedly on orders from their commanders in chief. The generally accepted explanation had to do with the then-popular notion of "the authoritarian personality," which hypothesized that certain kinds of childhood experiences of a strict, Teutonic cast produced people who would do anything to anyone if instructed. Milgram, a social psychologist, suspected that this explanation was too narrow. He purportedly believed the answer to destructive obedience lay less in the power of personality and more in the power of situation. In Milgram's view, any especially persuasive situation could cause any rational human being to abandon moral precepts and, on orders, commit atrocities. To test his hypothesis, Milgram set up one of psychology's grandest and most horrible hoaxes. He created a fake but convincing "shock machine." He recruited hundreds of volunteers and ordered them to deliver what they believed were lethal levels of electricity to an actor who feigned pain and even death. How far would people go under orders? What percentage of ordinary civilians would obey the experimenter's mandates to shock? What percentage would rebel? Here is what he found.

PART ONE: THE EXPERIMENT

Possibly you are late. You are running down a small side street in New Haven, Connecticut. It is June 1961, and ahead of you loom the spires of the Yale Episcopalian Church. The streets smell of summer, wet crushed flowers and spoiled fruit, and maybe, because of this, you already feel a little ill. In anticipation. Because of the odor. Something sweet and singed in the air.

Or perhaps you are not late. Perhaps you are the responsible type, with minutes to spare, and so you are strolling and there is no moon because it is raining, a summer rain darting down silver and sideways and making the streets smell strongly of sewage and cement. In this scenario, as well, you already feel a little sick, in anticipation, although of what you cannot say. There is that odor, something rotting in the air.

You are carrying the ad. Just two weeks ago you ripped it from its newsprint page: "We Will Pay You $4.00 for One Hour of Your Time. Persons Needed for a Study of Memory." And because it was Yale, and because of the cash, enough to buy a new blender to replace the one that went kaput, and because, well, it's all in the name of science, you said yes. Now you are on your way. On your way! The side streets are so . . . sideways; they curve and tip, the bricks buckling, green weeds thrusting up between the pavers. You trip. You straighten yourself up. You come to the address—Linsly-Chittenden Hall, a gray door—and you are just about to open it when it opens itself and a man comes from the other side, his face all red—and could those be tears streaming down his cheeks? He hustles off into the shadows, and you, it's your turn. You go in.

First off, you are paid. You go into a room, which is in worse shape than the sidewalk that led you here, walls flaking, naked pipes in a complex meshwork on the ceiling, and a stern man in a white coat who gives you three fresh smackers and four quarters, cold in your palm. He says, "Here is your compensation. It is yours to keep regardless of what happens," or some such thing. What, you wonder, is going to happen?

Another man comes into the room. He's got a round face and a silly grin and a straw hat sideways on his head. He's got blue eyes, but they're not the ice blue of intelligence or the cornflower blue of passion; they're a bland, boiled blue. Even before all that happens, you think, *This man does not look smart.* His name, he says, is Wallace something or other. Hi, you say, my name is Goldfarb, or Wentworth—pick a name, any name will do. Just remember, either way, whatever name, this is you.

The experimenter says, "We are interested in learning about the effects of punishment on learning. There has been very little systematic research into this subject, and we are hoping our findings will be of some help to educational systems." He says, "In this experiment, one of you will be the learner and receive shocks when you make a mistake in word pairs read to you, and the other one will be the teacher, who will administer the shocks when the word pair repetition is wrong. Now," the experimenter asks, "which one of you would like to be the learner, which one the teacher?"

You look at—what's his name?—Wallace. And Wallace shrugs. You shrug. The experimenter says, "We'll do a drawing." He holds out two pieces of folded paper. You pick one, Wallace picks one. You open yours: "teacher," it says. Thank god. Wallace says, laughing, "Looks like I'm the learner."

The experimenter motions for you and Wallace to follow him. You do. You go down a short dark hallway and into a room that looks like a cell. "Sit in this chair," the experimenter says to Wallace, and Wallace does. This is no ordinary chair. This is a goddamn electric chair, with a switch plate on the table and straps and strange suckers to put on the skin. "We've got to strap him down," the experimenter says, meaning strap Wallace down, and suddenly you're bending over this big man, buckling him into the seat as though he's just a baby, his skin, when you brush it, surprisingly soft. The experimenter takes a can of paste and says, "Rub this on his hands, for the electrodes," and before you know it, you are massaging grease into this loose-fleshed man, and you feel oddly ill and a tad aroused, and the experimenter says, "Tighten those belts," and so you do. You grease and tighten, pulling the straps on the black belts so Wallace is harnessed and wired up, and just before you leave, you look at him, a captured man, his pale eyes a little scared, just a glint of fear, and you want to say, "Shhh. Nothing bad will happen here."

NOTHING BAD WILL happen here. Nothing bad will happen here. You repeat that to yourself as you follow the experimenter out of one cell-like room and into another cell-like room where there is no electric chair, but instead a huge generator with dime-shiny buttons, beneath which are printed the voltages—15, 30, 45, all the way up to 450. "Danger, Extreme Shock, xxx," it says on the top-level levers. Jesus H Christ. Who is *H*? Did Jesus have a middle name? Haley, Halifax, Huston? You are starting to think seriously about Jesus' middle name; sometimes that happens to you—you think about the wrong thing, so you won't have to think about the right thing. Halifax. Haley. Huston. And meanwhile the experimenter is saying, "You will read these word sequences to Wallace through the microphone. For each mistake he makes, you give him a shock. You start at the lowest, 15, and go up. May I give you a sample shock?"

Oh sure, you've always liked samples, sample spoons of ice cream, sample fabric swatches, miniature shampoo samples in drug stores, so why not a sweet little sample shock? You offer your arm. It looks white and floppy in the fluorescent laboratory lights. It is an ugly arm, with dark dots where the hairs spring up. The experimenter lowers some pronged device onto your very own skin and you feel a pair of hot fangs, the kiss of a stingray. You flinch away. "That was 45 volts," the experimenter says. "Just so you'll know what the punishment is like."

Okay okay.

You begin.

LAKE, LUCK, HAY, SUN. *Tree, loon, laughter, child*. The word pairs have a kind of poetry to them, and now you are happy, all these lakes

and loons, and Wallace, whose voice comes crackling at you through
a tiny microphone, also seems happy. "Keep 'em coming boy!" he
shouts, and you lob him *chocolate, waffle, valentine, cupid*, and that's
when he makes his first mistake. He forgets the cupid, unlucky in
love. You give the first shock, just 15 volts, a kittenish tickle, nothing
to worry about.

But that first shock changes things. You can just tell. Wallace's
voice, when he repeats the next word pair, is somber, serious, but,
goddamn it, he makes another mistake! You give him 30 volts. Next
try, good boy, he gets it right, and then again, he gets it right. You find
you're rooting for him, and then he screws up *tree house*. Then he
screws up *dahlia* and *grass* and before you know it, you're up to 115
volts; you watch your finger land on the press-pad, the nacreous nail,
the knuckle, which is the hardest part of the hand. You press down.
Through the microphone comes the sound of a scream. "Let me out,
let me out! I've had enough, let me outta here!"

You're starting to shake. You can feel wet crescents under your
arms. You turn to the experimenter. "Okay," you say. "I guess we gotta
stop. He wants out."

"The experiment requires that you continue," this poker face says.

"But he wants out!" you say. "We can't continue if he wants out."

"The experiment requires that you continue," he repeats, as
though you're hard of hearing, which you're not, you're not! Your
hearing's fine, and so is your vision, twenty-twenty. You have the
absurd desire to tell this man all about your clean bill of health and
your excellent eyes and your good grades in college and your recent
promotion at work. You want to tell Mr. White Coat that you're a
decent person who has always wanted to help, who would do anything not to disappoint, but you're so sorry, so sorry, you cannot continue the experiment, you hate to disappoint but—

"Please continue," he says.

You blink. Sometimes the sun blinks in and out, on days when
clouds scuttle across the sky. That is the best kind of day, fresh blue
sky, clouds as white as bandages, a crisp flag snapping at the tip of its

pole. You continue. Somewhere between the cloud and the flag you found yourself going on. You don't know why, you hate to disappoint, and this experimenter seems so sure of himself and as you continue, you recall how once, when you were a child, there was an eclipse, and the sun and the moon merged in a golden burning minute.

Wallace makes a mistake. He makes three, four mistakes, and now you're up to 150 volts, and he's screaming, "I have a heart condition. Let me out of here! I no longer wish to be in this experiment," and the experimenter is standing right next to you and saying, "Go on, please, the shocks are painful but they are not harmful. There will be no permanent tissue damage."

You are fighting tears. Your name is Goldfarb, or Winegarten, or Wentworth. What is your name? You're not so sure. "But he has a heart condition," you say, you think you say, or is your mind just whispering to itself? "There will be no permanent tissue damage," he repeats, and you shout, "For god's sake, what about temporary damage?" and he says, "The experiment requires that you continue," and you say, you're crying now, or you're laughing now, your stomach's laughing hee-hee-haw while your eyes are dribbling tears, you say, "Why don't we just go in there and check on him? Let's just make sure he's okay," and Mr. White Coat shakes his head, you can hear the bones click in his neck—click click, no no, go on, you touch your own neck and you are shocked, no pun intended, you are shocked to feel how slippery wet it is, from sweat, and also how oddly boneless it is; you press and press, but you cannot find any scaffolding in your neck. Is this experimenter a doctor? "Are you a doctor?" you ask. "Are you convinced there will be no permanent tissue damage?" He seems so sure of himself, just like a doctor, which you're not, even though you got good grades in school, he knows what he's doing. You don't. He wears a white coat. So you continue up the ladder of levers, reading word pairs, and something strange has happened to you. You concentrate totally on your task. You read each word pair carefully, carefully, you press the levers like a pilot at his panel. Your range of vision narrows to the mechanics at hand. You are flying into something. You are flying through something, but what it is you cannot say. You have a job to do. This is not about the sky outside. This is not about sun, bones, blinks, flags. You have a job to do, and so flesh fades away, and Wallace fades away, and in his place, a gleaming machine.

At 315 volts Wallace gives one last, blood-curdling scream and then stops. He falls silent. At 345 volts you turn to the experimenter. You feel very odd. You feel hollow, and the experimenter, when he speaks, seems to fill you up with his air. "Consider silence a wrong answer," he says, and that seems so funny you start to sneeze and laugh. You just laugh and laugh and press those levers, because there is no way out, no way to say, "No! No! No!" In your head you can say it, but in your hands you can't, and you understand now how great the distance between the head and the hands—it is miles of unbroken tundra. With your head you say no and with your hands you tap-dance up and down the shock board, in and around the words—*skirt, flair, floor, swirl; goose, feather, blanket, star*—and all the while there is just this eerie silence punctuated by electric skillet sizzles, and no man. There is no man here.

IT IS LIKE waking up. It is like falling asleep and dreaming of loons and sharks and then waking up, and the whole thing is over. The experimenter says, "We can stop now," and through the door comes Wallace, his hat still sideways on his head, not a hair out of place. He looks fine. "Boy, you really shook me up in there," he says, "but no hard feelings." He pumps your hand. "Wow," he says, "you're sweating. Calm down. Geez I'm known for my melodrama, but I'm fine," and the experimenter echoes, "Wallace is just fine. The shocks weren't as bad as they seemed. The danger, lethal level, that's only for small laboratory animals, which is what we usually use the generator for."

Oh, you think.

Wallace leaves. A spry little man named Milgram enters the room and says, "Do you mind if I ask you some questions?" Then he shows you a picture of a schoolboy being flogged and takes down your education level and whether you've ever been in the army and what religion you are and you are so numb—you answer everything—and you are also so confused. So the shock generator was geared for mice, not men? Are you a mouse or a man? If Wallace really wasn't hurt, then why did he scream so loud? Why did he holler about his heart? You know about hearts. You know about bones and blood, which you happen to have on your hands. A rage rises up. You look at this nimble little Milgram and you say, "I get it. This wasn't about learning at all. This was an experiment about obedience, obedience to authority," and Milgram, who is only twenty-seven years old and terribly young to be pioneering such a controversial, damaging, illuminating, and finally famous setup, Milgram turns to you. He has green eyes, the color of lollipops, and a little red scribble of a mouth. "This was about obedience," you repeat, and Milgram says, "Yes, it was. If you hadn't guessed it, I would have told you later, in a standard letter I mail to my subjects. Sixty-five percent of my subjects behaved just as you did. It is totally normal for a person to make the choices you did in the situation we put you in. You have nothing to feel badly about," but you, you won't be taken in. You won't be reassured. He fooled you once, but he won't fool you twice. There are no reassuring words for what you've learned in his lab tonight. *Lake. Loon. Swan. Song.* You have learned you have blood on your hands. And a body built for the words of other men.

OTHER MEN. Maybe that one across the street or in the house next door, but not you. This is what *you*, the reader, may be thinking. Should *you* have had the outrageous luck to have found yourself in Linsly-Chittenden Hall at Yale University on a limpid June night in 1961, *you* would not have done such a thing. Your name, after all, is not Goldfarb or Winegarten or Wentworth. You are, perhaps, a Buddhist. A vegetarian. A hospice volunteer. You work with troubled youth, or donate money to the Sierra Club, or cultivate the most amazing phlox, purple-pink clusters of miniature flowers in a city garden. Not you. But yes, *you*. For Stanley Milgram proved it to be true, in Linsly-Chittenden Hall, and then later in a lab in Bridgeport, and then still later in replications all around the world. Sixty-two to sixty-five percent of us, when faced with a credible authority, will follow orders to the point of lethally harming a person.

This seems improbable, impossible, especially because you are—I am—a humanist at heart.

So were his subjects, many of them.

"I am a good worker. I provide for my family. . . . The only bad thing about me, I do get tied up in my work—I promise the kids to do something, take them somewhere, and then have to cancel because I get called out on a job."

"I enjoy my job. I have an enjoyable family, three children. . . . I like to grow flowers around my yard. I like to raise a vegetable garden primarily because I like fresh vegetables."

These were self-descriptions given by two of Milgram's fully obedient subjects after the testing. Fresh vegetables. Flowers. Those purple-pink phlox in our gardens.

Prior to beginning his experiment, Stanley Milgram, an assistant professor at Yale, took a poll. He asked a group of eminent psychiatrists how they thought subjects would behave in his simulated situation. He also polled Yale undergraduates and a handful of regular New Haven folks. All came up with the same prediction. People would not administer the shocks all the way. They would break off at 150 volts, maximum, save for the pathological fringe of crypto-sadists who would play every lever as the victim screamed. Even today, forty years after the lesson of Milgram has supposedly been learned, people still say, "Not me."

Yes you.

The power of Milgram's experiments lies, perhaps, right here, in the great gap between what we think about ourselves, and who we frankly are.

———

MILGRAM WAS CERTAINLY not the first psychologist to experiment with obedience, nor the first psychologist to deceive his subjects (the shock machine was utterly fake, the learner and the experimenter paid actors Milgram had hired to do the job), but he was the first to do so, on both accounts, systematically. However, before Milgram, there was a mysterious experimenter by the name of C. Landis, who in an unnamed laboratory in Wales in 1924 found that seventy-one percent of his subjects were willing to decapitate a rat at the experimenter's insistence. In 1944 a psychologist by the name of Daniel Frank realized that he could get his subjects to perform the oddest acts just because he wore the white coat when he made the request: "Please stand on your head," "Please walk backward with one eye closed," "Please touch your tongue to the window."

It is unlikely that Milgram was influenced by these peripheral blips of research. For one thing, Milgram, who had aspired to become a political scientist, had not taken a single psychology course in his four undergraduate years at Queens College, so he was by no means intimate with the literature of the field. For another, Milgram, a voluble little man, gave credit where credit was due. He points to the social scientist Solomon Asch as being the man who made him, if any one man can make another. While obtaining his graduate degree, Milgram served as Asch's research assistant at Princeton. Asch was hard at work on an experiment involving group pressure. In a study using lines of different lengths, Asch found that his subjects would capitulate to the group's perceptions, so if the group said line A was clearly longer than line B, even when it obviously wasn't, the baffled subject would say so too, abandoning his own beliefs in an effort to conform.

Back then, and still now, Asch was a giant in social science research, but Milgram, inches shorter than he and smaller in stature in all sorts of other ways, would soon outpace his mentor. Milgram admired Asch. But lines, well, lines lacked lyrical power, and Milgram, like Skinner, was a lyricist at heart. He wrote librettos and children's stories, quoted Keats and Rilke. He saw his fifty-one-year-old father die of heart failure and always believed he too would go early, so he was powered by a bright light. "When we married," says his widow, Alexandra Milgram, "Stanley told me he wouldn't live past fifty-one, because he looked just like his father. He always had a sense of his future as very short. Then, when Stanley developed heart troubles in his thirties, he knew, we both knew, his days were numbered."

And perhaps it was for this reason he didn't want lines, something straight and narrow. He wanted to devise an experiment that would cast such a glow, or a pall, over the earth it would leave some things simmering for a long, long time. He wanted something huge with heart. "I was trying to think of a way to make Asch's conformity experiment more humanely significant," he said in an interview with *Psychology Today*. "I was dissatisfied that the test of conformity was judgments about *lines*. I wondered whether groups could pressure a person into performing an act whose human import was more readily apparent, perhaps behaving aggressively towards another person, say by administering severe shocks to him."

Milgram was no stranger to shocks. Even before he'd seen his father die, he knew about fear. He had spent his childhood years in the South Bronx, where wildflowers grew in gutters and cockroaches scuttled across buckled linoleum. In his family's living room, heavy curtains clamped out sunlight and the radio was big and boxy, with a piece of bubbled glass protecting the channel pad. Milgram was fascinated by that radio. He was fascinated by its tiny plastic pores, its serrated dials that moved the white wand up and down, so there was music, now laughter, now weeping, now waltzing—so many sounds, but they always resolved into this: It was 1939 and Stanley was six. It was 1942 and he was just on the cusp of a certain sort of deepening. Through the radio, which his family listened to every day because they had relatives in Europe, came the death reports and the sounds of the SS and shovels on hot concrete. He grew into adolescence with this as his background music—bombs and burns—and meanwhile his body was doing its own detonations. How confusing: sex and terror. We can only guess; it says so nowhere.

IN 1960 MILGRAM left Princeton and his mentor Asch to take an assistant professorship at Yale. Soon after his appointment he began submitting expense reports for switches and electrodes; in the Yale archives are mock-up scripts and notes dated around that time in Milgram's handwriting: "audio cable through ceiling . . . sparks, practice electrode application procedure. James Justin McDonough, excellent victim, A+ victim, perfect as victim, mild and submissive." Reading these notes it is difficult to avoid the sense of Milgram as part imp, a little Jewish leprechaun, his science soaked in joke. In fact, Milgram did have a keen sense of comedy, and it may be he, more than any other scientist, who has shown us how small the space between art and experiment, between humor and heartlessness, between work and play. "Stanley loved, LOVED what he did," says Mrs. Milgram. How could he not have? He used to address letters, drop them on the New York City sidewalks, and then observe who would pick them up, who would mail them, how and why. He developed a technique called "queue barging," a kind of guerrilla social science in which Stanley sprung from a hiding place and darted into a queue, all the while observing the reactions of those he had cut in front of. He went outside, into a bright blue day, pointed at the sky, and timed how long it took to amass a crowd, all of whom stood there, staring at nothing. He was ingenious, subversive, absurd. But, unlike Sartre, or Beckett, Milgram measured absurdity. "He bottled it," says psychology professor Lee Ross of Stanford University. "He bottled absurd behaviors in his lab, so we could see them. Study them. That's what makes him . . . him."

SO MILGRAM PUT in orders for electrodes, thirty switches, black belts, and audio equipment—all the props for the dangerous play he was about to enact, the play that would, quite literally, rock the world and put such a dent in his career he would never quite recover. He started with Yale students, and, much to his surprise, every one of them complied, shocking their way blithely up the switchboard.

"Yalies," his wife Alexandra told me he said. "We can't draw any conclusions from Yalies."

Says Mrs. Milgram, "Stanley was sure if he went beyond the college community he would get a more representative sample, and
more defiance," so he did. Milgram put an ad in the *New Haven
Register*, an ad calling for able-bodied men between the ages of
twenty and fifty, "factory workers, skilled laborers, professionals,
cooks." He recruited a young Alan Elms, then a graduate student at
Yale, to help him find and keep a steady supply of volunteers. Elms,
who is now sixty-seven and teaching at the University of Davis,
clearly remembers his work with Milgram. Elms's voice is slow, tired.
I cannot help but think it is the voice of a man who has been
shocked himself, seen something bad. "Are you glad you were
there?" I ask him. "Oh yes," Elms says. He sighs. "It was a very, very
powerful thing. It is not something you would forget." He pauses. "I
will never regret being involved."

And so started the experiments, that summer of 1961, the summer
of abnormally warm weather, of a bat infestation in the church's bel-
fry, the summer you went stumbling down the side streets, ad
clutched in your hand. All together, Milgram recruited, with Elms's
help, over a hundred New Haven men. He tested them almost always
at night. This gave the whole thing a ghoulish air, which it did not
need, for there were mock screams and skulls on the generator.
Milgram alerted the area police: You may hear of people being tortured. It is not true. It is an act.

An act, apparently, that was quite convincing to the subjects, who
sweated and squirmed their way through at the experimenter's prod-
dings. Many were visibly upset at being told to continue administering the shocks; one subject had a laughing convulsion so severe the
experiment had to be stopped. Laughing? Why laughing? The odd
thing was, there was a lot of laughter going on, a lot of strangled hee-
haws and belly-aching bursts. Some have said the laughter indicates
that everyone knew Milgram the Imp had struck again, that this was
just a frivolous joke. Some say his subjects were laughing *at* him, such

an obvious bit of trickery. Elms disagrees. "People were laughing out of anxiety. *We* were laughing, Milgram and I, out of discomfort." Milgram and Elms observed the subjects behind a one-way mirror, and in between filming the unbelievable obedience they themselves could not have predicted, they dabbed at their eyes with hankies, for something here was horribly, horribly funny.

That scholars and writers have used the laughter present during the experiment as a sign of its essential frivolousness shows little about the experiment and a lot about the rather simplistic notions we hold in regards to comedy, tragedy, and the connections between the two. Comedy and tragedy are inextricably intertwined, in sign, in symbol, in etymology. Milgram himself laughed one moment, and said in another that what he had discovered was "terrifying and depressing." Alexandra Milgram reports, "The results, which he did NOT expect to be so high, made him cynical about people." Of course they did. Milgram had expected compliance, but not at the astounding rate of sixty-five percent of subjects willing to deliver what they believed were lethal shocks. No, he had not expected that. In an attempt to coax more defiance out of his subjects, he varied the conditions. He moved the learner into the room with the subject, removed the microphone, and had the subject deliver the shocks by forcing the learner's hand onto a metal plate. Compliance did drop then, but not by much. Terrifying. Depressing, yes. A full thirty percent of subjects were willing to repeatedly slam the learner's hand onto the shock plate, endure the sound of his screams, and watch him slump over, all under orders from the experimenter.

Milgram's experiment was funded by the National Science Foundation. The monies came in June. July and August passed in a sizzle of blue sparks. In September, only three months into the experiment, Milgram wrote to his backers, telling them of his results: "In a naïve moment some time ago, I once wondered whether in all of the United States a vicious government could find enough moral imbeciles to meet the personal requirements of a national system of death camps, of the sort that were maintained in Germany. I am now beginning to think that the full complement could be recruited in New Haven."

Imagine what it must have been like for Milgram, as he was making these discoveries. Was he up at nights? Did he touch his children's faces and feel how they were not so soft, the jutting ridge of his daughter's cheekbones, the tiny white teeth? Did the normal New Haven streets take on shadow and curve? Milgram's discovery was not that people will hurt or kill one another; we have always known that to be true. Milgram's discovery was that people will do so in the absence of aggression; he effectively disentwined murder from rage, for his subjects were not angry; they were quiet good folks with phlox in their gardens and children in cribs.

Milgram was a social psychologist, which means he had to understand his findings primarily in terms of the situation, for that is social psychology's clarion call. In the eyes of social psychology, personality—*who you are*—matters less than place—*where you are*—and Milgram said he was demonstrating this, how any normal person can become a killer if he finds himself in a place where killing is called for. He used his experiments, to greater and lesser degrees over the years, to explain the appalling behavior at My Lai in Vietnam, and in Nazi Germany, where his work is inextricably hitched to Hannah Arendt's thesis on the banality of evil, the beaurocratic Eichmann blindly taking orders, propelled by forces external to him. Today, years and years after Milgram's experiment, social psychologists still sound this bell, proclaiming that what matters is context, not psyche. Says Lee Ross, coauthor of *The Person and the Situation: Perspectives of Social Psychology*, "I wouldn't say there are no stable character attributes in a person that contribute to moral or immoral behavior, but they are far outweighed by where the person is, and at what time, and with whom." In other words, Ross and his colleagues claim that our behaviors do not result so much from a stable set of internalized preferences or beliefs, but rather from external influences that change, like wind and weather.

Milgram ascribed to this general worldview, yet on closer inspection there are glitches that suggest he was not so sure. For instance, if he believed it was all, or mostly, situation that propelled his volunteers, then why did he administer a personality test at the end of each shock session? Why did he gather data on education, religion, military service, and gender? Why did he later, as a professor at City College of New York, chair a doctoral dissertation that took as its subject the individual character traits of nonconformists, by a young Sharon Presley? Something in the subject must have interested him.

Not long after the initial experiments, Milgram and Elms went on a hunt for personality traits that correlate with obedient or defiant behavior. They did follow-up studies of their subjects, scrutinizing their lives and psyches for clues as to who did what and why. This, understand, is a no-no in the field of social psychology. Snorts Ross, "It's personality stuff, and we don't DO that. Milgram didn't DO that." But he did. He went with Elms and measured individual men, and wrote a paper or two. And he could only have done this because he knew the situation was not a total explanatory factor. Listen, if it had been, if Milgram had created a situation so all embracing and solidly persuasive, then he would have achieved one hundred percent obedience. But he achieved sixty-five percent, which means that thirty-five percent defied the experimenter and the situation. Why? WHY? This is a question no social psychologist can answer. It is at this critical juncture that social psychology breaks down. It can tell you about aggregate behavior, but it can tell you nothing about the naysayers, the exotic tendrils that curl off the main frame and give sprout to something strange. Here, Milgram had devised a study in which thirty-five percent of his plants, to extend the metaphor, came up crimson, hybrid—it was not the soil; it must have been something in the seed.

In the mid-1960s, Milgram and Elms called subjects back to the lab and administered batteries of personality tests. One was called the Minnesota Multiphasic Personality Inventory (MMPI), another the Thematic Apperception Test. Elms did extensive one-on-one interviewing, asking obedient and defiant subjects about their childhoods, their relationships with their mothers and fathers, their earliest memories. They found very little.

"Catholics were more obedient than Jews. We did find that," Elms tells me. "And the longer one's military experience, the more obedient. We also found that defiant volunteers measured higher on the MMPI's social responsibility scale, but," sighs Elms, "that scale supposedly measures not only greater concern for social and moral issues, but also a tendency towards compliance and acquiescence, so what do we learn from that? Not much? That could describe either an obedient or a defiant subject."

It was very difficult for Elms and Milgram to find any consistent character traits in defiant versus obedient subjects. They did find that obedient subjects reported being less close to their fathers during childhood than defiants did. As children, they found obedients received either spankings or very little punishment, whereas defiants had been punished by severe beatings or by some kind of deprivation—dinner, perhaps. Slightly more obedients had served on active military duty. Most obedients in the military admitted to shooting at men; most defiants denied it.

When you look at this information, what do you get? Not a whole lot. A defiant is beaten, an obedient is spanked. A defiant is close to his father, an obedient distant. A defiant scores high on a social responsibility scale that measures, among other things, acquiescence. Either the scale is wrong, or the defiant and the obedient have so many strands in them we cannot cleanly sort it out.

I, FOR ONE, want to sort it out. I clearly remember the first time I heard about the Milgram experiments. I was at Brandeis University, where I did my undergraduate work. I was sitting on the lawn on a May day and all the cherry trees were in bloom, petals of the palest, membranous pink. We were having class in the spring air, and the sociology professor said, "So they shocked and shocked," and a shiver went through me, because I recognized the situation. I knew intuitively, immediately, that I would have done it, obedient soul that I am. I could understand perfectly how you get bound into a situation, how you lose your own eyes, your own mind, how you empty out and just obey, obey, because who are you anyway? I remember looking at my hands, then, on the lawn, with the cherry trees all fluttery above. My hands are like your hands, three lifelines and tiny cross hatchings, and I said to myself, "What would I need to have within me in order to disobey?" I was skinny then, my hips sharp, my eyes shiny. I did what I could to fit in. I always have. Zap zap. I wanted to know what it would take to change me, grow me, up, away, an exotic tendril curling off the main frame, *no. No*. Such a simple word. So hard to hold in the mouth.

THAT WAS YEARS ago, but still today I want to understand. Elms says to me over the phone, "We didn't find any strong stable personality traits in either obedients or defiants," and I ask, "Are there any subjects from the Milgram experiments I can speak to, any that are still alive?" He answers, "The archives are sealed until 2075. The names are confidential."

I may be obedient, but that doesn't stop me from being nosy. I called this person, that person, who led me to this person and that person. Weeks went by. I called priests and rabbis and Milgram scholars, and during this search I read, in some reference I cannot relocate, that one of the defiant Milgram volunteers later turned up at My Lai and refused to shoot. I pictured this man, now sixty, now seventy, living in a clean simple house with pots of basil by his front door. I had to find him.

He called.

PART TWO: THE PEOPLE

I never saw the basil. I never saw his house. And he was not, it turns out, the My Lai man. But he was, this seventy-eight-year-old named Joshua Chaffin, in the Milgram experiments way back then, and he was, he promises me, defiant. The first thing he says to me over the phone is, "Yeah, I was there. I was in that lab, and I only went to 150 volts. If I'd gone any higher, believe me, I wouldn't be talking to you right now. That would be between me and my psychiatrist."

A defiant subject, and a funny one at that! Even before I meet Joshua in person, I can tell he's affable, a real sweetheart, his voice with a slight yiddishy lilt, his eyes, which I can just imagine, soft and sweater-gray.

Joshua keeps me on the phone for a long, long time. It's as though he's been just waiting for a reporter to call and ask him about his fateful role in those long-ago, now much-maligned experiments. He says, "You young people today just don't have an appreciation for how convincing the situation was. I didn't doubt it for a moment. Never crossed my mind it was a hoax. The generator had a gold plate on it that said 'Made in Waltham Massachusetts,' which is just the kind of place equipment like that would be made, if you see what I mean. And if you think the obedience had to do with Yale, like Yale's prestige, think again because Milgram moved his whole act to a storefront in Bridgeport and people still shocked. I shocked. I feel bad about that. I shocked but I only went to 150, I broke off at 150." He keeps repeating this, as though to reassure himself, and it is strange how fresh the whole thing is in his mind—the lab, the blue stutters of sparks, the learner's screams, all perfectly preserved in the bottle of this old man's body. He ages; the experiment stays still in time.

We make arrangements to meet. He lives, still, in New Haven, and many days he walks by Linsly-Chittenden Hall. Sometimes he even goes down to the basement, where it all took place. "It was a real mess then," Joshua says to me, "but I can see the scene just perfectly as it was, this gray door, and pipes. Pipes everywhere."

I drive up to see him on a beautiful summer day. The air and sky are incredibly soft, and the gulls' screams have the saddest sound. New Haven looks vacant, emptied of college students but littered with mattresses and trunks piled by the crumbling curbs.

We meet at a restaurant. Outside the light is bright and blinding.

And then there's the close dimness of the interior, where candles flicker on tiny tables in a perpetual evening. Everyone here is old, and eating fish. Joshua, who has described himself for me, waits at a table way in the back, where napkins are folded into the shapes of swans. I sit.

Our food comes. Joshua forks up a piece of breaded fish, pops it in his mouth, and chews vigorously.

"I was an assistant professor of environmental studies," Joshua says, "and I saw this ad, and I thought, why not? Back then, four dollars was some substantial sum of money, and I needed money. So I did it." He proceeds to tell me what the "it" consisted of, the story we now already know—how he rubbed electrode paste onto the learner's skin, how he heard the first grunt of pain somewhere around 75 volts, how the grunts got louder, how the scream was sharp and came crackling through the microphone, how Joshua turned to the experimenter and said, "This isn't right," and the damn experimenter, "The damn experimenter!" Joshua says, little flakes of fish flying from his mouth, his liver-spotted hands trembling with the memory of it, "The damn man tells me to continue."

"And you?" I say, leaning forward, although toward what I am not sure. Morality? As though that is a single concrete construct one can grasp.

"I said to that experimenter, 'No.'"

I watch Joshua's mouth as he forms the word *no,* the word I have such trouble uttering, tongue to the pink palette, spit it out. *No.*

"I said," repeats Joshua, "I said, 'I've been in a few experiments before and this isn't right,' and I was getting all wound up, hearing the learner's screams and I was getting sweaty and my heart was going really, really fast, so I stopped and I announced, 'Enough.'"

"And why did you do that?" I say. "I mean, what enabled you to break off, when so many others couldn't?"

I really want to hear his answer. I have driven all these miles to hear how a man makes himself autonomous. To hear how a man severs the strings that make our lives a performance of pure puppetry. Joshua is not a puppet. He moves his own muscles.

Joshua dabs his mouth with the starched white napkin. He pulls at the napkin's peak, the swan collapses, and he cleans his lips. He looks toward the ceiling, pauses, and then says, "I was worried about my heart."

"About your heart?" I echo.

"I was worried," Joshua says, lowering his head and looking at me, "that the experiment was causing me so much stress that I might have a heart attack, and also," he adds, almost as an afterthought, "and also, I didn't want to hurt a guy."

I nod. It is impossible not to notice that "the guy" came second, Joshua's heart first, although who could blame him? Still, this was not the answer I was expecting from my moral man. I was expecting something coated with Judeo-Christian gloss, something high-minded like, "There has always been a deep ethical imperative within me to do unto my neighbor as . . ."

No such luck. Joshua, it turns out, was worried about his heart, and his defiance came from this concern, at least in his retrospective rendition. He goes on to tell me how after the experiment he was so outraged that the next day he burst into Milgram's office at Yale and found the professor calmly behind his desk, grading papers. Joshua said, "What you are doing is wrong. Wrong! You are upsetting naïve subjects. You don't screen people for medical problems. You could give someone a heart attack, that experiment's so stressful."

Joshua recalls Milgram looking up at him. Milgram seemed unperturbed. He said, "I am sure we will not be giving any subjects heart attacks," and Joshua said, "You almost gave me one," whereon the two had a long talk. Milgram essentially calmed Joshua down and praised him for his defiant performance, and then, before he left, Milgram said, "Mr. Chaffin, I'd appreciate it if you, you know, kept it quiet."

"Kept what quiet?" Joshua said.

"The experiment," Milgram responded. "What it's really about. I'm still testing subjects and I don't want them, obviously, to know we're looking at obedience, not learning."

"Well," Joshua says to me, "I thought about that one for awhile, I mean, keeping it quiet. I thought maybe I should go to the police. Because I was really, really mad. I thought about it."

"And did you?" I say, "go to the police, or otherwise blow Milgram's cover?"

Chaffin's eyes flutter oh so briefly. The waiter comes over and whisks our plates away, so between us now there is just a white expanse of tablecloth and a candle in a pool of wax. "No," says Joshua.

"No what?" I say.

"No, I kept the real nature of the experiments a secret," says Joshua. "I didn't tell on Milgram." I think it odd, how he is so proud of defying Milgram, when at some other, larger level, he obeyed Milgram's most essential mandate. And now my eyes flutter, for it is confusing, the moral center I cannot find. I find, instead, a regular, charming, contradictory, complex man with liver spots on his hands.

I ASK JOSHUA about his life. The surprises keep tumbling out. There is absolutely nothing to suggest that Joshua's defiant laboratory behavior carried over in any way to his choices outside the lab. A corporate man, he spent many years working for Exxon. He calls environmentalists "tree huggers." At age twenty-five he joined the service and was shipped to the Philippines. "I was an excellent soldier," Joshua says. "We took those SOB Japs and locked them up."

"Did you kill anybody in the war?" I ask.

"It was World War II," says Joshua. "It was a different kind of war."

"I know, " I say. But the SOB comment, the caging of Japs, the tree huggers, the military man, the choice to keep Milgram's cover—it just doesn't fit with the otherwise low-voltage behavior Chaffin seems so proud of.

"Did you kill anybody in the war?" I ask again, and as I do, I recall Elms's comments, that obedients almost always shot at people during military service, defiants hardly ever.

"I don't know," says Joshua. He shifts uncomfortably.

"Did you do anything in the war you wished you hadn't?" I ask.

"I don't know," says Joshua. "I . . . Waiter!" he says, "I'd like some coffee," and so then comes coffee, and crème brûlée, which he eats too fast, his mouth full of sugar, and silence.

I CALL ELMS. "So," I say, "I found a defiant subject and it turns out he talks about locking up SOB Japs and being a good soldier, and overriding his own values to keep Milgram's cover" and Elms, whose voice today sounds more tired than ever, says, "Well, how people act in one situation is not necessarily how they act in another." I speak to a few other social psychologists who repeat that same idea to me, using phrases like "lack of cross-situational consistency." Lee Ross says, "Chaffin just proves that it's not personality that defines behavior, it's situation," but, frankly, that comment seems entirely unilluminating. To say that Chaffin behaved defiantly in one situation and obediently in another simply because people are a hodgepodge of unpredictable responses is a pretty piss-poor explanatory model, and I'm not going to accept it. Chaffin's case in no way proves that there are no personality traits associated with defiance and its opposite, obedience, but what it does prove, if a sample size of one could ever prove anything, is that how a subject acts in the laboratory does not necessarily generalize to how he or she will act in situations outside the laboratory, which is a whole different issue.

This issue, called external validity in the field of psychology, and better understood as generalizability, presents a serious problem for laboratory psychology. For what good does it do to demonstrate findings that cannot be replicated outside the clean white walls of a decidedly small scientific room? Picture a scientist discovering a new antibiotic that works amazingly well on male rats in super-sterilized cages with one testicle only. That discovery lacks external validity, for most men have two testicles and, as a general rule, keep their living conditions less than sterile.

Questions of external validity have plagued the Milgram experiments from their very inception. People have criticized the experiments for creating a situation that lacks any mundane realism, meaning a situation so unlike the conflicts of real life that the human drama it portrays is, in fact, irrelevant to the world in which we live. While the general public seized on the findings with fervor—going so far as to publish them in the *New York Times*, "65% in Test Blindly Obey Orders to Inflict Pain," and to incorporate them into an ABC televised movie called *The Tenth Level*, starring William Shatner as the wiry-haired, slightly mad Milgram—the smaller circle of psychology looked askance at the experiment. Scholar Bernie Mixon claimed that Milgram had not necessarily studied obedience at all; rather, he had studied trust, for the subjects that had "gone all the way" had every reason to believe in the experimenter's goodwill. Still others quibble with the trust hypothesis, and say, no, it's not trust that Milgram studied; what he did is create this entirely staged situation that tells us little about the decidedly unstaged lives in which we find ourselves. Some say the Milgram experiment "does nothing but illuminate itself," which is harsh criticism, essentially casting the complex setup as a piece of solipsistic theater that keeps eyeing its own machinations and murmuring, in the words of Henderikus Stam, "Aren't we clever?" Ian Parker, who wrote about the experiments for *Granta* magazine, eventually dismisses them as a piece of tragicomic theater, a view that the distinguished scholar Edward E. Jones upheld earlier when he rejected Milgram's first obedience paper for his journal because "we are led to no conclusions about obedience, really, but rather are exhorted to be impressed with the power of your situation as an influence context."

One of the most vocal Milgram detractors is Daniel Jonah Goldhagen, a former professor at Harvard University and author of the book *Hitler's Willing Executioners: Ordinary Germans and the Holocaust*. Goldhagen has serious doubts about both the generalizability of Milgram's specific obedience experiment and the resulting obedience paradigm as an explanation for why genocides occur. "The

Milgram experiment makes more mistaken assumptions about the Holocaust than just about anything else ever published," says Goldhagen. "His obedience theories just don't apply. People disobey credible authorities all the time. The American government says x. We do y. Even in the medical world where people assume benign motives on the parts of their physicians, patients still all the time neglect to follow orders. Furthermore, the situation Milgram set up, where subjects didn't have anytime to reflect on what they were doing, is not how the real world works. In the real world, SS officers were killing during the day and going home to their families at night. In the real world, people have plenty of opportunities to alter their course of behavior. When they don't, it's not because they're scared of authority, but because they choose not to. The Milgram experiments illustrate nothing about this factor of choice."

Well, this is a mouthful. And much of it was hard for Milgram to take, on the one hand, but on the other hand, it was fun. He got a lot of attention. Scholars puzzled over the meaning of his dark-hearted white-walled lab while Peter Gabriel composed a song for Milgram called "We Do What We're Told."

NO ONE, HOWEVER, could tell just what the Milgram experiments meant, what they measured or predicted, or how much meaning to ascribe to their findings. Was it obedience, trust, external compulsion, or something else? "Really," says Lee Ross, "the meaning of the experiments, what, exactly, they illuminate about human beings is profoundly mysterious."

Meanwhile, alongside the methodological critiques that were tumbling in, another sort of fervor was brewing. Milgram published his findings in 1963. In 1964 Diana Baumrind, a child psychologist, published in the field's leading journal a severe reprimand of Milgram on ethical grounds; he had deceived his subjects, failed to get informed consent, and caused trauma. A colleague at Yale tipped off the American Psychological Association and Milgram's membership application was upheld for a year, while he was investigated. "You have to understand," says Lee Ross, "this whole ethical thing was happening in the 1960s, the 1960s," he repeats, "when people were primed for it. The Tuskegee experiment of withholding treatment for syphilitic black men had just come to press, and the horrible Nazi experiments, and the general anti-scientism; it was in this light that Milgram was investigated."

Investigated he was. Held under the bright laboratory lights of his colleagues and found wanting. He squirmed and struggled. At parties, people recoiled when they heard who he was. Bruno Bettelheim, paragon of humanism, called Milgram's work vile. When it came time for tenure, Milgram was denied the ivy halls of Yale and Harvard; "Who would have him?" says his widow Mrs. Milgram. "In those days you needed to have unanimous approval for a tenure candidate and Stanley was so controversial."

Stanley, it seems, wanted it both ways: he wanted to be a maverick and he wanted acceptance; he wanted to shock the world and then be taken in to its forgiving embrace. University after university turned him down. He—not his subjects, not Joshua, but he, Stanley Milgram—began to have heart troubles. The thick blue aortal stem got clogged with grease; the flap muscles faltered. At thirty-one he was hired by the City College of New York as a full professor, not a bad move for such a young man, but at thirty-eight he had already suffered the first of five myocardial infarctions, his hand going up to his closing throat, a shooting ache in the shoulder, knees buckling under, revived, revived again, each time the pump a little weaker.

What killed Stanley Milgram is what kills all of us: life itself. The wear and tear, the tamp of time, the inevitable decay egged on by too many eggs, too much meat and fear and loss. He had a lot of loss: the loss of his father at a young age, a man who looked just like him and was a baker and every morning came home with two challas, their tops braided and buttered. He lost his father, and then he lost the prestige of Ivy League tenure, and then he lost an unvarnished reputation as he was attacked, and attacked again, for his inhumane laboratory practices. "It was awful for Stanley. Just awful," says Mrs. Milgram. I press her to say more, but she won't. In 1984, when he was fifty-one years old, he felt a wave of nausea while listening to a student's dissertation defense. "He hadn't eaten lunch that day," says Mrs. Milgram, "I'm just sure of it, and he had a real women's libber for an office assistant. She wouldn't even get him a glass of water if he asked," and so he sat there, parched and nauseous. His good friend Irwin Katz accompanied him home on the subway, and Milgram must have felt how the steady rhythm of the rails contrasted with the flopping of his own starving heart. Alexandra Milgram picked her husband up at the train station and drove him right to the emergency room. He was still walking at that point. He was pale in the face, and his hands shook. He went straight to the nurse's station and said, "My name is Stanley Milgram and I am having my fifth heart attack," and then he dropped to his knees. "He was gone," Mrs. Milgram explained to me, taken to another room, where his shirt was ripped open and suckers, electrodes, and paste were pressed onto his chest. *The experiment requires that you continue, continue, continue.* They shocked him once, twice, who knows how often his body rose into the air, flailing like a fish's, *shock shock*, the black cardiac cuffs beating down. But he was gone, and could not be shocked back into being.

HIS NAME IS *not* Jacob Plumfield; he *does not* have blue eyes or live in a part of Boston called Jamaica Plain. He is not seventy-nine, but he is somewhere near there. I will give him a beard, I think, silver-white stubble, and I will say, for the sake of the story, that his lover's name is Jim.

Jacob Plumfield will speak with me on the condition of one hundred percent anonymity. He was in the Milgram experiments and, unlike Joshua, was obedient to the end of the shock board. He says his hands still hurt with what he did.

People question what Milgram created: a false situation, an unethical situation. One thing is for sure: his situation made some powerful memories, for both Joshua and Jacob speak of it as though it were yesterday, their eyes ignited. If the laboratory is not a real situation, as many Milgram critics have cited, then why or how has it managed to stamp itself so solidly into these men's undeniably real lives, to take up residence alongside anniversaries, children's births, first sex?

"I was twenty-three," says Jacob, "a postdoc." He goes on to tell me a tale with Oscar Wilde flourishes. He was having a secret affair with a roommate, struggling with a burgeoning homosexual identity. "In high school and college I'd done everything to fit in," says Jacob. "Everything! I was the golden boy. I got great grades. I had a gorgeous girlfriend. All the while, though, I kept looking at boys' backs when we went swimming, their backs. I don't know why."

Finally, in his postdoc year, Jacob acted on his impulse, falling in love with and consummating a relationship with his roommate, who, it turned out, was just experimenting with homosexuality and soon left him for a girl. But Jacob remembers those nights of lovemaking, the room hot, the sucking sounds of their puddled chests coming together, the unbearable excitement. And then, the suite mate left him for a girl, and Jacob was devastated. "I felt it in my body, the shame of being gay. Why couldn't I like a girl?" He masturbated compulsively, picturing "awful things." And then he saw the ad. He answered it. "God knows why," he says to me. He went to Milgram's lab three days after the breakup, his appendages hurting and bruised, semen-sticky hands, and when the experimenter said, "There will be no permanent tissue damage, please continue . . ."

"Well," says Jacob, "I just continued. I was so depressed I almost didn't care, and I was thinking, 'No permanent tissue damage, he's got to be right, I pray he's right, I don't want any permanent tissue damage, do *I* have permanent tissue damage?'" He describes a scene where the screams of the learner merged with his own self-loathing, a joint pain, and up he went, utterly without a center, having spurted it all out in secret shames.

"Afterwards," said Jacob, "when I was debriefed afterwards, explained what had happened, I was horrified. Really, really horrified. They kept saying, 'You didn't hurt anyone, don't worry, you didn't hurt anyone,' but it's too late for that. You can never," says Jacob, "really debrief a subject after an experiment like that. You've given shocks. You thought you were really giving shocks, and nothing can take away from you the knowledge of how you acted. There's no turning back."

I recall, while speaking with Jacob, the words of Boston College sociology professor David Karp, who said to me, "Just imagine what it must be like for those subjects, to have to live their whole lives knowing what they were capable of . . ."

"So," I say to Jacob, "I would guess you think the experiments were essentially unethical, that they caused you harm."

Jacob pauses. He strokes his dog. "No," he says. "Not at all. If anything, just the opposite."

I look at him.

"The experiments," he continues, "caused me to reevaluate my life. They caused me to confront my own compliance and really struggle with it. I began to see closeted homosexuality, which is just another form of compliance, as a moral issue. I came out. I saw how essential it was to develop a strong moral center. I felt my own moral weakness and I was appalled, so I went to the ethical gym, if you see what I mean."

I nod. I see what he means. "I came out," he says, "and that took a lot of strength and built a lot of strength, and I saw how pathetically vulnerable I was to authority, so I kept a strict eye on myself and learned to buck expectations. I went from being a goody-two-shoes golden boy with a deep secret headed straight for medical school, to a gay activist teaching inner-city kids. And I credit Milgram with galvanizing this."

Argot, the dog, has laid his wet nose in Jacob's lap. Jacob strokes and strokes the snout. The room we are in has a bay window, a maple floor, a built-in hutch with a silver clasp. It's a lovely, peaceful room. I could sleep in a room like this. So much has been settled, stilled, in a room like this. It is painted white, with white sailcloth curtains and a passionflower plant on the windowsill. Jacob lives simply. Nearing the end of his life, he has minimal money saved, although his long-term partner, Jim, a lawyer, has more. Jacob shows me the first pink triangle he ever proudly wore.

Everywhere you look in this condominium, you can see signs of Jacob's alternative life—the inner-city teaching awards, the active resistance to material goods. He, the obedient one, has lived by far the more defiant lifestyle than Joshua, the defiant one, who worked as a top officer for Exxon, and then the army.

So what are we left with? Again, questions of validity, for if the experiment does little to predict how a man's choices in the lab will translate into choices outside the lab, and if we accept prediction, and generalizability, as one of the main goals of a scientific experiment, then, indeed, are not Milgram's critics right?

Douglas Mook, a social scientist, wrote an article called "In Defense of External Invalidity," in which he questions the whole notion of using generalizability as an indicator of an experiment's worthiness. "Unless a researcher's purpose is of a specifically applied nature . . . the representativeness of the laboratory in terms of mundane realism may be irrelevant." In other words, if you don't plan on using your findings in the real world, then who cares whether or not the findings are relevant to it. Well, I guess that's okay. But where, in terms of the mysterious Milgram experiments, does an argument like Mook's actually leave us? A person, say, a critic, comes to an experiment the same way a reader comes to a novel; there are similar aesthetic demands in terms of structure, pacing, revelation, lesson learned. You cannot close *The Brothers Karamazov* and say, "Very interesting, although I've no idea what it was about," because you just can't. A piece of literature makes its way into canon based largely on the meaning it imparts in our lives. Milgram's experiments are indisputably in the canon. And yet, no one can agree on the theme—a story of obedience? No. A story of trust? No. A piece of tragicomic theater? No. An example of ethical wrongdoing? No. What message has Milgram sent us, in what sort of bottle, on which sea?

Perhaps the best thing to do, then, is to turn to the subjects themselves, for they are, more than even Milgram, the bearers of his bad or
good news. And when you do that, when you turn to the subjects
and ask, "What was this all about for you?" you start to hear a similar
story that may finally pull the conflicting threads together: Did he
measure obedience or trust? Was his situation real or false? Did his
subjects know it was a hoax or were they fooled? Was this the work
of an imp or a scientist? Does generalizability matter or not?

Says Jacob, "The experiment changed my life, caused me to live
less according to authority." Harold Takooshian, a former student of
Milgram's and a professor at Fordham University, recalls a binder of
letters on Milgram's desk: "It was a big black binder filled with hundreds of letters from subjects, and many, many of the letters said how
much the obedience experiments had taught them about life, and
how to live it." Subjects claimed the experiment caused them to
rethink their relationship to authority and responsibility; one young
man even said that as a result of his participation in the Milgram
experiments, he became a conscientious objector in the war.

So this, perhaps, is what we're left with: an experiment that derives
its significance not from its quantifiable findings, but from its peda-
gogical power. Milgram's obedience experiments had the ironic
effect of making his subjects, at least some of them, less obedient.
And that is pretty stunning—an experiment so potent it does not
describe or demonstrate, so much as detonate, a kind of social psychology equivalent of the atom bomb, only this time in the service of
creation, not destruction, for as Milgram himself said, "From these
experiments comes awareness and that may be the first step towards
change."

As for the personality variables associated with obedience and
defiance, I cannot locate them, much, I'm sure, to the social psychologists' glee. Nevertheless, I believe they are there, for we are not simply the situations in which we find ourselves. Milgram, himself a
great believer in the power of the situation, went looking for traits—
so how great a believer was he?—and he wrote in an often over-

looked statement, "I am certain there is a complex personality basis to obedience and disobedience. But I know we have not found it."

But I remember on that late spring day at Brandeis, when I first heard of the Milgram experiments, how I felt a shock of recognition, and the immediate knowledge that I could do such a thing, unsteady as I am. And I knew I could do such a thing, not because some strange set of circumstances propelled me to, no. The impetus lay within me, like a little hot spot. It was not external. It was internal. A little hot spot. Up the shock board. How often had I, have *you*, heard a racial slur and said nothing in order to keep the peace? How often have I, have *you*, seen something wrong at work, maybe a mistreated colleague, and done nothing so your own job stays steady? The little hot spot travels inside us. Certain situations may make it glow brighter, and others dimmer, but the moral failing that lies at the heart of so many humans, well, there it lies, at the heart, which cannot, after it has failed one too many times, be shocked back into being. I feel my own heart, clippety clop, and I see my own hands, and I'd like to think, now that I've made such an intimate acquaintance with Mr. Milgram, with Joshua and Jacob and you, yes *you*, I'd like to think I'd do the dance a little differently when my number is called. I look at my hands, here, on this midsummer day, and I see how the lines go every which way, up and down, good and bad— there is no way to know for sure. Sixty-five percent did. Thirty-five percent didn't. And then the good are bad and the bad are good. It's all mixed up. My hands hurt, and are huge with possibility. Now it is evening. My two-year-old daughter has learned a new word in Spanish. "*Obscura! Obscura!*" she keeps shouting, which she says means "darker! darker!" She comes up to me, and with my hands, my hugely possible hands, I hold her.

On Being Sane in Insane Places

EXPERIMENTING WITH

PSYCHIATRIC DIAGNOSIS

In the early 1970s, David Rosenhan decided to test how well psychiatrists were able to distinguish the "sane" from the "insane." Psychiatry as a field is, of course, predicated on the belief that its own professionals know how to reliably diagnose aberrant mental conditions and to make judgments based on those diagnoses about a person's social suitability—performance as a parent, parolee's flight risk, prisoner's ability to be reformed. Rosenhan was conscious and critical of the huge amount of social control psychiatrists had, so he devised an experiment to test whether their actual skills were on par with their power. He recruited eight other people, and together they faked their way into various mental institutions, and then once in the ward, they acted completely normally. The goal: to see whether the psychiatrists would detect their sanity, or whether the psychiatrists' judgments would be clouded by presuppositions (i.e., if the patient is there, labeled a patient, then he must be crazy). Rosenhan's experiment elegantly explores the way the world is always warped by the lens we are looking through. His experiment implies we are inextricably immanent, suffused with subjectivity, and as such, it adds as much to the literature of philosophy as it does to psychology and psychiatry.

He lost his wife. He lost his daughter. He lost his mind to a series of small strokes and now David Rosenhan, Stanford professor emeritus of law and psychology, now he can barely breathe. He was standing a few months ago in his Palo Alto kitchen when he first felt it, a rising numbness in his legs. By the time he got to the emergency room, his legs were gone, and then his arms, and then his torso, and then, at last, his lungs. Doctors, confused, could not determine exactly what was ailing this renegade researcher, one who devoted the better part of his career to the dismantling of psychiatric diagnosis. Now here he was, a diagnostic question himself. Rosenhan's face froze. As of this writing, he still cannot say many words. His silence is a hole in the story that follows, a story itself about holes and how, in a series of stunning experiments, Rosenhan found them in what we thought was the firm field of psychiatry.

IT WAS 1972. Thomas Szasz had written *The Myth of Mental Illness.* R. D. Laing had challenged psychiatrists to rethink schizophrenia as a form of possible poetry. Only recently, flags had waved on the snouts of guns, signaling cease-fire in Vietnam. Rosenhan, a psychologist with a joint degree in law, did not go to Vietnam, but according to one colleague, he had observed how many men used mental illness as a way of avoiding the draft. It was fairly easy to fake some symptoms—how easy, exactly, was it? Rosenhan, who loved adventure, decided to try something out.

Almost on impulse he called eight friends and said something like, "Are you busy next month? Would you have time to fake your way into a mental hospital and see what happens, see if they can tell you're really sane?" Surprisingly, so the story goes, all eight were not busy next month, and all eight—three psychologists, one graduate student, a pediatrician, a psychiatrist, a painter, and a housewife—agreed to take the time to try this treacherous trick, along with Rosenhan himself, who could hardly wait to get started. Says pseudopatient Martin Seligman, "David just called me up and said, 'Are you busy next October?'" and I said, 'Of course I'm busy next October,' but by the end of the conversation, he had me laughing and saying yes. I gave him all of October, which is how long the experiment took."

Some of the hospitals Rosenhan had chosen were posh and built of white brick; others were state-run gigs with urine-scented corridors and graffiti-scratched walls. The pseudopatients were to present themselves and say words along these lines: "I am hearing a voice. It is saying thud." Rosenhan specifically chose this complaint because nowhere in the psychiatric literature are there any reports of any person hearing a voice that contains such obvious cartoon angst.

Upon further questioning, the eight pseudopatients were to answer completely honestly, save for name and occupation. They were to feign no other symptoms. Once on the ward, if admitted, they were to immediately say that the voice had disappeared and they now felt fine. Rosenhan then gave his confederates a lesson in managing medication, how to avoid swallowing it by slipping it under the tongue so it could later be blurted back to the toilet bowl. "It took me awhile," recalls Martin Seligman, "it took me awhile to get the pill thing right, and I was so nervous. I was nervous I'd accidentally swallow a pill if they forced one on me, but I was more nervous about homosexual rape."

The pseudopatients practiced for a few days. Much of the practice was, admittedly, passive, letting entropy and odor wend their way in. Their hair grew out and clumped. Their breath got a greenish tinge. They learned to tuck fat pills and pea-sized pills in the cavern beneath the tongue, and then to turn the head sideways and surreptitiously spit. It was autumn then, and a fat harvest moon hung in the sky. Goblins in bright capes drifted down the streets, witches carrying flickering pumpkins. Trick? Or treat?

THE ACTUAL DAY that Rosenhan departed for one of Pennsylvania's state hospitals was brilliant. The sky was a frosty pre-winter
blue, the trees like brushes dipped in pots of paint, turned upward
and wet with color.

Rosenhan pulled into the parking lot. The mental hospital had
Gothic buildings, every window caged. Orderlies in pale blue smocks
floated on the grounds.

Once in the admissions unit, Rosenhan was led to a small white
room. "What is the problem?" a psychiatrist asked.

"I'm hearing a voice," Rosenhan said, and then he said nothing else.

"And what is the voice saying?" the psychiatrist questioned,
falling, unbeknownst to him, straight into Rosenhan's rabbit hole.

"Thud," Rosenhan said. I imagine he said it a little smugly.

"Thud?" The psychiatrist asked. "Did you say thud?"

"Thud," Rosenhan said again.

The psychiatrist probably scratched his head. He could have been
confused, bemused. He could have put down his pen, his pad of
paper, and stared for a second at the ceiling. The problem is, we don't
know what exactly happened in any of the admitting rooms, because
Rosenhan has neglected to give any detailed reports. We do know
each pseudopatient, Rosenhan included, said the voice was of the
same sex as he or she, that it had been bothering the pseudopatient to
some extent, that he or she had come to the unit on the advice of
friends who had heard "this was a good hospital."

Robert Spitzer, one of the twentieth century's most prominent
psychiatrists, and a severe critic of Rosenhan, wrote in a 1975 article
in the *Journal of Abnormal Psychology* in retort to Rosenhan's findings,
"Some foods taste delicious but leave a bad aftertaste. So it is with
Rosenhan's study." He goes on to state, "We know very little about
how the pseudopatients presented themselves. What did the pseudopatient say." In a footnote to the article, Spitzer writes, "Rosenhan has
not identified the hospitals used in this study because of his concern
with confidentiality and the potential for ad hominem attack.
However, this does make it impossible for anyone at these hospitals to

corroborate or challenge his account of how the pseudopatients acted and how they were perceived." Spitzer later says, in a phone conversation with me, "And this whole business of *thud*. Rosenhan uses that as proof of how ridiculous psychiatrists are because there had never been any reports before of 'thud' as an auditory hallucination. So what? As I wrote, once I had a patient whose chief presenting complaint was a voice saying, 'It's okay, it's okay.' I know of no such report in the literature. This doesn't mean there isn't real distress." I don't want to challenge Spitzer, but a voice saying, "It's okay," sounds pretty okay to me.

Spitzer pauses. "So how is David?" he finally asks.

"Actually not so good," I say. "He's lost his wife to cancer, his daughter Nina in a car crash. He's had several strokes and is now suffering from a disease they can't quite diagnose. He's paralyzed."

That Spitzer doesn't say or much sound sorry when he hears this reveals the depths to which Rosenhan's study is still hated in the field, even after forty years.

ROSENHAN WAS LED down a long hallway. All across the country, unbeknownst to him, the eight other pseudopatients were also being admitted. Rosenhan must have been scared, exhilarated. He was a journalist, a scientist at the apex, putting his body on the line for knowledge. He wasn't looking through some microscope, some telescope; he was in actual orbit, damn it, he was walking on the moon. And the moon it was, the ward was a sterile place where sailors and mock professors and women with blotchy mouths floated in the weightless world of their visions. Rosenhan was taken to a room and told to undress. Did he note how his body was no longer his? Someone inserted a thermometer into his mouth, wrapped a black cuff around his arm, pressed on his pulse and read it: normal, normal, normal. Everything was normal, but no one seemed to see. He said, "You know, the voice isn't bothering me anymore," and the doctors just smiled. "When will I get out?" we can imagine Rosenhan asked, his voice perhaps rising now, some panic here—what had he done, my god. "When will I get out?"

"When you are well," a doctor answered, or something to this effect. But he was well: normal, normal, normal, 110 over 80, a pulse of seventy-two, a temp that hovered in the midzone of moderate, homeostatic, a machine well greased. It didn't matter. It didn't matter that he was totally lucid. He was diagnosed with paranoid schizophrenia and kept for many days.

THERE WAS A glassed-in office, which Rosenhan came to call the "bull pen." Inside nurses flurried about, busy as a blizzard, pouring cherry-red medicines into plastic cups. Pills abounded, pills as plentiful as candy, as fat as fireballs, as petite as the sugary pink dots on strips of long white paper. Rosenhan cooperated absolutely. He "took" the pills three times a day and then rushed to the bathroom to spit them back out. He comments on how all the other patients were doing this too, being fed their medication and heading en masse to the toilets, and how no one much cared so long as they were well behaved.

Mental patients are "invisible . . . unworthy of account," Rosenhan writes. He describes a nurse coming into the dayroom, unbuttoning her shirt, and fixing her bra. "One did not have the sense that she was being seductive," Rosenhan reports. "Rather, she didn't notice us." He saw patients being beaten. He describes how one patient was severely punished simply because he said to a nurse, "I like you." Rosenhan does not describe the nights, which must have been long, lying in that narrow bed while orderlies with flashlights did fifteen-minute checks, their gold beams illuminating nothing, absolutely nothing. What did he think of then? Did he miss his wife, Molly? Did he wonder how his two toddlers were getting on? That world must have seemed so far away, even though it was no more than a hundred miles away; this is what science teaches us. Osmosis is an illusion in the social world. Membranes are not semipermeable; they are solid sheaths separating spaces—you there, me here. Maybe in time only a second separates us, but in bias, in label, the distance is forever.

Rosenhan and confederates were given some therapy, and when they told of the joys and satisfactions and disappointments of an ordinary life—remember, they were making nothing up save the original presenting complaint—all of them found that their pasts were reconfigured to fit the diagnosis: "This white 39 year old male . . . manifests a long history of considerable ambivalence in close relationships . . . affective stability is absent . . . and while he says he has several good friends, one senses considerable ambivalence in those relationships." Wrote Rosenhan in *Science*, one of the field's most prestigious journals, in 1973, "Clearly, the meaning ascribed to his verbalizations . . . was determined by the diagnosis, schizophrenia. An entirely different meaning would have been ascribed if it were known that the man was 'normal.'"

The strange thing was, the other patients seemed to know Rosenhan was normal, even while the doctors did not. A number of the other confederates undergoing similar incarcerations all across the country also had this eerie experience, that the insane could detect the sane better than the insane's treaters could. Said one young man, coming up to Rosenhan in the dayroom, "You're not crazy. You're a journalist or a professor." Said another, "You're checking up on the hospital."

While in the hospital, Rosenhan followed all orders, asked for privileges, helped other patients deal with their problems, offered legal advice, probably played his fair share of Ping-Pong, and took copious notes, which the staff labeled as "writing behavior" and saw as a part of his paranoid schizophrenic diagnosis. And then one day for a reason as arbitrary as his admission, he was discharged. The air was burning with cold. He had learned something severe: he had learned about inhumanity in asylums; he had learned psychiatry was psychiatrically sick. He wondered, in how many hospitals all across this country were people being similarly misdiagnosed, medicated, and held against their wills. Did the label of *madness* beget madness, so that the diagnosis sculpts the brain, and not the other way around? Our brains do not, perhaps, make us. Maybe we make our brains. Maybe we are made by the tags affixed to our flesh. It was nearing winter, and I imagine all sorts of snow was falling, obscuring the supposedly fixed outlines of houses and cars and buildings. The grounds of the hospital were going fast, white as light, without substance.

IN 1966, YEARS prior to Rosenhan's adventure, two researchers, R. Rosenthal and L. Jacobson, did an experiment in which they administered to children in Grades 1 through 6 an IQ test with a bogus name: "The Harvard Test of Inflected Acquisition." The test was said to be an indicator of academic blooming, or "spurting," when in fact the test measured only some nonverbal skills. Teachers were told that students who did well on the test were expected to make unprecedented gains within the next year. In truth, the test could predict no such thing.

Meaningless results were released to the teachers, and in one year's time Rosenthal and Jacobson examined the children. They found that those assigned to the "spurting" group had, in fact, made larger academic gains than those not assigned. More worrisome, the spurting group had a significant rise in IQ scores, especially in Grades 1 and 2, indicating that one's "intelligence quotient" has as much to do with opportunity and expectation as it does with fixed capacity.

Even earlier, at the turn of the century, another "experiment" of this sort revealed the power of expectations in interpretation. This is, indeed, a very strange story that involves a horse named Hans, who everyone believed could do mathematics. If you gave Hans a math problem, this horse, who soon came to be called Clever Hans, would tap out the answer with his hoof! People paid money to meet Hans and to test him, experimenting over and over again with what is, undoubtedly, the largest lab animal known to psychology.

However, one skeptic in 1911, a man by the name of Oskar Pfungst, went to Hans and put him through his paces. He observed him with his spectacles and sticks over many days and nights, and found that the horse, indeed, did not know math but had simply learned to tap his foot based on subtle cues from the observers. For instance, as the horse reached the correct number of taps, the observers would give very subtle signals that the horse had learned to take in; an unconscious rise of the eyebrows, a tilt of the head, and Hans would stop. Lo and behold, it had nothing to do with knowledge of math; it had only to do with subterranean signals sent by the environment, absorbed by the oh so absorbent animal that both horses and humans are, and then interpreted to fit the existing schema, which in this case was so absurd it only underscores how far we will go to confirm whatever it is we want.

Rosenhan knew of Rosenthal and Jacobson. He knew of Hans the Clever Horse and O. Pfungst, the skeptic and savior of sanity. But he knew something else too. While all of these experiments showed the power of bias and context in determining reality, none had done so in reference to medicine, of which psychiatry so proudly claimed itself a part. These were genuine M.D.s at the Pennsylvania state hospital, and they had made very bad mistakes, but worse than that, they had made dumb mistakes. Upon meeting up with his confederates after the whole experiment had been conducted, east to west, Rosenhan discovered that all but one of them had been diagnosed as schizophrenic, based on a single silly symptom (the exception had been given the diagnosis of "manic depressive psychosis," an equally weighty label). Rosenhan found that the mean hospital stay was nineteen days, with the longest being fifty-two and the shortest seven. He found that all confederates had experienced a real reduction in status. And, lastly, Rosenhan found that all were released with their disease in remission, which means, of course, that their essential sanity was never detected and that their present sanity was understood as a temporary blip, to remit and remit again.

Rosenhan was a bald boxy man in his thirties when all this happened. He was known as an entertainer, holding at his house seders for as many as fifty people. He loved lavish parties and eventually installed two dishwashers in his kitchen to accommodate the plates for all those knishes. Says good friend and Stanford colleague Florence Keller, "David's the only man I know who enlarged his house *after* his kids left for college, so he could have more revelers over." Then Keller pauses. "He had a way with words," she says. "But you also never felt you really knew him. He had a mask on."

Indeed he did.

And, indeed, we are often eager to reveal in others the very tendencies we sense in ourselves. Therefore, it might have been with some glee that in the early 1970s Rosenhan took up his pen and wrote the paper that would burst like a bomb in the world of psychiatry, denuding it of its status, the paper describing his findings of the pseudopatient experiment. "On Being Sane in Insane Places" was published in the prestigious journal *Science,* which is ironic because Rosenhan was calling into question the very validity of science, at least as it applies to psychiatry. At one point early in the article, Rosenhan just lays it on the line. He claims that diagnosis is not carried within the person, but within the context, and that any diagnostic process that lends itself so readily to massive errors of this sort cannot be a very reliable one.

SCIENCE, A MAGAZINE still published today, has a circulation of about sixty thousand. In general, from what I can see, having perused many issues of it now, a lead article generates maybe a handful of anemic responses, letters lacking utterly in punch. Rosenhan's article, however, generated a flood of fluorescent missives enormously fun to read, the arguments incisively stated. Rosenhan dissed psychiatry as science, and in doing so, he egged many of America's psychiatrists to put their best foot forward and show the keen intelligence that runs beneath their often questionable claims:

> Most physicians do not assume that patients who seek help are liars; they can therefore, of course, be misled. . . . It would be quite possible to conduct a study in which patients trained to simulate histories

of myocardial infarction would receive treatment on the basis of history alone (since a negative electrocardiogram is not diagnostic) but it would be preposterous to conclude from such a study that physical illness does not exist, that medical diagnoses are fallacious labels, and that "illness," and "health" reside only in doctor's heads.

The pseudopatients did *not* behave normally in the hospital. Had their behavior been normal they would have walked to the nurse's station and said, "Look, I am a normal person who tried to see if I could get into the hospital by behaving in a crazy way or saying crazy things. It worked and I was admitted to the hospital, but now I would like to be discharged from the hospital.

And my favorite:

If I were to drink a quart of blood and, concealing what I had done, come to the emergency room of any hospital vomiting blood, the behavior of the staff would be quite predictable. If they labeled and treated me as having a peptic ulcer, I doubt that I could argue convincingly that medical science does not know how to diagnose that condition.

Robert Spitzer, that spry psychiatrist trained in psychoanalysis, who held his own prestigious post at the Institute for Biometrics at Columbia University, was by far the most distressed. He didn't write a letter. He wrote two entire papers devoted to dismantling Rosenhan's findings, totaling thirty-three pages of dense, extremely cogent prose. "Did you read my responses to Rosenhan?" Spitzer asks when I phone him. "They're pretty brilliant, aren't they?"

Spitzer argues many, many things. At root he is arguing for the validity of psychiatry, and its diagnostic practices, as sound scientific, *medical* procedures. "I believe in the medical model of psychiatry," he says to me, which means he believes psychiatric disorders are generally the same as disorders of the lungs or liver and can be viewed as such, and will someday be understood in terms of tissue and synapse, things that squirt in the brain's black box. Writes Spitzer in his response to Rosenhan: "What were the results? According to Rosenhan, all the patients were diagnosed at discharge as 'in remission.' A remission is clear. It means without signs of illness. Thus, all of the psychiatrists apparently recognized that all of the pseudopatients were, to use Rosenhan's term, 'sane.' "

Spitzer goes on to make a case for the credibility of psychiatry as a medical profession. Reading Spitzer's articles and the letters following Rosenhan's publication, I find myself swayed, as in a tennis match. On the one hand the study *was* flawed. *If* I drank a quart of blood and *if* I vomited it in the ER . . . , which must mean psychiatry really is no different from its supposedly more medical kin. But wait a minute, in the blood scenario, I wouldn't be held for fifty-two days, and besides, blood is not *thud*. I mean, blood is far more compelling a presentation— swayed, swayed, sanity and insanity, valid and invalid, here is where I am.

It is 1976 and *I* am the patient. This, by the way, is not a simulation. Just two years after Rosenhan presented his findings, I, a mawkish fourteen-year-old, entered an East Coast mental institution with all sorts of symptoms that definitely did not include hallucinations. I was doing things fourteen-year-olds do, and then some. I liked drama and fancied myself a burgeoning Virginia Woolf. On the other hand, I wasn't all act. My own symptoms aside, in the "bin"—as I came to call the hospital almost affectionately—I saw some things. I saw the glassed-in nurse's station, the candy stripers pushing chrome carts, the lunatic manic with sweat runnelling down his face, the woman named Rosa, found in the bathroom, neck bunched in a noose. I saw some things. I saw things that were definitely not in the doctor's heads, like that neck in the noose. For me, therefore, psychiatric illness is absolutely real. However, all of us patients used to gather in the dayroom, where the smoke was thick as yarn, and trade our doctor-given diagnoses like kids trade marbles: "borderline" was bright and blue; "schizophrenia" was scarlet with a smear of white; "depression" was a dull tinny green, cloudy as a cataract, not well respected. One

suicide attempt was pretty piss poor, three gave you some status, anything over ten gave you grave respect. Like criminals in a prison, we
swapped tricks of the trade, egged on, no doubt, by the labels and
medical attention we were given, so that at some point it became difficult to know whether we preexisted the labels, or the labels constructed us. I, for one, got sicker in the bin, the same way staph
infections spread in a hospital. And as for the claim that the pseudopatients did not act normally, because the normal thing would have been
to go up and cop to the experiment, well, I witnessed a lovely young
girl named Sarah, a Smith College student, meek and quiet and by all
accounts middle of the road, who every day asked gently to be
released, and every day she was denied. So who's to say? In Rosenhan's
study, the staff beat patients and woke them with, "You motherfucking
son of a bitch," and this in private as well as public facilities. I was in a
semipublic facility and no staff ever swore at me. It is true that the psychiatrist in charge of my case spent very little time with me, but actually I remember him in crisp detail, because I liked him so much. His
name was Dr. Su, and he came from another country, and he had a little broom of a mustache, and for some odd reason he often had a base-
ball mitt with him. We used to meet in a small office and he would lean
forward, look at the cuts on my arms, like little lips these cuts were,
because I kept them fresh and open with stolen shards. He would look
at the cuts and say with true feelings, "It's such a shame, Lauren. It's
such a shame you have to hurt yourself."

ROSENHAN'S EXPERIMENT, LIKE, perhaps, any piece of good art, is
prismatic, powerful, and flawed. You can argue with it, as in all of the
above. As in Dr. Su and his unquestioningly kind words: *it's such a shame*.

Nevertheless, there are, it seems to me, some essential truths in
Rosenhan's findings. Labels *do* determine how we view what we
view. Psychiatry *is* a fledgling science, if a science at all, because to this
day it lacks firm knowledge of practically any physiological substrates
to mental illness, and science is based on the body, on *measurable matter*.

Psychiatrists *do* jump to judgment, not all of them but a lot of them, and they can be pompous, probably because they're insecure. In any case, Rosenhan's study did not help this insecurity. The experiment was greeted with outrage, and then, at last, a challenge. "All right," said one hospital, its institutional chest all puffed up. "You think we don't know what we're doing? Here's a dare. In the next three months send as many pseudopatients as you like to our emergency room, and we'll detect them. Go ahead." Here was the gauntlet, thrown down.

Now Rosenhan, built like a boxer, liked a fight. So he said sure. He said in the next three months he would send an undisclosed number of pseudopatients to this particular hospital, and the staff were to judge, in a sort of experimental reversal, not who was insane, but who was sane. One month passed. Two months passed. At the end of three months the hospital staff reported to Rosenhan that they had detected with a high degree of confidence forty-one of Rosenhan's pseudopatients. Rosenhan had, in fact, sent none. Case closed. Match over. Psychiatry hung its head.

WE ONCE BELIEVED in psychiatry as a form of deity; those were the golden days, the 1930s, '40s, '50s, when psychoanalysis came to dominate the discipline with answers for pretty much everything. Your history could heal you; curl up and cry; mania was viewed as "a wish to eat, a wish to be eaten and a wish to go to sleep."

The strange thing was, psychoanalysis, which became one and the same as psychiatry so totally did it dominate the field, cared very little for the actual rigors of diagnosis itself. There was a manual; there still is. It's called the *Diagnostic and Statistical Manual of Mental Disorders*, "*DSM*" for short. The first edition was written in 1952, the second in 1968. The second was in use at the time of the pseudopatients' admission. In *DSM II*, the symptoms for schizophrenia are hazy, based on things like "reaction neurosis" and "attachment difficulties," and, as Rosenhan points out, the more ambiguous the language, the more room for error. It was in this context that prominent psychiatrists such as Adolph Meyer said, "I feel but rarely the urge to go far ahead of the attitude of inquiry to a need of finality which will take care of its own lack of necessity."

Despite such obvious obfuscatory language, psychiatry enjoyed a span of golden years when people believed in it deeply, and spent thousands upon thousands of dollars doing that believing on their backs. "David Rosenhan," says Florence Keller, Rosenhan's close friend, "was really one of the first of that era to announce, 'Guess what guys? The emperor has no clothes.' It might be fair to say he single-handedly dismantled psychiatry, and it's never recovered since." Keller pauses. She is chief psychologist at a Palo Alto inpatient unit. "I mean, look around you. Who's going into psychiatry today? You can't find a psychiatrist for your units anymore. There are no more psychiatrists because psychiatry as a field is pretty much dead, and it won't be revitalized until there's hard-core proof of pathogenesis, of the role neurons and chemistry play in all this. Then, maybe, it will make a comeback."

Spitzer disagrees. He has to. He's a psychiatrist. Spitzer disagrees now—"I think there are a lot of exciting things going on in our field"—and he disagreed in 1973, when the pseudopatient experiment was published. If Rosenhan single-handedly set out to dismantle psychiatry, Spitzer, back then, single-handedly set out to restore it. Together with a group of esteemed colleagues, he took that flimsy little diagnostic and statistical manual, the one that contained enough ambiguity to allow Rosenhan and confederates to get admitted, and gave it a good going-over. He plucked every ephemeral, subjective thing that he could. He scoured it for signs of psychobabble. He tightened diagnostic criteria so that each and every one of them was measurable, and in order to qualify for any diagnosis, there were very strict guidelines about which symptoms, for how long, for how often.

DSM III includes a lot of language like the following: "Patient must display at least four of the following symptoms from criteria A for at least two weeks, three of the following symptoms from criteria B, and one from criteria C." *DSM II* had no such guidelines. There were phrases like, "The chief characteristics of disorders is anxiety, which may be directly felt or expressed or which may be unconsciously and automatically controlled by the utilization of various defense mechanisms." Well, no more. Spitzer argued that the innovation of *DSM III*, two hundred some pages longer than *DSM II*, was "a defense of the medical model as applied to psychiatry." If patients met the extensive criteria, they had an illness. If they didn't, they were well. Ambivalence, potty training, ephemeral, untenable anxieties mattered not a whit.

PSYCHIATRY SINCE ROSENHAN has tried admirably to locate the physiological origins of mental disease—mostly, although not thoroughly, in vain. In the 1980s there was a promising new diagnostic test for depression called the dexamethasone suppression test in which a certain metabolite was isolated in the urine of some sad folks. This discovery was greeted with great enthusiasm. Soon, very soon, we could diagnose depression like we diagnosed anemia: squat over this cup, three amber drops on a prepared slide, and voila! You were or you weren't, and there would be no argument.

That test proved not very foolproof, so it went straight into the trash heap of history. Since then, psychiatrists have tried to develop other tests for diagnoses and failed. Recently the work of Charles Nemeroff, at Emory University, has taken the field a step forward by showing that the brain's hippocampus is some 15 percent smaller in depressed people and that rat pups deprived of their mothers develop a surplus of stress neurotransmitters. This is exciting stuff, but whether it illuminates cause or correlation is unclear.

If all this seems far afield of Rosenhan's study, it isn't. Much of the current-day research is a knowing or unknowing response to Rosenhan's challenge and the inherent anxieties it raises in "soft" scientists. Says Spitzer, "The new classification system of the *DSM* is stringent and scientific." Says Rosenhan, "Nothing underscores the consensual nature of psychiatric disorders more than the recent action by the American Psychiatric Association to delete homosexuality from the *Diagnostic and Statistical Manual on Mental Disorders* (DSM-II, 1968). Whatever one's opinion regarding the nature of homosexuality, the fact that a professional association could vote on whether or not homosexuality should be considered a disorder surely underscores both the differences between psychiatric/mental disorders and the context-susceptibility of psychiatric ones. Changes in informed public attitudes toward homosexuality have brought about corresponding changes in psychiatric perception of it."

To which Spitzer replies, "*All* diagnoses are manmade classifications, so that criticism is ridiculous. I'm telling you, with the new diagnostic system in place, Rosenhan's experiment could never happen today. It would never work. You would not be admitted and in the ER they would diagnose you as deferred." "Deferred," by the way, is a special category that allows clinicians to do just that, officially put off a diagnosis due to lack of information. "No," repeats Spitzer, "that experiment could never be successfully repeated. Not in this day and age."

I decide to try.

MANY THINGS ARE the same. The sky is a poignant blue. The trees are turning, each scarlet leaf like a little hand falling down on our green autumn lawn. In the stores there will soon be plastic pumpkins, and fresh pumpkins children will buy and carve with knives too huge for their hands, opening the circle of the skull, scooping out the innards, so many seeds in there, so many tangled dendritic fibers, and such a moist smell. My own child is too young for pumpkins; she has just turned two, and perhaps because of Rosenhan and all the research he has spawned into "etiology and pathogenesis," I often worry about her brain, which I picture pink-red and rumpled in its casement.

"You're WHAT?" my husband says to me.

"I'm going to try it," I say. "Repeat the experiment exactly as Rosenhan and his confederates did it and see if I get admitted."

"Excuse me," he says, "don't you think you have your family to consider?"

"It'll never work," I say, thinking of Spitzer. "I'll be back in an hour."

"And suppose you're not?"

"Come get me," I say.

He touches his beard, which is getting a little long. He is wearing a geek shirt, closer to plastic than cotton in its contents, with a Rorschach ink splotch from an uncapped pen on the chest pocket. "Come get you? You think they'll believe me? They'll lock me up too," he says, almost hopefully. My husband was born too late to enjoy the sixties, which is something he sorely regrets. He pauses, fingering his beard. A moth flies in through the open window and beats insanely against the lit orb in the center of our dusky room. On the wall the moth's shadow is as big as a bird. We watch the moth. We smell the season. "I'm coming too," he finally says.

NO, HE IS NOT. Someone has to watch the baby. I do my preparations. I don't shower or shave for five days. I call a friend with a renegade streak and ask if I can use her name in lieu of my own, which might be recognized. The plan is to use her name and then have her, later, with her license, get the records so I can see just what has been said. This friend, Lucy, says yes. *She* should probably be locked up. "This is so funny," she says.

I spend a considerable portion of time practicing in front of my mirror. "Thud," I say, and crack up, no pun intended. "I'm, I'm here . . ." —and now I feign a worried expression, crinkled crow's-feet at my eyes—"I'm here because I'm hearing a voice and it's saying thud," and then each time, standing in front of this full-length mirror, smelly and wearing a floppy black velvet hat, I start to laugh.

If I laugh, I'll obviously blow my cover. Then again, if I don't laugh, and if I tell the whole truth about my history save for this one little symptom, as Rosenhan and company did in the original experiment, well, then I might really go the way of the ward. There is one significant difference in my retest setup. None of Rosenhan's folks had any psychiatric history. I, however, have a formidable psychiatric history that includes lots of lockups, although, really, I'm fine now. I decide I'll fake my history, deny any psychiatric involvement in the past, and this lie, I know, is a radical departure from the original protocol. *Thud.*

I kiss the baby good-bye. I kiss my husband goodbye. I haven't showered for five days. My teeth are smeary. I am wearing paint-splattered black leggings and a T-shirt that says, "I hate my generation."

"How do I look?" I say.

"The same," my husband says.

I DRIVE THERE. There is nothing like a road trip in early autumn. Outside the city, the air is fragrant with feed and leaves. A red barn sits serenely in a field beneath a sky with scudding clouds and clear shots of sunlight. To my left a river boils, white with foam from the recent rains. It rears up, smashes itself hysterically onto the flat backs of rocks, like a woman flinging herself down, letting everything loose, alluvium, silt, pebbles from a murky ancient history.

I have chosen a hospital miles out of town with an emergency room set up specifically for psychiatric issues. I have also chosen a hospital with an excellent reputation, so factor that in. It is on a hill. It has a winding drive.

In order to enter the psych ER, you must stand in front of a formidable bank of doors in a bustling white hallway and press a buzzer, at which point a voice over an intercom calls out, "Can I help you?" And you say, "Yes." I say, "Yes."

The doors open. They appear to part without any evidence of human effort to reveal a trio of policemen sitting in the shadows, their silver badges tossing light. On a TV mounted high in one corner, someone shoots a horse—bang—the bullet explodes a star in the fine forehead, blood on black fur.

"Name?" a nurse says, bringing me to a registration desk.

"Lucy Schellman," I say.

"And how do you spell Schellman?" she asks.

I'm a terrible speller and I hadn't counted on this little phonetic hurdle; I do my best. "S-H-E-L-M-E-N," I say.

The nurse writes it down, studying the idiosyncratic spelling. "That's an odd name," she says. "It's plural."

"Well," I say, "it was an Ellis Island thing. It happened at Ellis Island."

She looks up at me and then scribbles something I cannot see on the paper. I'm worried she's going to think I have a delusion that involves Ellis Island so I say, "I've never been to Ellis Island; it's a family story."

"Race," she says.

"Jewish," I say. I wonder if I should have said Protestant. The fact is I am Jewish, but I'm also paranoid—not as a general rule, of course, but at this particular point—and I don't want the Jewish thing used against me.

Of what am I so scared? No one can commit me. Since Rosenhan's study, in part because of Rosenhan's study, commitment laws are far more stringent, and so long as I deny homicidal or suicidal urges, I'm a free woman. "You're a free woman, Lauren," I tell myself, while in the back of my mind is that rushing hysterical river with its buried alluvium and stink—smash smash.

I am in control. I tell this to myself while the rivers rush. I don't feel in control though. At any moment someone might recognize my gig. As soon as I say, "Thud," any well-read psychiatrist could say, "You're a trickster. I know the experiment." I pray the psychiatrists are not well read. I am banking on this.

This emergency room is eerily familiar to me. The nurse takes the name that is not my name and the address that does not exist; I make up a street with a lovely sound to it: Rum Row, 33 Rum Row, a place where pirates grow green things in their gardens. The emergency room is similar because in my past I have been in many that were just like this for undeniably real psychiatric symptoms, but that was a long time ago. Still, the smells bring me back: sweat and fresh cotton and blankness. I feel no sense of triumph, just sadness, for there is real suffering somewhere here, and a horse crumples into hay with a scarlet star on his forehead, and the smell is the smell and the nurse is the nurse; nothing changes.

I am brought to a small room that has a stretcher with black straps attached to it. "Sit," the ER nurse tells me, and then in walks a man, closing the door behind him—click click.

"I'm Mr. Graver," he says, "a clinical nurse specialist, and I'm going to take your pulse."

A hundred beats per minute. "That's a little fast," says Mr. Graver. "I'd say it's on the very high side of normal. But of course, who wouldn't be nervous, given where you are and all. I mean, it's a psych ER. That would make anyone nervous." And he shoots me a kind, soft smile.

"Say," he says, "can I offer you a glass of spring water?" And before I can answer, he's jumped up, disappeared, only to reemerge with a tall flared glass, almost elegant, and a single lemon slice of the palest white-yellow. The lemon slice seems suddenly so beautiful to me, the way it flirts with color but cannot quite assume it, the way its whiteness is tentative, how it comes to the cusp, always.

He hands me the glass. This, also, I had not expected—such kindness, such service. Rosenhan writes about being dehumanized. So far, if anyone's dehumanized here, it's Mr. Graver, who is fast becoming my own personal butler.

I take a sip. "Thank you so much," I say.

"Is there anything else I can get you? Are you hungry?"

"Oh no no," I say. "I'm fine really."

"Well, no offense but you're obviously not fine," says Mr. Graver. "Or you wouldn't be here. So what's going on, Lucy?" he asks.

"I'm hearing a voice," I say.

He writes that down on his intake sheet, nods knowingly.

"And the voice is saying?"

"Thud."

The knowing nod stops. "Thud?" he says. This, after all, is not what psychotic voices usually report. They usually send ominous messages about stars and snakes and tiny hidden microphones.

"Thud," I repeat.

"Is that IT?" he says.

"That's it," I say.

"Did the voice start slowly, or did it just come on?"

"Out of the blue," I say, and I picture, for some reason, a plane falling out of the blue, its nose diving downward, someone screams. I am starting, actually, to feel a little crazy. How hard it is to separate role from reality, a phenomenon social psychologists have long pointed out to us. I rub my temples.

"So when did the voice come on?" Mr. Graver asks.

"Three weeks ago," I say, just as Rosenhan and his confederates reported.

He asks me whether I am eating and sleeping okay, whether there have been any precipitating life stressors, whether I have a history of trauma. I answer a definitive no to all of these things; my appetite is good, sleep normal, my work proceeds as usual.

"Are you sure?" he says.

"Well," I say, "as far as the trauma goes, I guess when I was in the third grade a neighbor named Mr. Blauer fell into his pool and died. I didn't see it, but it was sort of traumatic to hear about."

Mr. Graver chews on his pen. He's thinking hard. I remember Mr. Blauer, an Orthodox Jewish man. He died on Shabbat, his yarmulke floating to the top of the pool, a deep velvet blue, just bobbing there.

"Thud," Mr. Graver says. "Your neighbor went thud into his pool. You're hearing 'thud.' We might be looking at post-traumatic stress disorder. The hallucination could be your memory trying to process the trauma."

"But it really wasn't a big deal," I say. "It was just . . ."

"I'd say," he says, his voice gaining confidence now, "that having a neighbor drown constitutes a traumatic loss. I'm going to get the psychiatrist to evaluate you, but I really suspect we're looking at post-traumatic stress disorder with a rule out of organic brain damage, but the brain damage is way far down the line. I wouldn't worry about that."

He disappears. He is going to get the psychiatrist. My pulse goes from 100 to 150 at least—I can feel it—for surely the psychiatrist will see right through me, or worse, he will wind up being someone I know, from high school, and how will I explain myself?

The psychiatrist enters the little locked room. He is wearing baby-blue scrubs and has no chin. He looks hard at me. I look away. He sits down, and then he sighs. "So you're hearing 'thud,'" he says, scratching the chinless chin. "What can we do for you about that?"

"I came here because I'd like the voice to go away."

"Is the voice coming from inside or outside your head?" he asks.

"Outside."

"Does it ever say anything other than thud, like, maybe, kill someone, or yourself?"

"I don't want to kill anyone or myself," I say.

"What day of the week is it?" he asks.

Now, here I run into another problem. It's actually a holiday weekend, so my sense of time is a little thrown off. Sense of time is one way psychiatrists judge whether a person is normal or abnormal. "It's Saturday," I say, I pray.

He writes something down. "Okay," he says. "So you're experiencing this voice in the absence of ANY OTHER psychiatric symptoms."

"Do I have post-traumatic stress disorder," I ask, "like Mr. Graver suggested?"

"There's a lot we don't know in psychiatry," the doctor says, and suddenly he looks so sad. He rubs the bridge of his nose, his eyes momentarily closed. With his head bowed, I can see a small bald spot, the size of Mr. Blauer's yarmulke on the dome of his scalp, and I want to say, "Hey. It's okay. There's a lot we don't know in the world." But instead I say nothing and the psychiatrist looks sad, and baffled, and then says, "But the voice is bothering you."

"Sort of, yeah."

"I'm going to give you an antipsychotic," he says, and as soon as he says this, the sadness goes away. His voice assumes an authoritative tone; there is something he can do. A pill is so much more than a pill. It's a point of punctuation. It breaks up the blurry long lines between this and that. Stop here. Start here. Begin.

"I'm going to give you Risperdal," he says. "That should quiet the auditory centers in your brain."

"So you think I'm psychotic?" I ask.

"I think you have a touch of psychosis," he says, but I get the feeling he has to say this, now that he's prescribing Risperdal. You can't prescribe an antipsychotic unless your diagnosis supports that. It becomes fairly clear to me that medication drives the decisions, and not the other way around. In Rosenhan's day it was preexisting psychoanalytic schema that determined what was wrong; in our days, it's the preexisting pharmacological schema, the pill. Either way, Rosenhan's point that diagnosis does not reside in the person seems to stand.

"But do I appear psychotic?" I ask.

He looks at me. He looks for a long long time. "A little," he finally says.

"You're kidding me," I say, reaching up to adjust my hat.

"You look," he says, "a little psychotic and quite depressed. And depression can have psychotic features, so I'm going to prescribe you an antidepressant as well."

"I look depressed?" I echo. This actually worries me because depression hits closer to home. I've had it before and, who knows, maybe I'm getting it again, and he sees it before I do. Maybe this experiment is making me depressed, driving me crazy, or maybe I chose to do this experiment as a way of unconsciously reaching out for help. The world is all haze.

He writes out my prescriptions. The entire interview takes less than ten minutes. I am out of there in time to eat Chinese with the real Lucy Schellman, who says, "You should've said, 'thwack' instead of 'thud,' or 'bam bam.' It's even funnier."

Later on, I fill my prescriptions at the all-night pharmacy. And then, in the spirit of experimentation, I take the antipsychotic Risperdal, just one little pill, and I fall into such a deep charcoal sleep that not a sound comes through, and I float, weightless, in another world, seeing vague shapes—trees, rabbits, angels, ships—but as hard as I peer, I can only wonder what is what.

IT'S A LITTLE fun, going into ERs and playing this game, so over the next eight days I do it eight more times, nearly the number of admissions Rosenhan arranged. Each time, of course, I am denied admission—I deny I am a threat and I assure people I am able to do my work and take care of my child—but strangely enough, most times I am given a diagnosis of depression with psychotic features, even though, I am now sure, after a thorough self-inventory and the solicited opinions of my friends and my physician brother, I am really not depressed. As an aside, but an important one, a psychotic depression is never mild; in the *DSM* it is listed in the severe category, accompanied by gross and unmistakable motor and intellectual impairments. "No, you don't seem depressed like that, or at all," my friends and brother tell me. Nevertheless, in the ERs I am seen as such, this despite my denying all symptoms of the disorder—and I am prescribed a total of twenty-five antipsychotics and sixty anti-depressants. At no point does an interview last longer than twelve and a half minutes, although at most places I needed to wait an average of two and a half hours in the waiting rooms. No one ever asks me, beyond a cursory religious-orientation question, about my cultural background; no one asks me if the voice is of the same gender as I; no one gives me a full mental status exam, which includes more detailed and easily administered tests to indicate the gross disorganization of thinking that almost always accompanies psychosis. Everyone, however, takes my pulse.

I CALL BACK Robert Spitzer at Columbia's Institute for Biometrics.

"So what do you predict would happen if a researcher were to repeat the Rosenhan experiment in this day and age?" I ask.

"The researcher wouldn't be admitted," he says.

"But would they be diagnosed? What would the doctors do about that?"

"If they only said what Rosenhan and his confederates said?" he asks.

"Yeah," I say.

"Thud, hollow, or empty as the only symptoms?" he says.

"Yeah," I say.

"They would be given a diagnosis of deferred. That's what I predict would happen, because thud, hollow, and empty as isolated symptoms don't yield enough information."

"Okay," I say. "Let me tell you, I tried this experiment. I actually did it."

"You?" he says, and pauses. "You're kidding me."

I wonder if I hear defensiveness edging into his voice. "And what happened?" he says.

I tell him. I tell him I was not given a deferred diagnosis, but that almost every time I was given a diagnosis of psychotic depression plus a pouch of pills.

"What kind of pills?" he asks.

"Antidepressants, antipsychotics."

"What *kind* of antipsychotics?" he asks.

"Risperdal," I say.

"Well," he says, and I picture him tapping his pen against the side of his skull, "that's a very light antipsychotic you know."

"Light," I say. "The pharmacological rendition of low fat?"

"You have an attitude," he tells me, "like Rosenhan did. You went in with a bias and you found what you were looking for."

"I went in," I say, "with a thud, and from that one word a whole schema was woven and pills were given despite the fact that no one really knows how or why the pills work or really what their safety is."

Spitzer, in his biometrics lab at Columbia, doesn't say anything. I wonder what a biometrics lab really is. It hadn't occurred to me until now to question that title, or question what in the world a psychiatrist was doing there. *Bio metric*. The measurement of life. I see him, now, surrounded by bottles, test tubes, each one filled with a chemical color—Atlantic blue for depression, electric green for mania, plain old happiness a lavender mist.

And still Spitzer is silent. I want to ask, "What exactly is it that you *do*, on a day-to-day basis?" but then, he clears his throat. "I'm disappointed," he says, and I think I hear real defeat, the slumping of shoulders, the pen put down.

"I think," Spitzer says slowly, and there is a raw honesty in his voice now, "I think doctors just don't like to say 'I don't know.' "

"That's true," I say, "and I also think the zeal to prescribe drives diagnosis in our day, much like the zeal to pathologize drove diagnosis in Rosenhan's day, but either way, it does seem to be more a product of fashion, or fad."

I am thinking this: In the 1970s American doctors diagnosed schizophrenia in their patients many times more than British doctors did. Schizophrenia was in vogue this side of the sea. And now, in the twenty-first century, diagnosis of depression has risen dramatically, as have those of post-traumatic stress disorder and attention-deficit hyperactivity disorder. It appears, therefore, that not only do the incidences of certain diagnoses rise and fall depending on public perception, but also the doctors who are giving these labels are still doing so with perhaps too little regard for the *DSM* criteria the field dictates—the criteria to ensure against sloppy guesswork, the criteria out of which grow the treatment plan, the prognosis, the construction of the person's past, the future, folding toward them.

HERE'S WHAT'S DIFFERENT: I was *not* admitted. This is a very significant difference. No one even thought about admitting me. I was
mislabeled but not locked up. Here's another thing that's different:
every single medical professional was nice to me. Rosenhan and his
confederates felt diminished by their diagnoses; I, for whatever reason, was treated with palpable kindness. One psychiatrist touched my
arm. One psychiatrist said, "Look, I know it's scary for you, it must
be, hearing a voice like that, but I really have a feeling that the
Risperdal will take care of this immediately." In his words, I heard my
words, the ones I, as a psychologist, often use with patients: *You have
this. The medication will do this*. And I speak such words not to prome-
nade my power, but just to do something, to bring a balm, somehow.
If we can only fix a mystery in space—Atlantic blue depression, the
haziness of happiness and where on the continuum it lies—if we can
only pin these things down for just the time it takes a neuron to
pulse, well then maybe we could get our hands and heads around
emotion, sculpt it to bring some solace. I believe this is what drove
the psychiatrists I saw, not pigheadedness. One psychiatrist, upon
handing me my prescription, said, "Don't fall through the cracks,
Lucy. We want to see you back here in two days for a follow-up. And
know we're here twenty-four hours a day, for anything you need. I
mean that. ANYTHING."

I felt so guilty then, so touched. "Thank you so much," I said. "I
can't tell you how much your kindness means."

"Be well," he said.

Then he disappeared through the swinging glass doors, and I went
out into the night, where the stars were numerous and accusing, like
cold coins pressed against black tin, and when I turned back to look at
the ER, its windows were blazing, and there was a sharp scream—
human pain in so many forms, and one person's desire to keep another
company, to keep kin, to break bread, and bring lemons in water. This
is the human side of psychiatry, and it should be celebrated.

NOW, THREE WEEKS have passed since my last ER debacle, and out
of the blue, my daughter has developed an obsession with Band-Aids.
Her dolls have many hurts not visible to the human eye. I come home
at the end of the day and find Band-Aids applied to the exposed floor
joists, the kitchen cabinets, the walls, as though the walls themselves
are wounded. Our house hurts, and it is old. In the night it creaks.
My daughter cries. Sometimes she cries for no reason at all, except, I
think, that there are thuds we cannot capture, and when this knowledge dawns on her, she throws herself to the floor and screams, "I just
want to go to the zoo!" I comfort her, then, with Band-Aids. One for
you, one for me, until we are wrapped. She loves to see me slide the
Band-Aids out of their contained cardboard boxes, lift the paper
wrapper to my teeth, tear a slit, and then, moments later, peel back the
plastic layers to reveal the sticky tabs, the plump cotton pad smack in
the tape's taupe center. I lay it on her skin. The Band-Aids soothe,
even though we don't know just what or where her wound is.

ROSENHAN USED THE results of his study to discredit psychiatry as
a medical specialty. But are there not many, many diseases or wounds
in our country's pain clinics, oncology centers, pediatric wards,
where etiology, pathogenesis, even label itself, are hazy? Does the
woman have fibromyalgia or Epstein-Barr virus? Does the person
have epilepsy or a brain tumor too small to be detected? For a time
Rosenhan himself was suffering from a mysterious disease that could
be given many names, depending on the practitioner. What we
knew: He could not speak. He could not breathe without his exte-
rior lung. What we don't know: why, how, the millions of ways a
body goes bad, how to heal or even help.

I'd like very much to help Rosenhan, who as of this writing is still
in a West Coast hospital, paralyzed, even his vocal cords. His friend
Florence Keller says to me, "He's had so many tragedies. Three years
ago his wife Molly died of lung cancer. Then two years ago his
daughter Nina died in a car crash in England. It's been too much for

him." Therefore, I'd like to tell him I redid his study and had a grand old time, because I think it would please him to know this. He is, now, at seventy-nine-years old, at the eve of his life and will soon perform the greatest experiment of all, the stepping over into another world, from where the results are never ever returned.

I would like to go visit Rosenhan. "I don't think now would be a good time," Jack, his son, says. "He still can't talk and he's very tired." But it's not talking I'm after. I'd just like to see him. I picture, right now, a nurse bathing him. I picture what I would bring to him, this essay, perhaps, my copy of his original article, all underlined and starred, to show him how we last, how our words fold into the future. I don't even know the man, but I have an unreasonable fondness for him. I'm partial to jokesters, to adventures, to people in pain. As an ex-mental patient, I'm impressed with anyone who cares to understand the intricacies of that distant world. So I would bring Rosenhan gifts, this essay, an apple, a watch with a face large enough to see the swirl of time, and from my daughter, boxes and boxes of Band-Aids.

In the Unlikely Event of a Water Landing

DARLEY AND LATANÉ'S TRAINING
MANUAL—A FIVE-STAGE APPROACH

In 1964 there occurred a bizarre crime in New York City that cat-alyzed two young psychologists to investigate witness behavior. Although John Darley and Bibb Latané were not Jewish, and never explicitly or implicitly tied their work to Nazi Germany, the results of their experiments in human helping behavior have been used in the service of a particular twentieth-century Western obsession: compre-hending the Holocaust. Darley and Latané devised a series of experi-ments wherein they tested the conditions necessary for people to ignore one another's cries for aid, and the conditions wherein compassion holds sway. In some ways similar to Milgram's experiment on the sur-face, Darley and Latané's work has deeper significant differences. Milgram was looking at obedience to a single authority. Darley and Latané were looking at the opposite: what happens when, in a group crisis, there is no authority to take charge.

1. YOU, THE POTENTIAL HELPER, MUST NOTICE AN EVENT IS OCCURRING

Yesterday I ordered my gas masks, one for the baby, one for me. My husband thinks this is crazy and refuses to be included. It

is September 26, 2001, early fall, lyrical light, the Twin Towers down
but still smoldering. Not long ago I received an email that read:

Warning: Germ Warfare

   Do not open any blue envelope from The Klingerman
Foundation if it comes to you in the mail. These supposed "gifts"
contain small sponges loaded with the Klingerman virus, which
has so far killed twenty Americans . . .

Probably a hoax, but still. In a congressional white paper of far more
authority I recently read how easy it would be to disseminate anthrax:
put the virus in an aerosol bottle, depress the plastic nozzle, and watch
the white mist rise into the air. My husband says, "Let's focus on the
real emergency, which is the decline of civil liberties and the buildup
of troops in the Persian Gulf." But what is the real emergency? The situation in this country is suddenly so ambiguous, difficult to decipher.
Therefore, I have ordered my gas masks—it has come to this—from a
military supply store in Virginia. They arrive at my door in a swift
twenty-four hours, and now I unpack them. I am surprised to see that
beneath the plain cardboard carton, the masks are delicately, even lov-
ingly wrapped, the way some soaps are, in pale green tissue paper that
emits a soft lavender scent. I unwrap the tissue paper, layer after lus-
cious crumpled layer, until I get to the source, until I see the shock of
black rubber, the canisters shaped like snouts, the straps with big buck-
les, and the shield for the eyes. Here they are. Perhaps I have over-
reacted. John M. Darley and Bibb Latané, two psychologists who have
studied the human propensity to deny emergencies, might say no.
"Given the work of Darley and Latané," says psychiatrist Susan Mahler,
"we should now know that the best way to respond to possible crisis is
to err on the side of caution." Now I pick up my gas mask and try it
on. It fits to my face with a loud sucking sound. The gas mask for my
daughter is really unbearable. It is so small, such a dense miniaturization
of horror. I hold it in my hand. I call her over and try to put it on her,
but she backs away, cries out, of course. Help is so hard to give.

2. YOU MUST INTERPRET THE EVENT AS ONE IN WHICH HELP IS NEEDED

In 1964, John Darley and Bibb Latané had little interest in studying styles of crisis management. They were two young psychologists, assistant professors trying to rise through the ranks of academia. Then something happened. I offer the details here not for their obvious shock value, but because they underscore how bizarre were the responses of the thirty-eight witnesses who saw the scene and offered no assistance.

It was March 13, Friday the thirteenth actually, in the year 1964. The early predawn hours in Queens, New York, were cool and moist, breezes carrying the scent of snow. Catherine Genovese, commonly called Kitty, was coming home from her late-night shift at the bar where she worked as a manager. Genovese, twenty-eight, was a slender woman with punkish black hair and a delicate pixy face. Her eyes were gem-green. She drove her car into a parking lot adjacent to her apartment, where she lived alone.

She pulled her car into a space and stepped out. It was 3 A.M. She noticed, just after her first strides toward her building, a hunched figure in the distance, a suspicious-looking man, so she quickly veered right, toward the police call box on the corner.

Catherine Genovese never made it to the call box. The man, later identified as Winston Moseley, screwed a knife deep into her back, and then, when she turned to face him, deep into her gut as well, and there was blood. She screamed. She said, specifically, these words: "Oh my god! He stabbed me! Please help me! Please help me!" Immediately, lights flickered on in the crowded urban neighborhood. Moseley saw them. In his trial he said he saw the lights but he "didn't feel these people were coming down the stairs." Instead of coming down someone yelled, "Let that girl alone," and so Moseley ran off and Catherine, stabbed in several places, dragged herself into the shadow of a bookstore door, where she lay.

The apartment building lights went off then. The street was silent.

Moseley, headed toward his car, heard the silent streets, saw the windows darken, and decided to turn back to finish his job. First, however, he opened his car door and exchanged his stocking cap for a fedora. Then he prowled down the street again, found the woman curled and red and wet, and started to stab where he'd left off, slotting open her body at the throat and genitals. Again, she screamed. And screamed. Minutes passed. Again, lights came on in apartment windows—imagine them—dabs of yellow both Catherine and Winston must have seen, so *there* and yet so absent. Again, Moseley retreated, and now Catherine managed, somehow, to stumble into the hall of her building, where, once again, minutes later, Moseley found her and set out to finish the job. She cried for help and then stopped crying. She moaned. He lifted her skirt, cut off her underclothes, and reported in his trial, "She was menstruating." Then, not knowing whether she was dead or alive, he pulled out his penis, but was unable to achieve an erection. So he lay down on top of her body and had an orgasm then.

This crime occurred over a thirty-five-minute period, between 3:15 and 3:50 A.M. It occurred in a series of three separate attacks, all of them drawn out and punctured with screams for help. People, the witnesses, those who flicked on their lights, could both hear and see. They did nothing. There were thirty-eight witnesses in all, watching from their windows as a woman was stabbed and snuffed. Only when it was over did one of them call the police, but by then she was dead, and the ambulance came to cart her away, and it was four in the morning, and those who saw went back to sleep.

At first, the murder was reported like any other murder of any other working-class woman in Queens. It received a four-line mention in the Metropolitan section of the *New York Times*. Soon, however, the editor of that section, A. M. Rosenthal, who has since written a book called *Thirty-Eight Witnesses: The Kitty Genovese Case*, learned that there had, indeed, been a sizable group of people watching the murder and doing absolutely nothing to help. Thirty-eight people, Rosenthal reports, stood by windows, normal men and

women, who "heard her scream her last half hour away and did nothing, nothing at all to give her succor or even cry alarm."

When the *Times* reported not the murder, but, later, in a series of
separate articles, the bizarre behavior of the bystanders, the nation
went into moral overdrive. Letters from readers poured in. "I feel it is
the duty of *The New York Times* to try to obtain the names of the witnesses involved and to publish the list," one reader wrote. "These
people should be held up for public ridicule since they cannot be
held responsible for their inaction." Another woman, the wife of a
professor wrote, "The implications of their silence—and of the cowardice and indifference it revealed—are staggering. If the laws of
New York State do not prescribe some form of punishment, then we
believe your newspaper should pressure the state legislature for an
amendment to these laws. And since these people do not choose to
recognize their moral responsibility we feel it would be appropriate,
as a form of censure, for the *Times* to publish, preferably on page 1,
the names and addresses of all thirty-seven people involved."

John Darley of New York University and Bibb Latané of
Columbia University, like so many other New Yorkers, read these letters. They, like everyone else, wondered why no one had helped. Was
it apathy, or were there other psychological forces at work? Darley
recalls hunkering down for a while to focus on this singular, quite
current event. Experts from all corners offered hypotheses to explain
why the witnesses did what they did. Renee Claire Fox of Barnard
College's sociology department said the witnesses' behavior was a
product of "affect denial"; they had been, in other words, shocked
into inaction or numbness. Ralph S. Banay hypothesized that TV was
to blame; Americans, he said, are so subject to an endless stream of
violence from the television that they can no longer separate real life
from the screen. The same Dr. Banay also offered up the proverbial
psychoanalytic explanations, the sort of thing that, a decade later,
Rosenhan would so discredit in his pseudopatient study. Banay said,
"They [the witnesses] were deaf, paralyzed, hypnotized with excita-
tion. Persons with mature, well integrated personalities would not

have acted this way." Karl Menninger wrote, "Public apathy is itself a manifestation of aggressiveness."

Darley and Latané were not happy with these explanations, in part because, like Milgram, they were experimental social psychologists who believed less in the power of personality than in the power of situation, and in part because the explanations defied intuitive sense. How does an ordinary person stand by while a young woman is raped and murdered in a crime that stretched out over half an hour? It would have been so easy to seek help, so easy to merely pick up the phone and call in. There was no risk to life or limb for the witnesses. There could have been no damaging legal implications for "getting involved." A portion of the witnesses, we can be sure, had children, and some were in the helping professions, so these people were no strangers to compassion. Something mysterious was at work that night, the night Kitty Genovese was killed, the night spring was careening around the corner of what had been a mild winter, green buds coming early to all the trees, tiny nippled branches, opening up.

3. YOU MUST ASSUME PERSONAL RESPONSIBILITY

Some experiments start with a hypothesis, others with just a question. Milgram, for instance, did not have a hypothesis as to how his subjects would react; he just wanted to see. The same for Rosenhan, who knew something would happen but was not sure what. Darley and Latané, on the other hand, had been following both the crime and the nation's responses, and something didn't fit. They may have thought about other similar incidents, for instance, how, if you're in a building and the fire alarm goes off, and no one seems worried, you too might decide it's okay; or if you're walking down the street, and someone falls, and no one offers to help, you too might keep walking on. For the two psychologists, these mundane examples could have held clues as to what really happened that early spring night, behind the windows.

So they set about constructing an experiment. For obvious reasons they could not replicate a murder, so instead they replicated a seizure. They recruited naïve subjects at New York University (NYU) to participate in what appeared to be a study of student adaptation to urban college life. A student sat in a separate room and spoke into a microphone for two minutes about the challenges at NYU. In a series of separate but audio-wired rooms were tape recorders carrying other students' stories, but the naïve subject didn't know the voices were pre-recorded; the subject believed there were actual neighbors. The instructions were very specific. The naïve subject was to wait in turn while each pre-recorded voice carried on about its troubles. When the subject's turn came, he or she could speak for two minutes. When it was not the subject's turn, the microphone would be off, and the subject was to listen in a sort of tag-team group therapy. In the original experiment, fifty-nine women and thirteen men participated.

The first voice to speak was the pre-recorded voice of the supposedly "epileptic" student. He confessed to the "group" that he was prone to seizures. He spoke with a halting embarrassment. He said the seizures were especially bad when studying for exams. He said New York was a tough place to live and NYU a tough college to master. Then his voice blinked off. Another voice came on. The naïve subject, understandably, thought this was another live person, not a tape recorder whirring in an adjacent room. This voice spoke. It was robust and hearty. Then the naïve subject spoke, and the disembodied voices went round and round, until at last this happened. A seizure started. The naïve subject, of course, could not see the seizure, because he or she was in a separate room, nor could the subject see or hear the reactions of the other supposed subjects, because they were supposedly in separate rooms, although really they were all on a tape next door. The epileptic actor began speaking in a normal voice, which became increasingly scrambled, louder, more insistent, until it reached a crescendo of pleas: "I-er-um-I think I-I need-er-if-if could-er-er somebody er-er-er-er-er-er give me a little-er-give me a little help here because-er-I-er I'm er-er- h-having a-a-a- real problem-er-right now and I-er-if somebody could help me out it would—it would-er-er-er s-s-sure be good . . . because I've got a-a one of the-er-sei———er-er things coming on and-and-and I could really use-er-use some help so if somebody would-er-give me a little h-help-uh-er-er-er-er-er c-could somebody er-er-help- er-uh-uh uh (choking sounds) . . . I'm gonna die-er-er-I'm . . . gonna die-er-help-er-er-seizure-e," and then a final choke, and silence.

Now the one live listener, who of course thought there were at least one, or two, or five other live listeners, could, at any point, get up and go down the hall and ask the experimenter for help. Before leaving the group to their discussion, the experimenter said, in the interest of privacy, he would exempt himself and would get the subject's reactions later, by microphone. However, the examiner had also told the subject to please follow protocol and speak in order.

Darley and Latané had been careful to set up their experimental conditions so they mimicked the Genovese murder. In the Genovese murder, the witnesses had seen the other witnesses but were unable to communicate with them, separated as they were by panes of glass. In this experiment, the witness was able to hear other confederates, but was prevented from seeing or communicating with them due to the separate rooms and the microphones, which were only on when it was a particular "person's" chance to speak. So when the seizure happened, the subject knew others could hear, and also knew he or she could not confer with the others, because the sound system was off.

The concocted seizure in Darley and Latané's experiment lasted for a full six minutes, similar to the Genovese murder, which was not a single stab but a series over the arc of a night. The students had a chance to think, and then to act. Here are the results: very few acted—thirty-one percent to be exact, similar to Milgram's thirty-two to thirty-five percent disobedience rate.

But then it gets more complicated.

Darley and Latané varied the size of the "groups." When a subject believed he or she was in a group of four or more, the subject was unlikely to seek help for the victim. On the other hand, eighty-five percent of subjects who believed they were in a dyad with the epileptic student, with no other bystanders, sought help and did so within the first three minutes of the crisis. Darley and Latané also found that if subjects in any size group did not report the emergency within the first three minutes, they were highly unlikely to do so at any point. So, if you are on a plane when it is hijacked, and you do not act within the first 180 seconds, you are unlikely to act at all. In the case of emergencies, time is never on your side. The longer you wait, the more paralyzed you become. Keep that in mind, and body.

More interesting, however, than the relationship between time and helping behavior is the relationship between group size and helping behavior. You would think that the larger the group, the more emboldened you would become, the less fearful, the more likely you would be to reach out across danger. After all, do we not feel most intimidated alone, in the dark, in the back ally, where no light shines down? Are we not, as animals, most afraid and hesitant when we singularly roam the Pleistocene plains, our predators everywhere, the protective herd dispersed? Latané and Darley's experiment challenges the evolutionary adage of safety in numbers. There is something about a crowd of bystanders that inhibits helping behavior. If you have the unlucky experience of, say, falling off a Ferris wheel at a carnival, you might just be ignored, as Icarus was ignored when he fell through the blue skies while the city teemed beneath him and people turned so casually away. However, if you find yourself in the desert with one other person, and a sandstorm comes, you can count on his help, eighty-five percent of the time, at least according to these findings.

When subjects first heard the phony fit, they became scared. Not one subject displayed the kind of apathy so many hypothesized was at work within the Genovese witnesses. The examiner heard over the microphone subjects saying, "My god, he's having a fit." Others gasped or simply said, "Oh." Some said, "Oh god, what should I do." Subjects were sweaty and trembling when the examiner finally entered the room, after six minutes of seizure had resulted in no call for help. "Is he all right, is he being taken care of?" the bystanders asked, clearly upset. We don't know who they are, but the Genovese witnesses were probably upset too, more frozen in fear or indecision, than in the syrupy urban lassitude people suspected.

When police asked the Genovese witnesses why they did not help, they were at a loss for words. "I didn't want to get involved," they said, but none could really give a coherent report of their internal monologue during those thirty-five minutes of horror. Darley and Latané's subjects also had no idea why they hadn't acted, and these were NYU college students with advanced verbal skills.

Darley and Latané surmise that, far from feeling apathy, subjects "had not decided not to respond. Rather, they were still in a state of indecision and conflict concerning whether to respond or not. The emotional behavior of these nonresponding subjects was a sign of their continuing conflict, a conflict that other subjects resolved by responding."

Because response rates were so consistently tied to group size, Darley and Latané understood what no one else yet had: a phenomenon they came to call "diffusion of responsibility." The more people witnessing an event, the less responsible any one individual feels and, indeed, is, because responsibility is evenly distributed among the crowd. Diffusion of responsibility is further compounded by social etiquette so strong it overrides even life-and-death situations; it would be terrible, after all, to be the only one to make a fuss, and perhaps for nothing as well. Who is to say what's a real and what's a false emergency. "We thought it was a lover's quarrel," said one Genovese witness. "I didn't know exactly what was happening," said several Darley and Latané subjects. I understand this. So, probably, do you. A poorly clad man falls on the street. Is he having a heart attack or did he just trip? Is he a "bum," who is drunk and might cop a feel if you reach out? Supposing he doesn't want your help, your bleeding-heart-liberal help, and he yells at you, and you are shamed in the marketplace, the public square, your politics and tendencies revealed for what they truly are, self-righteous and discriminatory. We doubt ourselves. Do we ever doubt ourselves! Feminist psychologists like Carol Gilligan have written at length about how girls in this culture lose their "voice" and their perceptions once they turn the treacherous corner into adolescence, but experiments like Darley and Latané's suggest this loss of confidence is spurious. We never had it. We are animals cursed with a cortex that has bloomed so big above our snake brains that instinct and it corollary—common sense—get squelched.

4. YOU MUST DECIDE WHAT ACTION TO TAKE

The story is not over. It gets still stranger. We are unlikely to help others, Darley and Latané discovered, more because of the presence of other observers than because of ingrained apathy. What happens, however, when the "other" in need of help is now us? What happens if we find ourselves in a social setting, and in possible danger? Will we act on behalf of our own bodies, at the very least?

The critical phrase here is "possible danger." In clear danger, as in conflagrations, the snake brain uncoils and hisses its directives. But most of life, and most emergencies, reside in some more nuanced place, in twilight times where interpretation is difficult. You feel a lump on your breast: what is it? The house smells like gas, or is it tea? Darley and Latané's work shows us that even something as supposedly stark as a crisis is really malleable narrative; emergencies are not fact, but conscious construction, and this may be why we fail. Our stories, writes psychiatrist Robert Coles in his book *The Call of Stories: Teaching and the Moral Imagination*, give meaning to our lives. The flip side of the story about stories is this: they lead us absurdly astray.

A second experiment conducted by Darley and Latané occurred in a room with a vent. The two psychologists recruited two college students as actors. One college student was the naïve subject. All were to sit in a room together and fill out a questionnaire on college life. Several minutes into the experiment, the psychologists, crouched deep in the building's ductwork, released a form of nonhazardous but entirely convincing smoke through the room's vent. Picture it. At first the smoke wisped up slowly, but not so slowly that it wasn't immediately recognized by the naïve subject. The confederates were instructed to keep filling out their forms, to display no fear. They did. The smoke started pouring like cream, coming faster, heavier, smearing the air and blotting out figures, faces. The smoke was an irritant and caused one to cough. Each time, the subject looked alarmed, looked at the smoke going from wisp to waft, looked at the calm confederates, and then, clearly confused, went back to filling out the questionnaire. A few subjects went over to the vent and inspected it, and then looked at the confederates, who did not seem to care, and then went back to filling out the form. How odd! A few of the subjects asked whether it was unusual, smoke pouring from the vent, but the confederates just shrugged the question off. In the entire experiment, only one subject reported the smoke to the experimenter down the hall within four minutes, only three reported the smoke within the entire experimental period, and the rest not at all. They decided, based on the social cues of the confederates, rather than the material evidence, to interpret the emergency as a harmless failure of the air-conditioning system, and under the spell of that story, they just hacked away until many minutes had passed, and there was a fine white film in their hair and on their lips, and the examiner came in and called it off.

Now, this is funny. This perhaps more than any other experiment shows the pure folly that lives at the heart of human beings; it runs so counter to common sense that we would rather risk our lives than break rank, that we value social etiquette over survival. It puts Emily Post in a whole new place. Manners are not frivolous; they are more forceful than lust, than fear, more primal—that deep preening. When Daley and Latané varied the experiment so the naïve subject was alone in the room, he or she almost always constructed the story of smoke as an emergency and reported it *immediately*.

SOCIAL CUING. The bystander effect. Pluralistic ignorance. The scientific-sounding phrases belie the absurdities they describe. Across the street from me is a beautiful church with emerald moss tamped between the stones. Sometimes I go to this church, for the singing. After Sunday sermons, a collection basket gets passed around. One day, while in the midst of reading the stories of smoke and stabbing, I noticed that the basket, before reaching the first person in the first pew, was already mysteriously plied with a flurry of folded dollar bills. A few weeks later, my sister, a bartender, confessed to me how she "salts" her tip cup at the beginning of each evening with a few fives and tens: "I get a lot more tips that way," she told me. "People think people before them have given. And so they do too." We are driven by imitation.

The Darley and Latané experiments galvanized ethologists to look for similar tendencies in "the wild." Do giraffes, for instance, give a lot of sideway glances before eating from the top of that tree? Do primates depend on the reactions of the pack before figuring out how to proceed? Here's a tale about turkeys: Turkey mothers know to care for their young only when they hear the babies make a very particular chirping sound. If the chicks fail to make that sound, the mother is suboptimally cued, and the chicks die. So strong is the influence of that particular social cue that scientists have been able to attach tape recordings of the chicks' cries onto polecats, the turkey's prime predator, and thus fool the mother into maternity while she is murdered by the wired beast. Ethologists claim social cuing, or fixed patterns of behavior, in animals like birds is instinctual, a part of the brain's paste and circuits, while in humans it exists in another plane, a product of learning. Scientists doubt we have any particular "cuing" gene. I, for one, think we might. I remember being pregnant and how shocked I was that my body could make a baby, a whole separate other, with no conscious instruction from me. How did it know what to do? Cells, it turns out, are engaged in continuous conversation with one another, sending each other chemical cues to then set off a looping cascade of events that, over time, become particular human parts and then the complex whole. The human heart is made when one single cell cues another, and then that cells nudges yet another, and so here is the hand, the tongue, the bones, which are fine white wires eventually sheathed with the silk of flesh. In my case, the cues were all correct and so I have my girl, and she is good.

IN A WORLD where ever complex signals—cellular, chemical, cultural—cascade through us and around us with amazing alacrity, we simply don't have time to sift through all the evidence and take considered action. We would be paralyzed if we did. Thanks to social cuing, and its chemical components, we can build babies and sit silently when silence is called for. Because of social cuing we know when to waltz, when to break bread, when to make love. On the other hand, as Darley and Latané have demonstrated, our interpretive gear, like the turkey mother's, is far from foolproof. Based on the smoke experiments, David Phillips, a sociologist at the University of California, has discovered a particularly bizarre side to the story. Data from the FBI and state law enforcement agencies clearly show that after any well-publicized suicide, the number of fatalities from plane and car crashes rise. Phillips has dubbed this phenomenon "the Werther effect," because after Goethe published *The Sorrows of Young Werther*, about an overwrought fictional character who killed himself for unrequited love, a rash of suicides rippled through eighteenth-century Germany. Phillips examined the suicide statistics in the United States between 1947 and 1968. He found that within two months after every front-page suicide story, an average of fifty-eight more people than usual killed themselves. More disturbing is the data that shows the rise in car and plane wrecks following such well-publicized suicides. Writes Robert Cialdini, a social scientist at the University of Arizona, "I consider this insight brilliant. First [the Werther effect] explains the data beautifully. If these wrecks really are instances of imitative suicide, it makes sense that we should see an increase in the wrecks after suicide stories appear. . . . For several reasons—to protect their reputations, to spare their families the shame and hurt, to allow their dependents to collect on insurance policies—

they do not want to appear to have killed themselves. . . . So purpo-
sively, furtively, they cause the wreck of a car or a plane they are
operating . . . a commercial airline pilot could dip the nose of an air-
craft . . . the driver of a car could suddenly swerve into a tree."

This is hard for me to believe. Imitative single suicides I can
understand, but is the Werther effect, or social cuing, so strong that it
would really cause a rise in commercial plane crashes following, say,
Kurt Cobain's death? Would pilots of planes or trains who have har-
bored suicidal impulses, but never been able to act on them, be so
liberated into imitation by a front-page story that they would bring
down other lives as well? Darley says, in a phone conversation, "Well,
there are certainly a lot of instances of people being cued into suicide, but maybe the plane crash thing is an exaggeration." On the
other hand, Cialdini, one of the most cited living social psychologists,
swears by the accuracy of the data. "Truly frightening," he writes in
his book on influence, "are the number of innocent people who die
in the bargain. . . . I have been sufficiently effected by these statistics
to begin to take note of front page suicide stories and to change my
behavior in the period after their initial appearance. I am especially
cautious behind the wheel of a car. I am reluctant to take extended
trips requiring a lot of air travel. If I must fly during such a period I
purchase substantially more flight insurance than I normally would.
Dr. Phillips has done us a service by demonstrating the odds for survival when we travel change measurably for a time following the
publication of certain kinds of front page stories. It would seem only
prudent to play those odds."

How, I wonder, is Cialdini planning to play the odds now that
suicide stories have been in the front page for well over a month, and
show no signs of dispersing? He must be hiding in a hand-built
bunker somewhere. I call him up. A woman named Bobette tells me
he's in Germany and won't be back for quite some time. "Is he afraid
to fly back?" I ask her. "Oh," she says, "these are scary, scary times. Of
course Dr. Cialdini knows there will be more attacks, the principle of
cuing makes it inevitable."

"Would he think it's strange that I purchased a gas mask?" I ask her.

"Of course not," she says. "But he would also say to you that in light of what happened, you have to live your life and live it better."

"Does he have a gas mask?" I ask.

She doesn't answer.

IT ALL APPEARS grim. These are glorious autumn days, a sudden Indian summer, the air smelling of warmed fruit pulp from the apple trees, where every orb is flush. I pick apples with my daughter, holding her high in my arms so she can pluck the fruit from its tentative tether on the tree, hold it in her hand, bite it open, her tiny teeth puncturing the skin—sweet juice and bees. The bees drive us inside. The mosquitoes are having a renaissance, their nosy noses burrowing into our exposed skin, and welts swell. I spray DEET and other chemical things, but the bugs are of some strange, strong strain; they go on humming, higher and higher. These are glorious days but for the bugs and the DEET and the dead mouse I find beneath the stove, just its furred husk and the debris of decay here and there—its last breath was long ago.

Who could feel happy in such times? The Dow slides, the dogs are restless, and then the Cialdinis and Darleys and Werthers of the world are claiming how bad builds on bad, stupidity begets stupidity, publicity drives the day until we are all wrapped in a media movie where the reel won't stop. What hope for us is there, really? You read about Milgram and feel badly. You read of Skinner and feel confused. You read Rosenhan's findings and feel our folly, but you read these experiments and you feel something far more lethal than even the lethal shocks: You feel contagion. You feel how we infect one another with our immobility, our diffusions, our confusions. Is there a gas mask for that?

5. YOU MUST THEN TAKE ACTION

His name is Arthur Beaman and he's not famous, although maybe he should be. Beaman, a social scientist at the University of Montana, made an interesting discovery that he and his coauthors reported in 1979 in *The Personality and Social Psychology Bulletin*. I went in search of the actual study and found it in the expected, dusty library tome, the paper extremely short, dense with correlation coefficients and two-tailed tests and quantitative symbols like $\wedge$, $\#$, $+$, $-$, and $=$, which may be why no one knows of their findings. An experiment, in order to break beyond the container of science, needs to have some poetry in its presentation, some smoke, some shock, a verbal trill or two.

But let's try to shuck our way through Beaman's weighty writing style and try to find the fruits of the work, which are this: if you educate a group of people about the concepts of social cuing, pluralistic ignorance, the bystander effect, then you in some sense inoculate them against these behaviors in the future. Thus, what you have just read, these twenty or some odd pages, these eight thousand words, is as much a piece of pedagogy as it is description or report. According to Beaman's findings, now that you know how prone you are to miss the crucial beat, you are far less likely to fall victim to interpretative mishaps. It might even be fair to say that I bought one kind of gas mask and wove another, with words, to protect against a different sort of threat.

Beaman took a group of college students. He showed them films of Darley and Latané's seizure and smoke experiments, films that clearly articulated for the viewer what Darley and Latané developed as the five stages of helping behavior:

1. You, the potential helper, must notice an event is occurring.
2. You must interpret the event as one in which help is needed.
3. You must assume personal responsibility.
4. You must decide what action to take.
5. You must then take action.

The students who saw the films and learned the necessary stages that culminated in good citizenship were nearly twice as likely to offer help than those without such education. Students so exposed, or inoculated, held out their hands to ladies who slipped on the ice, to people in fender benders, to the epileptic with a sudden seizure— accidents are everywhere, these water landings. One has to wonder why, if education is so effective in changing the rates of helping behavior and promoting effective crisis management, it isn't a permanent part of our national pedagogy. It would be so easy to slip it into the mandatory course on first aid, or CPR certification, or even public service billboards. Five simple things you need to do. Especially now, as our nation appears to be rounding some critical bend, we need to know. If the bus blows up, we need to know.

Now that I know, I feel I am better prepared. We are instructed by politicians to go about our business, but to be alert for strange signs. I decide it is time, and go downtown. One week has passed since this country's largest terrorist attack, and there are rumblings that another one is coming this weekend. "You must go about your business," everyone says, and, really, what else can you do? So I go downtown, despite the fact that crowds now put me on edge. Boston in the autumn is lovely, gilded with warm sunlight, the grass in the city graveyard a teal Atlantic green. The city, however, is oddly quiet, and what sounds there are have a heightened significance, everything saturated with meaning. A child screams as his swing arcs high into the air. A newspaper left on a park bench twitches in the wind. Up on Beacon Hill I see my favorite Boston site, the one I have loved since I was a little girl, the statehouse's gold dome, beneath which I used to imagine all manner of strange winged creatures convened, and I was right. Now, the politicians are nowhere to be seen, but what I do find, by the iron gate, is a bad-looking boy, of about eighteen, with an aggressively bald head sporting an etched blue cross. He is in his uniform, those lace-up black boots, the Aryan hair on his arms giving off a glint. He looks very suspicious. A knife handle, or what appears to be a knife handle, juts from his pocket. He is hunched in a corner, clearly trying not to be seen, and sketching something fast—a route into the statehouse, a route out, who knows. We heard, just the other day, that sketches of embassies and airports, along with crop-dusting manuals, were plucked from dens in Detroit. The boy is muttering something to himself. He says, "Air." He says, "Swallow." Despite all I have read and studied about being a bystander, I am still not at all sure what to do. The safest thing would be to report him, but how really ridiculous that would be! This is the problem with education. Step number one. You have to recognize that help is needed. In a world more shadow than sun, this is not easy to do. Instead, I go a little closer to the bad-looking boy, the neo-Nazi, or someone's kind rebellious son, and then all of a sudden, sensing my prying presence, he whips his head toward me, and I see his eyes are a cut-glass green, in liquid.

I smile at him, a little shaky smile.

He ponders me up and down and then smiles back.

We say not a word, but he knows what I am thinking: the fast, furious sketches, the military crouch, the baldness, the badness, every-where.

The pencil he is using is short, with a thick charcoal nose, and it gives off lush fuzzy lines of design.

This I know because the boy now, understanding my thoughts (that we can hear each other sometimes without any words exchanged, yet at other times not even a scream helps us make sense—how odd this is, how confusing the multiple languages of life), turns his sketch pad toward me so I can see what he is up to, and on it there are no exit or egress routes or anything suspicious. There is just a drawing of the single tree on the statehouse lawn, its leaves in the picture so intri-cately rendered, so multiply veined. And then I see it, how inside every leaf there is the slightest suggestion of a human face, life at the very beginning or at the very end. It is not clear. But the picture is lovely. Now the boy rips it from his sketch pad and gives it to me. I take it home. I hang it here, above my desk, and sometimes as I type these words, I stop to stare into the branches where those half-born human faces hover, the leaves' webwork so loaded with message and mystery and multiple meanings. I know the five stages, and still the story swerves.

Quieting the Mind

THE EXPERIMENTS OF
LEON FESTINGER

Leon Festinger was born May 8, 1919, to parents of Russian descent. He studied psychology at City College of New York, and then pursued a graduate degree at the University of Iowa, where he was mentored by the well-known German psychologist Kurt Lewin. Eventually Lewin and Festinger moved to MIT, and in 1957, Festinger published his best-known work, A Theory of Cognitive Dissonance, *in which he writes, "The psychological opposition of irreconcilable ideas (cognitions) held simultaneously by one individual, created a motivating force that would lead, under proper conditions, to the adjustment of one's belief to fit one's behavior—instead of changing one's behavior to fit one's belief (the sequence conventionally assumed)."*

Festinger was a rigorous researcher and experimentalist. In order to test his theory of "irreconcilable ideas," better known now as "cognitive dissonance," he constructed a series of small, strategically complex, and surprising experiments that were the first of their kind to illuminate the rationalizing machinations of the human mind.

Her name was Marion Keech. His name was Dr. Armstrong. They lived in Lake City, Minneapolis, a cold windy place where the winters were all white, where snow fell from smeared clouds, each flake like a little message, a design to be decoded.

And in this vast landscape Marion Keech, an ordinary housewife, received one day a letter from a being named Sananda. It came not in an envelope, but in a high-density vibration that caused her hand to shiver across the notebook page, and the words said this: "The upris-ing of the Atlantic bottom will submerge the land of the Atlantic seaboard; France will sink. . . . Russia will become one great sea . . . a great wave rushes into the Rocky Mountains . . . for the purpose of purifying it of the earthlings, and creating the new order." The mes-sages, after that, came to Marion Keech fast and furious. They warned of an impending flood, on midnight, December 21. But all who believed in a god named Sananda would be saved.

Marion Keech believed. Dr. Armstrong, a physician who held a prestigious post at a nearby college, and who met Mrs. Keech at a fly-ing saucer club, also came to believe. So did Bertha and Don and Andrew and quite a few others. They became a cult and made their preparations. It was November and nights fell fast, darkness slamming down, as tactile as tar. The group put out a single press release to a news agency, but other than that they shunned publicity, for only a few were chosen by Sananda, and to spread panic seemed cruel. Nevertheless, word got out, and midwesterners from Idaho to Iowa were curious, bemused. Leon Festinger, a thirty-one-year-old psy-chologist at the nearby University of Minnesota, heard about the cult and decided to infiltrate it. What would happen, he wondered, when midnight on December 21 came around and no spaceship landed, no rains came? Would the group lose faith? How do human beings react, Festinger wanted to know, when prophecy fails?

Festinger organized a few cohorts to go under cover, posing as believers and gaining entry into the cult. They observed the mem-bers' intense preparation for the solstice event. Kitty, a cult member, quit her job, sold her home, and left with her infant daughter to take up residence with Mrs. Keech. Dr. Armstrong, too, was so convinced of the imminent flood that he jeopardized his job as a doctor by preaching in the examining room, and so was summarily fired, left high and dry with a simple stethoscope and a reflex hammer—it didn't matter. Worldly goods, prestigious titles, they were irrelevant to the savior Sananda, and to the new planet where these people were going, far, far from here, invisible in the sky except for an occasional flash of light, like a red rent opening up and then sucked back into blackness.

On the eve of the actual flood, believers and the incognito researchers gathered in Marion Keech's living room for instructions, which came in the form of automatic writings and phone calls from spacemen posing as people playing practical jokes, but who really had coded messages to deliver. For instance, one caller said, "Hey, there's a flood in my bathroom, wanna come over and celebrate?" and this was so obviously a secret signal from Sananda's special assistant that the group expressed delight. A message came in the form of a mysterious piece of tin found in the weave of the living room rug. The tin was a warning that group members must remove all metal from their clothing before entering the spaceship, which would park at the street curb in just ten more minutes! Frantically, the women began tearing the eyelets and clasps from their brassieres; the men plucked out buttons; one of the researchers, who had a metal zipper in his pants, was hastily removed to a bedroom, where Dr. Armstrong, in a surge of panic, breathing heavily and eyeing the clock, cut out the crotch so there was a great gash where the midwestern wind seeped through.

It was 11:50 P.M. then, ten minutes to touch down. People had quit jobs, sold homes, alienated family members—they were heavily invested. The two clocks in Mrs. Keech's house clicked loudly, first a sound as steady as a heart and then a sound more and more ominous as midnight came, and went. Click click went the clock, the tsking of a tongue, not a drop falling from the frozen sky, the land outside as parched as Canaan, as dense in its darkness. Some cult members, visibly shocked, wept into their hands. Others just lay on couches, staring blankly into the empty air. Still others peered between the curtains at the great spotlights sweeping the yard, spotlights not from a spaceship, as they had so hoped, but from news stations, come to have some fun.

PRIOR TO THE Great Event, the cult members had eschewed almost all publicity, save for a single warning in a press release, this despite the fact that news of the coming catastrophe had spread across the Midwest and members received many requests to speak on camera. Now, however, as the night wore on and the sky stayed dry, Festinger observed a strange thing starting to happen. The cult members swept open the curtains to the camera crews. They invited them in, gallantly, manically, offering them tea and cookies. Marion Keech, sitting in the living room chair, received an urgent message from a high-density being that said, once she had scribbled it out, to contact as many media stations as possible and report that the flood did not come because "the little group sitting all night long had spread so much light that god saved the world from destruction." Mrs. Keech called ABC, CBS, and the *New York Times*, and this was a complete about-face; now, she wanted to talk. Around 4 A.M. a newsman phoned. He had phoned just a few days earlier and asked, with much sarcasm, if Mrs. Keech would like to come on his show and celebrate an end-of-the-world party, to which she had responded by slamming down the receiver, heated, furious. Now, when he called back to bait her over the failure of the prophecy, she said, "Come right out! This minute!" Cult members phoned *Life*, *Time*, and *Newsweek*, and in the ensuing days gave dozens of interviews to reporters, all in an attempt to convince the public that their actions and beliefs were not in vain. They greeted news of a December 21 earthquake in Italy with joy and dancing. "The earth's skin [is] slipping."

Dissonance. A million rationalizations, fault lines in the earth, in the brain, and all sorts of ways to sew them up. We can only imagine

Festinger's fun, and also his sorrow, as he saw the way people leap to lies, overlook, sift through, sort out, tamp down. To Festinger, the dramatic increase in public proselytizing following such an obvious failure was completely counterintuitive and became the basis for a theory and a set of experiments he designed to test the theory: cognitive dissonance. What Festinger found, in his infiltration of the cult and in his readings of the history, was that it is precisely when a belief is disconfirmed that religious groups begin to proselytize, a sort of desperate defense mechanism. The disjunction between what one believes and the factual evidence is highly uncomfortable, like scratching on slate. Soothing can come only if more and more people sign onto the spaceship, so to speak, because if we are all flying this thing together, then surely we must be right.

IT SEEMS FITTING that a man like Festinger would discover cognitive dissonance. Festinger had a grumpy manner and wherever he went, he grated.

Elliot Aronson was one of Festinger's graduate students way back in the 1950s, when behaviorism still dominated the day. "Festinger was an ugly little man," says Aronson, "and most students were so afraid of him they wouldn't take his seminars. But he had a certain warmth about him. He was also the only genius I have ever met."

After the cult study, Festinger and his colleagues set out to explore cognitive dissonance in all its dimensions. In one experiment, they paid some people twenty dollars to lie and other people only one dollar to lie. What they found is that those who had lied for one dollar were far more likely to claim, after the fact, that they really believed the lie, than those who'd earned the twenty dollars. Why would that be? Festinger hypothesized that it is much harder to justify lying for a dollar; you are a good, smart person, after all, and good, smart people don't do bad things for *no real reason*. Therefore, because you can't take back the lie, and you've already pocketed the measly money, you bring your beliefs into alignment with your actions, so as to reduce the dissonance between your self-concept and your questionable behavior. However, those folks who were paid twenty dollars to lie, they didn't change their beliefs; in effect, they said, "Yeah, I lied, I didn't believe a word of what I said, but I got paid well." The twenty-dollar subjects experienced less dissonance; they could find a compelling justification for their fibs, and that justification had double digits and a crisp snap.

Dissonance theory took American psychology by storm. "By storm," says Aronson. "It was THE THING. It was so elegant. It offered such elegant explanations for such mysterious behavior." Dissonance theory explained, for instance, the long baffling fact that during the Korean War, the Chinese had been eerily efficient at getting American POWs to espouse communism. The Chinese did this, not through torture or through big gilded bribes, but merely by offering the prisoners a bit of rice or candies for writing an anti-American essay. Subsequent to writing the essay and getting the prize, many soldiers came to convert to communism. This is odd, especially because we tend to believe brainwashing is accomplished through a series of fierce scrubbings with caustic soap, or piles of glittering prizes. But dissonance theory predicts that the *more paltry the reward* for engaging in behavior that is inconsistent with one's beliefs, the more likely the person is to change his or her beliefs. It makes a kind of crooked sense. If you sell yourself for a piece of candy, or a single cigarette, or a scatter of rice, you had better come up with some convincing reason why you did this, lest you feel you are, just simply, a schmuck. If you can't take back the essay, or the lie, then you change your beliefs so they no longer scrape and scratch and you are saved from schmuckdem. The Chinese were masters at intuitively understanding cognitive dissonance; they held tiny trinkets in their palms and, from the force of these, got grown men to open and change their very moldable minds.

Festinger and his students discovered several different forms of dissonance. What he observed in the cult, he called the Belief/ Disconfirmation Paradigm. What he observed with the lying for money, he called the Insufficient Rewards Paradigm. Another type, the Induced Compliance Paradigm, is best illustrated by an experiment in which college freshman, attempting to get into a fraternity, went through severe or mild hazing rites. Those who went through the severe hazing rites claimed much more allegiance to the group than those who hadn't. With these simple experiments, Festinger turned all of psychology on its head. He turned Skinner hard on his head. After all, Skinner had said rewards reinforce and punishment extinguishes, but this little man Leon, this shedding sloppy scholar, had, with a few swift strokes, shown behaviorism was wrong. Wrong! We are driven by punishment and paltriness; at the center of the human universe sits not a big chunk of cheese but a tiny scrap of something, and there are no pigeons, no rats, no boxes. There are only human beings motivated by minds that must be made comfortable. Skinner took mentalism right out of the picture, leaving us with just our mechanistic conditioned responses, and then along came Leon, cranky, acerbic Leon, and he handed us back our complex brains, and he said, in effect, *human behavior cannot be explained by reward theory alone. Human beings THINK. They engage in the most amazing mental gymnastics, all just to justify their hypocrisy.*

Festinger did not have a happy view of human nature. He smoked two packs of unfiltered Camels a day and died of liver cancer at age sixty-nine. It is no surprise that Festinger's tastes ran to the existentialists: Sartre with his hollowed universe; Camus, who believed man spends his entire life trying to convince himself that he is not absurd. Man, thought Festinger, was not a rational being, but a rationalizing being. He lived with his second wife, Trudy, in a village apartment, where, I imagine, his cigarette glittered orange in the low light, where books lined the study walls, where a single mezuzah was pinned to the door frame, a tiny silver scroll, inside, some story.

I KNOW A story. It's one Festinger would probably like. Not far from me, in the small city of Worcester, Massachusetts, lives a walking talking epitome of rationalization. Her name is Linda Santo. Fifteen years ago, her three-year-old daughter, Audrey, fell into the family swimming pool and was discovered floating face down, in the deep end. She was rescued and resuscitated, but her brain had been blotted out, just a few electrical squiggles at the base, where the heartbeat is controlled, where the sweat glands send their signals, that sort of thing. The base.

Fifteen years ago Linda Santo—about whom I have read many articles and who has appeared many times on local television as half-hero, half-oddity—fifteen years ago she brought her baby Audrey home, hooked up to life support, a tracheotomy hole drilled in her throat, and she bathed the child and turned her ten times a day so her skin stayed rosy and not a single bedsore puckered, and she propped her girl's head on white satin pillows, shaped like hearts, and she surrounded her girl with religious relics, because Linda's Catholic faith had always been strong. Audrey lay in bed while on a ledge above her, Jesus held his heart and Mary looked on in an attitude of ecstasy—tiny statues, huge statues, stigmata on porcelain palms, the blood beet-red and dried.

A few months after the accident, according to various newspaper articles, her husband left her. Now she had no money. She had three other children. The religious relics around Audrey's bedside began to move. They would, of their own accord, turn and face the tabernacle. Real blood oozed out of Christ's cracked wounds. Strange oils began to track the faces of the saints. And Audrey herself, well, her eyes opened and ticked back and forth, back and forth, and every Lent she screamed in pain, and then fell into a deep, deep sleep, on Easter.

People began to come to Audrey, people with multiple sclerosis and brain tumors and heart disease and depression. They began to come and take home with them some of the miraculous holy oils dripping from the relics. In the Santo household, miracles occurred fast, one after the other, as the ill pilgrims kneeling by the girl's bedside went from blindness to sight, as Audrey herself began to bleed from every orifice as though she were suffering the sins of the whole world. Linda claims that she was not mystified. She knew her daughter was a saint, that God had chosen Audrey to be a victim soul, to take on the pains of other people so that they could be healed. Linda had seen it with her own eyes. Furthermore, the date of Audrey's drowning was August 9, at 11:02 in the morning, and only forty years before that, on August 9, at 11:02 in the morning, the United States had dropped the bomb on Nagasaki. One incident, according to Linda, had shamed all of humankind; now this incident was to redeem it.

The Santo story is classic Festinger, the way the mother's mind twists to turn a terrible tragedy into something of salvage, consonance achieved through a series of rapid rationalizations. How, I wonder, would a person who so embodies Festinger's theory actually react to its explication?

LINDA'S VOICE ON the phone is hoarse and slow; something in its sound surprises me. I'm a writer, I tell her. I've seen her on TV. I'm exploring belief and faith and a man named Festinger—

"What is it you want to know?" Linda asks. Perhaps what I hear is simply celebrity fatigue. One more interview in the thousands she's given, but she'll do it again if she has to—for Audrey, to spread the word.

"If you're a journalist who wants to come photograph my girl, I can tell you right now, you have to ask the church—"

"No," I say. "I want to know if you know of a man named Festinger, and his experiments . . . "

"Festinger," she says, cackling, and then she doesn't say anything else.

"There was once this group," I say, "and they believed a savior would come for them on December 21, and Festinger, a psychologist, studied what happened when December 21 came around and they weren't saved."

There's a long pause on the phone. What I'm doing seems suddenly cruel. *When they weren't saved.* In the background I can hear mysterious sounds, a knocking, the screech of a crow flying skyward.

"Festinger," Linda says. "Is that a Jewish name?"

"Absolutely," I say.

"Jewish people ask good questions," she says.

"And Catholics?" I say.

"We can question. Faith in our God," Linda says. "It isn't always absolute. Even if you have a direct email to Jesus, the line goes down sometime." She stops speaking; I can hear something clotted in her voice.

"For you?" I say. "Has the line gone down?"

"I have breast cancer," Linda continues. "I've had it for the last seven years. I just found out I'm in my fifth recurrence, and I'll tell you, today I'm tired."

I lift my hand to my own chest, which has its own chiseled spots from multiple biopsies, the cells beneath the skin squirming recklessly.

"Can Audrey, would you ask her to heal—"

Linda interrupts me. "You want to know the truth?" she says, her voice sharp. "Do you and Festinger want to know what's what? On a bad day, a day like today, I doubt whether suffering has meaning. Write that down," she says.

WHAT FESTINGER WROTE: the seeking of consonance is a "drive state." We spend our lives paying attention only to information that is consonant with our beliefs, we surround ourselves with people who will support our beliefs, and we ignore contradictory information that might cause us to question what we have built.

And yet, Linda Santo points to the flaws in this theory, and the experiments designed to test it. Somewhere, not far from me, right this minute, sits a woman in semidarkness, and she can cling to nothing. Her cancer, and her daughter's failure to heal it, are dissonant with her prevailing paradigm, but instead of seeking consonance through rationalization, as Festinger, and I, predicted, Linda seems to be in some suspended place, where beliefs break up and form new patterns we cannot yet quite see. Who knows what new shapes of faith might emerge from Linda's willingness to withhold rationalization for real revision? Festinger never explored this phenomenon—how dissonance leads to doubt and doubt leads to light. Nor does he explore why some people choose rationalization as a strategy, and others choose revision. I think about Linda. I think about others. What allowed Isaac Newton to exchange the palm of god for gravity, or Columbus to come away with a curved rimless world? Throughout all of history there have been examples of people who, instead of clapping their hands over their ears, pushed into dissonance, willing to hear what might emerge. Festinger, actually, is one of those people. His ideas and experiments were highly dissonant with the Skinnerian wisdom of his day. And he pursued it. Why?

"Dissonance," says Elliot Aronson, leading dissonance researcher and Professor Emeritus at University of California, Santa Cruz, "dissonance is really not about looking at how people change. The theory just didn't concern itself with that."

"Don't you think that's a shortcoming to the theory?" I ask. "Understanding why some people resolve dissonance creatively, while others duck and cover, could illuminate a lot."

Aronson pauses. "In Jonestown," he says, "nine hundred people killed themselves as a way of resolving dissonance. A few people didn't kill themselves, that's true, but nine hundred did and that's remarkable. That's what the theory focuses on, the vast, vast majority who hang onto their beliefs even until death."

I am not a great psychologist, like Leon, but after talking to Linda, I have an opinion, and it is this: Dissonance theory falls a little short because it accounts only for the way we reify narratives, and not for the way we revise them. In doing so, dissonance is presented as a unidimensional state, a kind of senseless clanging, when, in fact, the sound of something out of tune can also sharpen our ears and seed new songs.

"Don't you think," I say to Aronson, "that in failing to explore the people who respond to dissonance by creating new paradigms to incorporate new information, the theory misses an important aspect of the human experience?" Why, I ask Aronson, does he think some people rationalize, while others more deeply revise? And more importantly, how do those people in the midst of a major paradigm shift deal with the long days, weeks, months of grating, and what can their ability to tolerate such sounds and sensations teach us about how we might do the same, in search of a wider life? "Has anyone studied these types of people?" I ask.

"That's human growth stuff," Aronson says to me. "I would speculate that the types of people who respond to dissonance with honest introspection would have high, well-grounded self-esteem, or they might also have really low self-esteem, so they've got nothing to lose by saying, 'Geez, I guess everything I invested in really doesn't make much sense; I'm really a jerk.'"

"But have you actually done any experiments where you've looked at who these people are, and how they experience the dissonance? Do you have any data?"

"We don't have any data," Aronson says, "because we don't have people. People like you're talking about are few and far between."

I GO TO visit Linda. Worcester, Massachusetts, is about an hour from my home. An old sooty mill city, it houses hollowed-out factories and decrepit stores. If Linda were to revise her narrative of the saint daughter, of the suffering in all its supreme sense, what would she have left? What new narrative could possibly bring comfort in her situation? I've been asking how dissonance leads one deeper, but depth is dangerous; it's where the octopi live, where the sharp shark teeth are buried.

The Santo home is on a cheery side street. The modest ranch house is painted the color of flesh, each window sporting a pair of plastic shutters. I ring the doorbell, which chimes merrily inside the house, and then a voice calls out, "Meet me next door, in the chapel."

I assume that was Linda's voice. For a moment I press my ear to the door and hear guttural breathing sounds, the clanging of a bed-pan—Audrey. She is eighteen now. She bleeds monthly. Her mother is dying.

I find the chapel in the garage. It is damp and everywhere I look are statues dripping oil with tiny Dixie cups tied to their chins to catch the royal runoff. A woman comes in with strangely unfocused eyes, in her hands a container loaded with cotton balls. "My name's Ruby," she says, "I volunteer here." She presses the cotton balls to the wet saints and then drops each swab into a Ziplock bag. "People order these," she says. "It's holy oil. It can cure just about anything."

I want to ask Ruby how she justifies the startling fact that the holy oil cannot cure its keeper, Linda, mother of the saint, but I don't. I watch Ruby walk around the chapel dabbing up oil with swabs of cotton and then I say—I just cannot help myself—"How do you know someone doesn't come out here at night and put oil on these statues when you can't see?"

She spins to look at me.

"Like who?" she says.

I shrug.

"I've seen it myself," she says. "I was standing by Audrey's bed the other day and one of the religious relics just started gushing oil, *hemorrhaging* oil, so I know."

The door to the chapel opens, a wedge of bright afternoon sunlight in the dim damp space, and in steps Linda. Her hair is brittle, purposefully curled, and she wears large hoop earrings set against a pale lined face.

"Thank you for agreeing to see me," I say. "Thank you for agreeing to discuss your faith with me in this difficult situation."

Linda shrugs. She sits, one leg swinging back and forth, like a child. "My faith," she says, "my faith started when I was in utero. If I didn't have my faith, I'd be a turnip in a padded cell right now."

"What does your faith mean?" I ask her.

"It means," she says, "it means I have to turn things over to God, which is hard, because I'm short and so are you—we're both Napoleonic types—so it's hard." She cackles, this Linda.

I study her face. There is, to be sure, glitter in her eyes, but behind the glitter, a flat pool of fear.

"Well," I say, "you told me over the phone that maybe you were starting to question your faith, question your understanding that your daughter is a saint, that sort of thing . . ." I trail off.

Linda raises her eyebrows, each one tweezed into a perfect peak. "I didn't put it quite like that," she says.

"You told me you were having some doubts, and I wanted to talk about how you—"

"Those were inconsequential. Essentially, I have no doubts." She sounds angry.

"Oh," I say.

"Listen," she says. "I know who I am and I know who my daughter is. Audrey, she has a direct email line to God. Audrey goes to God with requests from sick people, and God takes away the sickness. It's not Audrey who takes away the sickness," Linda says. "It's God, but Audrey has his fax number, if you see what I mean."

I nod.

"Let me tell you," Linda continues. "Once we had a chemo patient come to see Audrey. A few days later Audrey developed an intense red rash, like she was on fire. Where could this rash have come from? We called a dermatologist to the house. He was Jewish, but a very nice man. And he says, 'This is a rash that a chemo patient gets,' and when we contacted the chemo patient, her rash was gone. You see," says Linda, "Audrey took the patient's painful rash, that's what my daughter does."

Linda goes on to tell me another story, about a woman with ovarian cancer who, after visiting Audrey, had a sonogram that showed a shadowy angel on her ovaries and all the cancer gone. I don't believe these things. Linda goes over to the tabernacle, lifts up a covered cup, and shows me what's inside. Oil, and floating within the oil, a bead of blood. "We've had this oil analyzed," she says, "by over thirty different chemists. And it's of no variety known to mankind."

"Why," I say softly, "then why, Linda, can't the oil or Audrey's intercessions to God, why can't they heal you?"

Linda is quiet. She is quiet for a long time. I see her eyes move back into her head, into some very private place I cannot get to. I don't know where she is, if she has died a small death, if she is sitting in senselessness, if she's making new sense—the weaving wheels are turning and turning. She looks up at the ceiling. Ruby, who is still in the chapel, looks up at the ceiling too. Then at long last Linda says, "It's spread to the bone."

"There goes Jesus," Ruby says, and points to a relic in front of us, and sure enough, I see it: Jesus is weeping grease, two tiny drops sliding down his figurined face, collecting in the creases of his neck.

I stare at this phenomenon. I have my own little fit of cognitive dissonance right there: (1) I do not believe in the Catholic faith or its rather cheesy-looking miracles, but (2) that statue is oozing, although of course it could be butter someone put on it that's now melting, but how am I to know for sure? I observe my own mind, to see if it leaps to cognitive closure. Butter. Butter. Butter. According to Festinger's theory, I will reduce this dissonance by explanation. But I don't really have an explanation. It's probably butter. But it might not be butter. Who's to say how god appears, in what signs, what symbols? Who's to say for sure? We three stand in the chapel watching Jesus cry. From inside the house I can hear the moan of a brain-dead girl, a nurse shushing, and I imagine Linda's horror, fifteen years ago, seeing her three-year-old drifting in the deep end. I don't know if there's a reason these things happen, or if there are saints who can see into heaven, or if pain has a divine purpose. I don't know why the statue weeps, why the bead of blood is in the chalice. I came here looking for Linda's willingness to tolerate dissonance, but what I have found, in some very small sense, is my own, for my mind right now is open, and all I can do is ask.

"It's in my bones," Linda repeats, "and I don't know how long I have left."

"You're her mother," I say then. "You've taken care of her for eighteen years. She has healed thousands upon thousands of people. She should heal you."

Linda smiles wanly. "Lauren," she says, "Audrey hasn't healed me because I've never asked her to. And I never would. She might be a saint, but she's also my girl, my baby. I would never ask her, or allow her, to take on my pain. A mother doesn't ask that of a child. A mother doesn't give suffering. She takes it away."

THE WOMEN LEAVE. Linda tells me she will be going to Sloan-Kettering Cancer Center soon. I sit for a little while longer in the chapel, by myself. Clearly, whatever doubts Linda expressed on the phone were so fleeting she can barely acknowledge them. Now, I want to pray. But no prayers come. "A mother doesn't request that of her child," Linda said, "A mother doesn't give suffering. She takes it away." This might be a rationalization, a way for Linda to avoid her daughter's failing her by simply never asking her, and thus the story stays intact. But it's more than that. It's also an act of deep caring. From inside the house I hear Linda now, crooning to her daughter, and someone gurgles in return, and for almost two decades now, she's done this, day in, day out, ministered. Did Festinger ever consider how our justifications are to save not only ourselves, but others too? Did he ever consider how lies and love are intertwined?

I LEAVE LINDA. The day is extravagant, backward, summer in winter, buried bulbs spearing upward through the ground, flaunting their purple flags.

When I was in graduate school studying psychology, I once worked on the neurological unit of a large hospital. There were a few people there like Audrey, curled into comas, their limbs stiff and cold.

Sometimes I'd stand over these people—a boy I particularly remember—and I'd say the alphabet, wondering if the letters would wend their way in, if there are parts of us deep underground that nevertheless still stay awake, watching the world while buried.

It was in graduate school that I first learned some scientists are actually studying the neural basis of dissonance theory. V. S. Ramachandran, one of the most well-known neurologists of this century, is investigating the neural substrates responsible for denial and revision. He claims we have a neuronal "devil's advocate" device located somewhere in our left lobe. The devil's advocate signals a little neurotransmitter alarm when it detects jabs at our sealed belief systems, and that's what allows us to even experience dissonance. In our right lobe, however, we have a Scheherazade of synapse and cell, a gleeful and powerful confabulator that often overrides its horned opponent.

"But not all brains," says Matthew Lieberman, assistant professor of psychology and social psychology at the University of California, Los Angeles, "not all brains engage in rationalizations, in such intense single-themed storytelling." Lieberman has repeated Festinger's lying-for-one-dollar-versus-lying-for-twenty-dollars experiment with East Asians, "and East Asians engage in far fewer rationalizations than Americans do." Lieberman is pretty sure that the East Asian brain, based on years and years of Zen practice, or simply because it has matured in a culture that can tolerate paradox (what is the sound of one hand clapping?), has a different "neural signature" than the American brain. "It's not that East Asian people don't experience dissonance," Lieberman says, "but they have less of a need to reduce it, probably because the structures that seek linear thought patterns have been rewired through spiritual exercise." Lieberman wonders if the anterior cingulate gyrus serves as the human "anomaly detector," or "devil's advocate," and if, in East Asian people, that brain part has fewer pathways to the prefrontal cortex, where we make our game-plans. "If this is the case," says Lieberman, "then East Asians experience the same amount of cognitive dissonance that we do, but they feel less compelled to act on it." In other words, East Asians may be better able to sit with it, hold in their cupped hands a thing that makes no sense—a carp without water, a tree without roots, a beautiful brain-dead girl.

I AM WORRIED about the weather. It is December 3, and the temperature is sixty-two degrees. The sky looks melted, the single rose blooming in our garden is apocalyptic. My husband carries my daughter outside, his feet sinking into the damp loamy lawn, and they pick the rose, breaking it off and bringing it to me. Festinger claimed that, ironically, worry could be a way of reducing cognitive dissonance. You feel afraid for no good reason, so you create a reason, and thereby justify your worry. How can one tell the difference between the just and the justifications? Perhaps if I were East Asian, I wouldn't even try. But the fact of the matter is, the planet appears to be warming. It is early December, and the wind smells like rot, and I find a beetle on the ground, its jointed hooked limbs waving in the warm air, a clear pool of ooze flowing from its segmented belly.

Linda has gone to the Sloan-Kettering Cancer Center and is back home by now. Since my visit with her a week ago, I've thought a lot about her—or perhaps I should say, my anterior cingulate gyrus has thought a lot about her. I've done some sleuthing, and there are serious medical experts who claim Audrey is, indeed, a rarity. The Jewish dermatologist said, "I cannot explain her skin condition in any way except to say it was caused by chemotherapy, a chemotherapy the mother says she never had." Audrey's pediatrician says, "I don't know. I have seen crosses on her palms, crosses of blood, what you could call stigmata, but they are under a layer of skin, so they couldn't have been cut there. I don't know. Medicine wants to put round things into round holes, but in Audrey's case, it's a square thing and it doesn't fit."

Currently, according to Linda, the Catholic Church is formally investigating Audrey for possible sainthood. "Oh, I hope she makes saint," Ruby says to me, like it's a cheerleading squad.

I call Linda Santo. She has had her breast operation by now and should be recovering. Her voice sounds weak, wavering. "Stage four," she tells me, "they cut out my breast and found it everywhere, everywhere." I picture it, the cancer, eel-black, beetle-black. I picture it. They cut it out. Now she is home, and hobbling, nursing herself on the one hand and her small saint on the other.

I drive back out to see her. It is nearing the solstice; already the sun is sliding down the sky when I arrive, and my shadow is long on the gold ground. Fifty years ago, Marion Keech and Dr. Armstrong and Bertha and Don and all the rest waited for Sananda and his silver rains, and when they didn't come, they found a way to explain it. Fifteen years ago, Audrey Santo fell into her pool, and when she never recovered, they found a way to explain it. Now, approaching the Santo home, I don't go to the front door or the chapel door. Instead, I creep around to the side and peer in one of the windows, and then I see her, Audrey herself, lying in a bright pink bedroom, her hair, so long and full of shine, massed across the satin pillows, falling to the floor in a single black sheet. Her eyes are fixed, open. She looks radiant, except for her mouth, where a single string of drool drops down.

To tell the truth, I don't know why I'm here. I came to Linda because I wanted to observe someone entering dissonance and putting together a new paradigm because of it, but she didn't show me that. She clung, instead, to her justifications, her rationalizations, but with so much love! Is it the love I am drawn to, this mother and daughter woven together by years of breath and touch? Or is it that I am drawn by the dissonance I am experiencing, the fact that the weird things happening here, in this house, rankle against my notion of how the world works, and I want to figure it out? I see a shadow to my left and I turn. I swear it is Leon himself in the dusk of this December day, scampering around, scowling and leprechaun-like at the same time. What would *he* say about the Santo miracles? He'd remind me that all of Christianity is the result of cognitive dissonance and its subsequent rationalizations. Writes Festinger in *When Prophecy Fails*, the Messiah was not supposed to "suffer pain," so the followers experienced great distress when they saw him crying out on the cross. It was at this moment, Festinger speculates, that followers quelled their doubts by beginning to proselytize.

I think this is funny, Christianity recast as cognitive dissonance. I also think it's a little sad. It speaks only of constriction, defensive people with blinders on their eyes. But, in fact, Christianity was also an opening, a doorway that millions upon millions streamed through.

Now, I ring the Santos' doorbell and then wait for Linda in the chapel. It is dark in the chapel, and the walls reek of saturated oil, of old clothes and incense. I go to the chalice, lift up the cup, and stare down into it, where the oil with the bead of blood sits just as it did weeks and weeks before. Who will take care of Audrey if Linda dies? When Linda dies? I touch the tiny, pointed face of a Jesus and my hands come away glossy and wet. I stare at my hands. The light is really going now, the day is so short, but my hand is glowing and glossy with this oil. I lift up my pant leg and rub the oil on a razor nick I got the other day, while showering. My skin soaks it up and the cut closes over, so there is no mark there anymore, or is it just too dark to really see? Perhaps I am seeing things, but the nature of those things I cannot quite tell. Who knows, maybe God makes himself known through a cheap plastic relic, in a ranch-style house. I really, really cannot say for sure. I am between stories, pending a paradigm, without justification or rationalization, a rich and profound place to be. Here, for this moment, hanging between dissonance and consonance, I am quiet. I am peaceful. This is what Festinger's experiments missed, what it's like to live in the gap between consonance and dissonance, where new theories take shape, new beliefs are about to be born, or something much smaller, just a person, just me, with my hands held out, my body held high, wide open—no ending.

6

Monkey Love

HARRY HARLOW'S PRIMATES

Harry Harlow's experiments with wire monkeys are central demon-
strations in the psychology of attachment. Harlow was able to show
that infant monkeys cared more for a soft surrogate mother than a
metal milk-bearing one, and with this finding, a whole science of touch
was born. His experiments, many captured on film, are chilling and
underscore the power of proximity in our lives.

*O*bedience. Conformity. Cognitive. Cuing. These were the words
and Harry Harlow didn't like them. He wanted to talk
about love. He was at a conference one day, speaking about love, and
every time he used the word, one of the scientists would interrupt
and say, "You must mean *proximity*, don't you?" until at last Harlow, a
brash man who could also be strangely shy, said, "It may be that proximity is all you know of love; I thank God I have not been so
deprived."

That was just like him, to make such a statement, in public no less;
he was prickly, impolite, a man who is remembered by some with
real distaste and by others with fondness. "My father," says his son
James Harlow, "I remember how he took me on all these trips; he

took me to Hawaii where we got to eat dinner with Gregory Bateson and his gibbon; he bought me ice cream cones; we flew on double decker planes." But it doesn't take much probing to find the story's other side. "Harlow was a real bastard; he tried to ruin me," a former student says. "He hated women, he was a PIG," says another, both of whom ask not to be identified. But there he was, the PIG, up on the podium, in 1959, speaking science in a way no one had dared to before, injecting statistics with hemoglobin and heart, the Nabokov of psychology. His experiments were long meditations on love, and all the ways we ruin it.

LITTLE IS KNOWN of Harlow's childhood. He was born in 1905 as Harry Israel, to Lon and Mabel Israel, of Fairfield County, Iowa. His father was a failed inventor, his mother a determined woman who perhaps found the midwestern town a little small for her tastes. She was, Harlow recollects in a partly finished autobiography, not a warm woman—Mabel Israel, standing by the living room's picture window, looking out onto the street, where it was always winter, the sky the color of something soiled, the land flat, wet snow falling in clumps from the tangles of black branches.

Harlow experienced bouts of depression throughout his life; maybe here is where they began, in the long midwestern winters, the land flat and forever stretching out, the days feeble, a meager sun lanced of its light by four o'clock each afternoon. Or maybe it was in the distance between his mother and he; he must have longed for something soothing. At school, he did not fit in. "He was a weird little misfit," says his biographer Deborah Blum. Harlow was interested in poetry and drawing. The Iowa school curriculum offered courses like "Farm Management and Crop Rotation" and "How to Cook to Please Your Man." One day, his fourth-grade teacher gave a poetry writing assignment, and this was so exciting for he would fit into this, he could be a part of this—until the subject was revealed: the beauty of brushing your teeth. Brushing your teeth. Brushing your teeth. By age ten, Harlow had begun to draw every free minute he had. Bending over the large sketch pad, tonguing his own teeth in fierce concentration; he made a strange and beautiful land called Yazoo, and this land he populated with winged animals and horned beasts, everything fluid, flying, swooping, and when he was done with the picture, he would bisect the beasts with sharp black lines, halve them, quarter them, so the animals lay on the page, all bloody color and still somehow beautiful, vivid, and vivisected.

Harlow graduated from the Fairfield County High School, went to Reed College for one year, and then completed his undergraduate and graduate work at Stanford, where everyone was eloquent and where Harlow, who had a speech impediment, felt too shy to talk. No place, Harlow often said, made him feel more insecure than Stanford. Therefore, he worked like a dog. He studied with Lewis Terman, the famous IQ researcher who was just then probing into gifted children. There was Harlow with his lisp and there were these shining children coming into the lab, putting together bright blocks and puzzle pieces. Terman told Harlow he would amount to nothing, that the most he could expect for himself was a job at a community college. But Harlow pleaded, and at last Terman said something to the effect of, "Change your name from Israel to something, something else . . . and we'll see what we can do." So Harlow picked *Harlow*, and Terman, in 1930, got him a job at the University of Wisconsin, where the lakes are like big blue eyes in the middle of the land-locked land, and the winter wind is full of teeth.

Harlow would go wherever he was sent. He lisped and limped his way from sunny Palo Alto to Madison, Wisconsin. He married one of Terman's gifted children, who was now not a child, Clara Mears, with her IQ of 155, and Terman wrote a letter of congratulations: "I am happy to see the joining of Clara's extraordinary hereditary material with Harry's productivity as a psychologist." A nice letter, I suppose, though it sounds more like animal husbandry than human bonding, and the put-down is ever so slight. Clara has the amazing genetic potential. Harlow, what does he have? What does he HAVE?

This was a question that plagued Harry Harlow for all of his life, a question he asked over and over again—in the darkest days, in the sheer yellow days when he was happy—still he asked the question, always suspecting that his gifts were fleeting, acquired only because of a great and stubborn and finally strangulating grip.

When Harlow came to Madison, he planned to study rats, but he wound up with monkeys, rhesus monkeys, a small agile breed. Ever Terman's student, he began by devising a test of monkey intelligence, a sort of simian IQ profile, and he was extremely successful at proving that these little primates could solve problems in ways far more complex than prior primate researchers had ever thought. His reputation rose. Madison gave him an old factory for a primate lab, and students sought him out. When studying the monkeys, Harlow would separate the infants from their mothers and peers, and this is how he stumbled into fame. He was studying the monkey head, but he observed the monkey heart, and he wondered. The infant monkeys, when separated, became extremely attached to the terry cloth towels covering the cage floors. They would lie on them, grip them in their tiny fists, tantrum if they were taken away, just like a human infant with a ratty blanket or a stuffed bear. The monkeys loved these towels. Why? This was a huge question. Attachment had previously been understood in terms of nutritive rewards. We love our mothers because we love their milk. A baby clings to its mother because it sees the swollen breasts, the tan aureole and the nub of nipple rising from its pleated folds, and it feels thirst or hunger. Clark Hull and Kenneth Spence themselves had said all of human attachment is predicated on drive reduction: hunger is a primary drive and we want to reduce it; so are thirst and sex. From the 1930s through the 1950s, the theory of drive reduction and its link to love went unquestioned.

Harlow, however, began to question it. He fed the baby monkeys by hand, with little plastic bottles, and when he took the bottles away, the infants just smacked their lips and maybe wiped a white dribble off their hairy chins. But when Harlow tried to take the terry cloth towels away, well, the simians screamed like a slaughterhouse, throwing their small bodies down and clutching at bunches of cloth. This fascinated Harlow. The simians screamed. (Somewhere else, in another time, Mabel had stood by the window, her son just two feet from her plush but cool side. Animals flew in a personal forest, slashed with black lines, bleeding blue and red.) He watched the monkeys scream and thought love. What is love? Then Harlow saw. As his biographer Blum writes, the best way to understand the heart, was to break it. And so started his brutal and beautiful career.

RHESUS MACAQUE MONKEYS share roughly ninety-four percent of their genetic heritage with humans. Another way to put this is that humans are ninety-four percent rhesus macaque monkey, six percent people. Moving up the phylogenetic scale, we are approximately ninety-eight percent orangutan or approximately ninety-nine percent chimpanzee, with just the barest fleck of flesh as solely human. This is precisely why psychological researchers have long gravitated toward the use of primates in their experiments. Says primate researcher Roger Fouts, "Monkeys have a whole repertorie of language, an entire, complex intelligence that we fail to value only because of our Cartesian view of the world." Obvious to Fouts, maybe, but not to Harlow, who said, "The only thing I care about is whether a monkey will turn out a property I can publish. I don't have any love for them. I never have. I don't really like animals. I despise cats. I hate dogs. How could you love monkeys?"

The experiment required wire cutters, cardboard cones, hot coils, steel nails, and soft cloth. Harlow used the wire cutters to fashion a wire mother, its torso patterned with small squares everywhere, a single inflexible breast "on the ventral front." Affixed to this breast, a steel nipple pierced with a tiny hole through which the monkey milk could flow.

Then, Harlow fashioned a soft surrogate, a cardboard cone bunted in a terry cloth towel.

We designed the mother surrogate in terms of human-engineering principals. . . . We produced a perfectly proportioned, streamlined body stripped of unnecessary bulges and appendages. Redundancy in the surrogate mother's system was avoided by reducing the number of breasts from two to one and placing this unibreast in the upper thoracic sagittal position, thus maximizing the natural and known perceptual and motor capabilities of the infant operator. . . . the result was a mother, soft, warm, and tender, a mother with infinite patience, a mother available 24 hours a day. . . . furthermore we designed a mother-machine with maximal maintenance efficiency since failure of any system or function could be resolved by simple substitution of black boxes and new component parts. It is our opinion that we engineered a very superior monkey mother, although this position is not held universally by monkey fathers.

So, they started. They took a group of newborn rhesus macaque babies and put them in the cage with the two surrogate mothers: the wire mother full of food, the cloth mother with an empty breast and a sweet smile. Lab assistants' notes detail the trauma of the experiment: the real mother macaques, realizing their babies were being stolen, screaming and banging their head against the cage; the infants choo-chooing as they were hurled into a separate space. Hour after hour this animal fear going on, and the lab filled with the stench of it, anxious scat, soft stools indicating, Harlow writes, high emotionality. The cages were smeared gold with grief, the infant macaques all balled over themselves with their tails held high to show their tiny oozing anuses.

But then, Harlow observed something amazing start to happen. Within a matter of days, the baby macaques transferred their affections from the real mother, who was no longer available, to the cloth surrogate mother, to whom they clung, over whom they crawled, manipulating her face in their miniature hands, biting her gently, spending hours upon hours on her belly and back. The cloth mother, however, had no milk, so when the youngsters were hungry, they would scamper off, dart over to the steel mammary machine—the

chicken-wire mother—and then, having had their fill from the foun-
tain, run back to the safety of the soft towel. Harlow graphed the
amount of time the monkeys spent nursing versus cuddling, and his
heart must have pattered fast, for he was on the brink of discovery,
and then he was over discovery's edge. "We were not surprised to discover that contact comfort was an important basic affectional or love
variable, but we did not expect it to overshadow so completely the
variable of nursing; indeed, the disparity is so great as to suggest that
the primary function of nursing . . . is that of insuring frequent and
intimate body contact of the infant with the mother."

Here Harlow was establishing that love grows from touch, not
taste, which is why, when the mother's milk dries up, as it inevitably
does, the child continues to love her, and then the child takes this
love, the memory of it, and recasts it outward, so that every interaction is a replay and a revision of this early tactile touch. "Certainly,"
writes Harlow, "man cannot live by milk alone."

The 1930s to 1950s was a cold era in childrearing. The famous
pediatrician Dr. Benjamin Spock advised feeding by schedule;
Skinner understood the infant in terms of its prior patterns of reinforcement and punishment, so that if you wanted to stop a baby from
crying, you were to stop rewarding it by picking it up. Nestlé and
Ross laboratories discovered formula, white powder, plastic nipples,
tepid water from the faucet. John Watson famously wrote, in his
books about how to rear children, "Do not overindulge them. Do
not kiss them goodnight. Rather, give a brief bow and shake their
hand before turning off the light."

Well, Harlow was going to take all that dreck to the dreck bin and
replace it with the REAL truth, which was that you should never
shake a baby's hand. You should not hesitate to hold him. Touch is critical, not a spoiler but a saver; however, the good news is, any old palm
will do. "Love for the real mother and love for the surrogate mother
appear to be very similar. . . . As far as we can observe, the infant monkey's affection for the real mother is very strong, but no stronger than
that of the experimental monkey for the surrogate cloth mother."

In Harlow's lab, at this time, there rose an air of great excitement. The researchers had stumbled into a major love variable and had discounted another love variable—feeding—as of minimal importance, and they could show all this on a graph. It was winter in Madison, then, dead in the middle of a very cold winter, the trees encased in ice like chandeliers. Students watched snow fall, saw it pile up in loose drifts on the ledges of the laboratory windows, and felt it was a time of pure excitement.

Harlow and company had identified "contact comfort" as an essential component of love. Surely there were other components. What about motion or facial features? When we are first born, we see our mother's face as a series of shifting shadows, triangles sliding one over the other, a swirl of something that might be hair, the nub of something that might be a nose, or a nipple, we do not know. We open our eyes and look upward, and there is the woman in the moon, a planet beaming back at us, with beautiful blue spots.

Surely, Harlow hypothesized, the face is another love variable. The original surrogates had primitive faces with black bicycle reflectors for eyes. Now Harlow ordered his lab assistant, to make a really good monkey mask. The plan was to take yet another newborn macaque and give it a surrogate with some beauty and see what sort of attachment followed. However, the experimental monkey was born before the face was finished, so in a rush, Harlow dropped the newborn in the cage with its terry cloth mom, who had only a blank featureless flatland for a face. No eyes. No nose. Nothing. It did not seem to matter. The little monkey loved the faceless mother, kissing it, nibbling it. When the ornamental monkey mask—so much prettier, so much more interesting—was finally finished, the baby would have none of it. The researchers tried to attach the masked ball to the surrogate mother, and the infant screamed in horror, rushed to a corner of its cage, rocked violently, grasping its raw genitals. They brought the masked mother closer, closer, and the little monkey reached out its hand, flipped the ball around, so the blank side was staring. Only then did he come forward, ready to play. No matter how many times they turned the masked mother toward the baby, the baby turned the mask away, and then at last he learned to remove the head completely, returning himself to the blank, featureless face, preferring the original view, imprinted—some might say, inscripted, the template for all that follows. Many have called Harlow's experiments cruel—to yank apart mother and child, to devise wire feeding stations with sharp nipples, to listen to primates cry in grief, to watch them cling to mannequins because they have nothing else—it may be cruel, yes. But there is also something powerful and affirmative about what he gave us: the sure knowledge that our needs are more complex than simple hunger, that we seek to connect at all costs, that we care not a whit for conventional beauty, and will always find the first face the loveliest face—no matter how far we go.

THIS ALL OCCURRED during the late 1950s and 1960s. Harlow was studying love and had earlier fallen out of love. He was always at his lab, never at home. Clara, with the high IQ, well, she was at home taking care of their two babies, while night after night her husband was out in the old factory, devising test after monkey test. It was a cold, cold winter in Madison, and Harry Harlow had an affair. "That's why my parents broke up," says Harlow's oldest son, Robert Israel. "It's very simple, my father had an affair."

Clara left with her two children, later to marry a construction worker and live in a trailer in the southwest part of the country. Harlow barely seemed to notice. There was a woman—we don't know who she is, possibly a student—and then there was this other woman whom he called the Iron Maiden. The Iron Maiden was a special surrogate mother Harlow had designed; she shot out sharp spikes and blasted her babies with air so cold and forceful the infants were thrown back against the bars of their cages, clinging and screaming. This, claimed Harlow, was an evil mother, and he wanted to see what would happen.

Here is where Harlow begins to earn his darker reputation. Here is where he steps from science into fairy tales—brutal stepmothers, the Brothers Grimm, the Iron Maiden in a magic forest where trees put down their second legs and start to walk away. Why did Harlow want to see such things? Animal rights activists say he's a sadist, pure and simple. I, myself, don't think that's it, although what drove him—the variables—I cannot quite detect. Did Mabel have sharp spikes? Too easy. Was his nature essentially, serotonergically tilted toward the difficult? Perhaps, but too easy. Was it that he had seen some things? He did a stint with the army where he went to New Mexico and observed soldiers setting off atomic blasts. He saw the firecloud, the black fallout in the distance, the huge horrific light. He has never written about that.

But the Iron Maiden, he has written about her, almost with glee. He made many variations: some iron maidens pumped freezing cold water over their children; others stabbed them. No matter what the torture, Harlow observed that the babies would not let go. They would not be deterred; they would not be thwarted. My god, love is strong. You are mauled and you come crawling back. You are frozen, and yet still you seek heat from the same wrong source. There is no partial reinforcement to explain this behavior; there is only the dark side of touch, the reality of primate relationships, which is that they can kill us while they hold us—that's sad. But again, I find some beauty. The beauty is this: We are creatures of great faith. We will build bridges, against all odds we will build them—from here to there. From me to you. Come closer.

LIKE MILGRAM, HARLOW had a flair for the dramatic, the lyrically perverted, and so he filmed his monkeys clutching their mothers of wire and snow, pricked by iron maidens. The movies are powerful, powerful demonstrations of desperation, and he was not afraid to show them. He knew that popular science has an element of art, even entertainment.

In 1958, he was elected president of the American Psychological

Association, a not insignificant honor. So he went to Washington, D.C., with his monkey movies and prepared to take the podium. He was jubilant. He had remarried a fellow psychologist, Margaret Kuenne; he called her Peggy. He stood on the dais in a cavernous convention room, looking out at a crowd of serious, bespectacled faces, and he said, "Love is a wondrous state, deep, tender, and rewarding. Because of its intimate and personal nature it is regarded by some as an improper topic for experimental research. But whatever our personal feelings may be, our assigned mission as psychologists is to analyze all facets of human and animal behavior into their component variables. . . . Psychologists, or at least psychologists who write textbooks, not only show no interest in the origin and development of love or affection, but they seem to be unaware of its very existence."

It's a grand statement, made for a grand occasion by a man who knows how to market himself. He interspersed his speech with black-and-white film clips of the sci-fi–looking surrogates and the babies who depended on them. At the end of his speech, which he titled "The Nature of Love" and later published in the *American Psychologist*, Harlow operatically came to a crescendo and a conclusion all at once:

If the research completed and proposed makes a contribution, I shall be grateful; but I have also given full thought to the possible practical applications. The socioeconomic demands of the present and the threatened socioeconomic demands of the future have led American women to displace, or threaten to displace, the American man in science and industry. If this problem continues, the problem of proper child rearing practices faces us with startling clarity. It is cheering in view of this trend to realize that the American male is physically endowed with all the really essential equipment to compete with the American female on equal terms in one essential activity: the rearing of infants. We now know that women in the working classes are not needed in the home because of their primary mammalian capabilities; and it is possible in the foreseeable future that neonatal nursing will not be regarded as a necessity, but as a luxury, a form of conspicuous consumption, limited perhaps to the upper classes. But whatever course history may take, it is comforting to know that we are now in contact with the nature of love.

I imagine a moment of stunned silence, then thunderous applause. The lights flicker on. Harlow holds up his hands: No more. *Please more.* More was to come. Harlow had released research that effectively showed a cloth surrogate mother was more important than a nursing mother and could stand in just as well as the real mother, for the infants came to "love" their bunting and appeared to mature well in her presence, playing and exploring. Soon after that speech, the University of Wisconsin at Madison put out a press release: "Motherhood Obsolete," it announced. The popular press followed. And Harlow? Well, his career leapt up, or crossed over, from the professional realm into the culture at large. He was on *To Tell the Truth*, and CBS made a documentary of his work, narrated by Charles Collingwood. The essential message was murky in its meaning for women: your babies don't need you, on the one hand; go out and get free, on the other. It was a feminist put-down, a mixed-up, snarled, multilayered missive that oozed both love and longing, a potent combination.

Harlow had two more children with his new wife. Peggy had an advanced degree in psychology and, like Clara, she too dropped out of the workforce to raise her babies. Harlow is quoted saying, later in his life, "Both my wives had the good sense not to be women's libbers; they knew a man was more important than anything else."

Pamela Harlow was born, and then her younger brother Jonathan. Today, the children are middle-aged. Pamela makes metal sculptures in Oregon, her work striking and severe. Jonathan is a woodworker; he makes, among other things, tiny pine boxes that he sells to craft stores: "Boxes," he says—

Boxes.

———————

SOMETHING WAS NOT going well. Something bad was happening. A cloth mother was just as good as a real mother; touch was central to the primate heart, and yet, here it was: Over the following year Harlow noticed the cloth-mothered monkeys were not thriving— this, after he had made such a bold pronouncement in front of all his peers. When he took the cloth-mothered monkeys out to play and mate, they were violently antisocial. The females attacked the males and knew nothing about correct sexual posturing. Some of the cloth-mothered monkeys began to display autistic-like features, rocking and biting themselves, sores blossoming open on their black arms, the blood rising up through the fur like bright pulp. Infections set in. One cloth-mothered monkey chewed off its entire hand. Something, now he saw, something had gone terribly, terribly wrong.

"Of course he was disappointed," says Harlow's biographer, Deborah Blum. "He thought he'd isolated the one variable essential to mothering, touch, and that this was a traveling variable, so to speak; anyone could provide it, and he'd made that announcement public, and then, over the next year, he saw his monkeys get very fucked up." A *New York Times* reporter came out to Madison to do a follow-up on the soft mother surrogate and Harlow led him to his lab, where a troop of rocking, head-banging macaques sat in cages, eating off their fingers, and Harlow admitted he had made a mistake.

Len Rosenblum, one of Harlow's students at the time and now a renowned monkey researcher in his own right, says, "So we came to understand there were other variables to mothering; it wasn't just touch, and it wasn't just face. We hypothesized it had something to do with motion too. We made a surrogate that could rock, and the babies were almost normal then, not completely, but almost. We then tried a rocking surrogate with one half hour a day when the baby could play with a live monkey and that produced an absolutely normal kid. What this means is that there are three variables to love— touch, motion, and play—and if you can supply all of those, you are meeting a primate's needs."

Rosenblum goes on to repeat that "the kids" only needed one half hour a day of play with a live monkey. "It's amazing," says Rosenblum, "it's amazing how little our nervous system needs in order to turn out normal."

In some respects I'm glad to hear this. I interpret these results to mean: it's incredibly hard to mess up your child. A little jiggle, a soft sweater, and only thirty minutes of actual primate interaction. Any mother can do this: lazy, working, wired, iron—we can do it! Harlow said we can.

But why, if Harlow's findings are seemingly so reassuring, so all about love, why do they lodge in the gut like one of his experimental spikes? Why, in exploring research about affection, do we shiver through the results?

And it's not just me or you. It's Harlow himself. He's shivering. He's having affairs again—he cannot be faithful to one woman—and now, maybe as he discovers that the soft-mothered monkeys are actually autistic, he begins to drink more heavily. Days are so short out in Wisconsin, early evening blotting out what little light there is, except for the yellow gleam in the shot glass. Harlow felt tremendous, tremendous pressure. He felt the applause of his original findings and he had to keep it up. He scrambled, and between 1958 and 1962, he published multiple papers. He bravely published the fact that his surrogate-raised monkey children were emotionally disturbed, and from there he went on to identify the variables essential to avoiding this fate—motion and a dollop of live play—using scores of infant macaques to prove his points.

"Harry always had to top himself," says Helen LeRoy, his assistant. "He was always looking for the next peak to conquer." Like others of similar disposition, he conquered his peaks with a bladder of wine, a pen poised, a do-better demon in the background. He never lost his lisp. Anne Landers began to write about him in her advice-to-mothers column. What would his next experiment be? His wife came down with breast cancer, the tapestry of milk ducts infiltrated—carcinoma—a sickly discharge from her nipples. She had a few years left to live. Harlow worked harder. Where could he rest his head? The motherless monkeys lost their minds, chattered madly. His published, powerful research made its way into baby care products— most notably the sling and the Snugli, which have added warmth to the ways we parent infants. William Sears, the famous attachment parenting advocate, a pediatrician who preaches sleeping with your babies, keeping them close at all times, is a Harlow-made man, whether he knows it or not. Orphanages, social service agencies, the birthing industry all had critical policies altered based in part on Harlow's findings. Thanks in part to Harlow, doctors now know to place a newborn directly on its mother's belly after birth. Also thanks in part to Harlow, workers in orphanages know it's not enough to prop a bottle; the foundling must be held, rocked, see, smile. Thanks to Harlow and his colleagues in the study of attachment, we have been humanized—we possess an entire science of touch, and some of this came from cruelty. There's the paradox.

CANCER IS ALWAYS bad, but in the 1960s it was worse than it is today. Radiation came in high volts and beams, the body marked with a black-inked X, bull's-eye. Chemotherapy was practically primitive; the doses, in huge green caustic vials, were mainlined into the arm, sending waves of heat and nausea through the body. Harlow and his wife went several times a week. I hope he held her hand. He must have seen the doctor clearing the syringe of air, a graceful arc of water landing like a tear splash on the tiled floor, and then into the vein, Peggy leaning over a basin he held for her, her stomach deposit-ing its contents in a rush of pure nausea.

"Those were dark, dark years," says Harlow's son Jonathan, who was eleven when his mother was diagnosed, seventeen when she died. Peggy became visibly more and more ill, the cancer doing its cancer dance, moving from breast to lung to liver, the woman turn-ing saffron yellow, her mouth pulled back in a masked grimace, her teeth peculiarly sharp looking, monkey teeth, mad. This is how I imagine it. It must have been bad, because during that time Harlow's already dangerous drinking turned worse. Students recall having to stop by the local bar at the evening's end and scoop Harlow off the stool to drive him home. Colleagues say there were more than a few occasions when, at hotel conferences, they'd have to put him to bed, his heavy head sinking into the sheets.

Years went by and the original surrogate-raised macaques grew older and older. They did not know how to play or mate. Now, the females were fertile, adolescence kicking in, the follicles ripening eggs. Harlow wanted to breed the females because he had a new idea, a new question. What kinds of mothers would motherless mothers make? The only way to tell was to get them pregnant. But damn bitches, they wouldn't raise their tails and bend their hairy hips. He tried putting, as he put it, very experienced, older male monkey gentlemen into the cages, but the females clawed their faces. At last he devised what he called "a rape rack," wherein he tied the females down so the males could mount them. It was a successful device, in that twenty of the motherless mothers were inseminated and gave birth. In an article published in 1966 called "Maternal Behavior of Rhesus Monkeys Deprived of Mothering and Peer Associations in Infancy," Harlow reported his results. A portion of the rape-rack mothers killed their infants; others were indifferent; a few were "adequate." This, again, is powerful stuff, but I, for one, am unsure whether it provides us with new knowledge, or simply confirms what we all intuitively knew, at the expense of many monkeys' lives.

Roger Fouts feels strongly that the information Harlow "discovered" in his deprivation experiments was not only obvious but derivative. "Harlow never referred to Davenport and Rogers," Fouts says. "Before Harlow, Davenport and Rogers put chimpanzees in boxes and when they saw what happened, they never did it again."

"The problem with Harlow," says primate researcher Len Rosenblum, "is the way he described things. He did it to get a rise out of people." Rosenblum goes on to tell this half-amusing story: Harlow was accepting an honor before a large crowd of psychologists. In the audience were three nuns, white habits, winged head-pieces, heavy crucifixes on chains. From his position at the podium, Harlow saw the nuns and then proceeded to show the audience pictures of two monkeys copulating. "He looked directly at the nuns," Rosenblum says, chuckling, "and announced, 'Here it is, the sermon on the mount.' " The nuns, they just withered. They sank straight into their habits.

"It was vintage Harlow," Rosenblum says. "He always wanted to get a rise out of people. He would never say 'terminated.' He would say 'killed.' Why couldn't he have called the rape rack a restraining device? If he had, he wouldn't have such a mixed reputation today."

It is clearly true that Harlow preferred the dramatic, but I think Rosenblum has it wrong. The issue, after all, is not what we call our devices, but what we do to animals with them. The animal rights movement was partly born out of Harlow's work. Every year, at the University of Madison Primate Research Center, the Animal Liberation Front has a demonstration where they sit shiva in the presence of thousands of stuffed Kmart monkeys. This seems absurd to me—the use of the Hebrew word *shiva*, for "grief," the Kmart animals. It makes ridiculous something that is not ridiculous, and that something is a question: What are psychologists' rights in the use of animals for research? Harlow can be credited for fomenting that question straight to the boiling surface of animal science.

ROGER FOUTS IS a research psychologist who is also an animal rights activist, a rare combination. He lives in Washington, in a tiny mountainous town where aqueous trees are always green and dewed with drops of rain, where the land smells like leaves, mulched and rich. Fouts spends most of his time with his good friend and chimpanzee Washoe, who drinks coffee every morning and likes to play tag. Over the years, Fouts has grown fond of the animals he studies, and could never harm them for the sake of science. Fouts studies chimpanzee language acquisition, an area of inquiry that does not demand knives or blood. Says Fouts, "Any researcher who is willing to sacrifice his animals is morally questionable." William Mason, one of Harlow's students in the 1960s and now a primate researcher at the University of California at Davis, says he is not at all sure whether the ends justify the means. Mason claims he has never quite been able to integrate his desires as an investigative scientist working on animals with his personal moral proclivities. In other words, Mason feels it's wrong to hurt an animal, but he still can see the reasons for doing so.

Animal rights activists are not moved by expressions of ambivalence. They are a fierce, determined bunch who regularly cite Harlow in their literature as a fascist torturer. Moving beyond the inflamed language and into the heart of the issues, animal rights activists claim that the use of animals in research delivers very little valid information. They are quick to cite the thalidomide fiasco. In the 1950s thalidomide was tested on animals and showed no teratogenic effects, but when humans took it, babies with serious birth defects were born. Along these same lines, the human immunodeficiency virus (HIV) administered to chimps for the purposes of studying the disease produces no symptoms whatsoever; penicillin is toxic in guinea pigs; aspirin causes birth defects in mice and rats and is virulently poisonous to cats. As for monkeys, well, they may be a lot like us, but they are not carbon copies, not by a long shot; the brain of a rhesus macaque is one tenth as large as a human's, and it develops at a far faster clip. A baby rhesus macaque is born with two thirds of its brain already adult-sized; a human infant's brain is only one fourth its adult size. So how far, if at all, can you generalize from one species to another? That, of course, depends on who you ask. No one will deny that the monkey is a model, and a model is an approximation of the domain it is attempting to describe. But *approximation*—that's a tricky, murky word that slip-slides on the page, swells and shrinks depending on who interprets it.

Animal rights activists like Roger Fouts and Alex Pacheco might say the primate brain is a piss-poor approximation and doesn't justify the squalor and pus and pain we heap on the animals of laboratory science. But someone like Stuart Zola-Morgan, a well-regarded memory researcher in California, obviously feels the monkey brain is a treasure trove of secrets that illuminate how the human mind might work. Zola-Morgan probes the monkey mind with scalpel and shears so as to locate the regions responsible for recollection, simple crude recollection like phone numbers and the lyrical recollections that give shadow and shape to our lives: the picnic table, the cream cheese sandwich, the smell of the our mother's mink coat.

Zola-Morgan's surgical explorations have deepened our under-standing of memory. There can be no question about that. And memory is crucial to who we are, as ensouled prismatic people. And yet, to achieve this knowledge, Zola-Morgan must anesthetize his monkey patient, then wrap a cord around the neck to cut off all blood supply to the brain, wait until the cells undergo apoptosis, and then wake the monkey up to study its ability to recall. Sometime later, the monkey is "sacrificed," and its brain examined for areas of damage, blighted, dead areas, lobes white with scar and stump.

"I think human life is more valuable than animal life," says Zola-Morgan. In an interview with Deborah Blum, he says, "We have a real obligation to care for these animals well. But is my son's life worth more than a monkey's life? I don't even have to think about that answer."

I DO. I do have to think about that answer. It's not at all as clear to me that human life has some intrinsically higher worth—no, not as clear to me at all. Not when I see a dolphin arcing out of the water, blowing jets of froth from that hole in its head. Not when I see how, as the earth's environment changes, the demise of one species alters the next, so even the algae in the ocean we must respect, for it keeps us, quite literally afloat. This is just what I think, right here, right now, today, the birds in the gutter of my home having hatched a few noisy slick chicks with their beaks spayed open. I am disturbed by a cuff strangling a monkey's neck. I am disturbed, of course, by the Iron

Maiden, the rape rack, despite the knowledge it gave us—and Harlow, perhaps he was disturbed as well. For all his pronouncements about how he didn't care for his monkeys and didn't like animals, some of his students suggest that the nature of his work began to really bother him. Certainly, as the years went on, and the drinking increased, something—many things—were bothering him.

In 1970 Harlow's wife Peggy died. Around the same time, he won the National Medal of Science Award. His eyes were blank and hooded. His mouth was an anemic pink, the barest slit for a smile. He said to Helen LeRoy on the eve of accepting his medal, "Now I have nothing left to strive for." Things turned precipitously worse. Without his wife, Harlow could not cook or clean or make his bed or get out of bed. He felt he had reached the pinnacle of his career, that he was standing on the farthest, finest peak, looking out, and there was nowhere to go but down. "I had to cook for my father," says Jonathan. "He was helpless without my mother." Harlow dragged his way into his lab, all those cages, stacked one on top of the other, all those bland bars and the white clouds in the sky and the scat. The scat. He was just so tired. The rape rack. The scat. The cries of despair and the chicken-wire surrogate and the terry cloth, which may have seemed terrible to him just then, its nubbly surface like sandpaper, irritating the skin, rub it.

He was so tired then, Harlow was. He buried his wife Peggy. At school, talking to students, this incredible, forceful fatigue would come over him, and he'd just have to sleep. So he did. In the middle of a conversation with a student, Harlow started to put his head down on his desk and take a nap. It was so easy to sleep on his desk! He just closed his eyes and let their talking lull him.

He was not well. It became obvious to everyone that he was breaking down and in desperate need of repair. So then Harry Harlow went off to the Mayo Clinic in Minnesota, where he submitted to a series of electroshock treatments, now he the animal strapped down on the table, his head shaved, gel applied here and there, dab it on the temples, smear it over the eyes, his body no longer his. Today, electroshock therapy is streamlined and toned; back then it was all AC, blasts of current squiggling through the wires, igniting the sluggish neurons. Here was Harlow, anesthetized, scrubbed, succumbing to a procedure that could be called experimental, for no one knew why it worked or how, or when, or if. His body jerked a hundred times. He woke up with cotton and clouds in his mouth, and no memory, and somewhere his wife walked with his mother in a midwestern town, and winged beasts were in the sky.

THEN HE LEFT. The treatments were over. He went back to Madison, but people said he was never the same again. He was pronounced "recovered," but he talked a little slower and didn't make wise cracks and became the slightest bit softer in his interactions. Without a wife, he was lost. He called Clara Mears, out in her trailer in Arizona. "Come back," he said. The years had been hard for Clara, too. She had had a son who drowned in a river outside the trailer home. Her second husband had also died. Widow and widower joined together and walked the aisle once more, remarried. And Terman? What did he think? His gifted children, with such promise, all of them with such high IQs, they had amounted to very little. But that's another story.

We are almost done. Harlow and Clara, loop de loop. Back at the beginning, except for this: Harlow's interests had shifted slightly. He no longer wanted to study maternal deprivation. In the 1960s there was the rise of biological psychiatry and the hope that medications might alleviate mental conditions. That interested Harlow. Possibly he hoped if he had another bout of depression, he could get a pill and not a shock. Possibly he was already on some pills, and they were only half helpful. In any case, he wanted to know what caused depression and what cured it, so, once again, he turned to his rhesus macaques.

He built an isolation chamber in which the animal crouched, his head hung down, unable to move or see the world for up to six weeks, fed through a grid at the bottom of the V-shaped device. This

Harlow called "the well of despair." Indeed, it was successful in creating a primate model of mental illness. The animals, once removed, after months or years, were shattered and psychotic. Nothing Harlow did could bring them back. There appeared to be no cure. No way to contact, to comfort.

In the end, Harlow died of Parkinson's disease. He could not stop shaking.

EVERYWHERE I GO there are animals. A squirrel leaps from wire to wire. Slugs, huge and indecent, crawl out of the garden and laze on the concrete steps. Touch them, and your fingers are sticky with gel. Cats cry. A white dog finds its way into our yard and sits there, sphinx-like, licking its pink paws. I would like to get a monkey, but my husband says this is a bad idea. He works in a lab and says monkeys smell. I say, putting down a book of Harlow's selected papers, *From Learning to Love*, "You have no idea how much I LOVE monkeys," and I'm surprised to hear real emotion, if not passion in my voice.

"Are you turning into an animal activist?" he asks.

"I'll tell you," I say, "after reading what this man did to those animals, and what we do to monkeys today, infect them with HIV, give them brain tumors, when they're so obviously our cousins, I'll tell you I'm against it. It's wrong. Harlow was wrong. All the monkey research he spawned is wrong."

"So you're telling me," he says, "that if you had to choose between a cure for Clara, if she got sick, and a monkey's life, you'd choose the monkey over your kid?"

I knew it was going to come to this. It's what Harlow would have said, what Zola-Morgan does say: our human lives are intrinsically more valuable; monkey studies yield information that helps those lives.

"Of course I'd choose Clara," I say slowly, "but that's because ninety-nine percent of me is a monkey, and any monkey would choose its child." But what I can't quite explain to him is that while ninety-nine percent of me may be instinct, or animal impulse, or mammalian love, there's that one percent of me that's not from the forests, and this fragment of self can see that to hurt one is somehow, somewhere, to hurt all. This one percent is maybe where my reason resides, and my reason tells me it is rarely defensible to cause suffering to sentient beings, especially if that data can be extrapolated by other means.

What, I wonder, is the one percent of us that's not chimpanzee, the two percent that's not orangutan, the mere six percent that's not rhesus macaque? I'd like to know. Is that where our spirit resides? Is that a sliver of angel, or god, mandating us to see the forest for the trees, the whole huge interrelated tapestry of life? It's such a small percentage, so hard to live there, where we are human, and thus responsible.

Today, I go to a primate lab. Harlow's primate lab is still up and running, housing over two thousand monkeys in Wisconsin. I go to another lab, located in Massachusetts. I won't describe it; we've heard enough. Here is where cure and death and sheer discovery sit side by side. The cages are stacked one over the other, with the animals in pairs inside. It smells of cleaning solution and dog treats. I kneel down next to a cage and slip my hands between the bars, and a primate comes up to me, mouths me like a horse might mouth my palm, lips all dry and velvety. I recall reading that once Harlow was working at night among his monkeys, and he accidentally locked himself inside one of the cages. For hours and hours he sat there and couldn't get out. The Wisconsin sky was dark; in the distance he heard revelers. "Help," he shouted from behind the bars. "Help help." At last someone heard, but by then Harlow was cold, and scared.

"Can I hold a monkey?" I ask my guide. He lets me, and I can't believe how lucky I am, to hold a monkey, to hold human history, the Pleistocene era, the Neolithic era, the dinosaurs long before that, roaming flat fields and brine. I gather the little brown ball of fur and muscle up into my arms. It is a young one. It wraps its incredible musty arms around my neck. Its heart is beating fast; it is scared. Scared of me? Scared of captivity? Scared of being free? "Shhh," I say to the monkey, my monkey, and I look into its wrinkled face, an old man, a baby, the saddest, wettest eyes, and suddenly I feel it is Harlow himself I am holding. This is funny to me—Harlow reincarnated as a monkey, in my arms right now—it's funny and it's not. I stroke the hard head. I look at the lifelines on the palm. They wind back to Wisconsin, to a small house in Iowa, to many drives and desires. The lines are pink and tangled. The animal shivers in my arms. "Just rest," I say, and I try to bring him close, as close as I can.

7

Rat Park

THE RADICAL ADDICTION
EXPERIMENT

In the 1960s and 1970s scientists conducted research into the nature of addiction. With animal models, they tried to create and quantify craving, tolerance, and withdrawal. Some of the more bizarre experiments involved injecting an elephant with LSD using a dart gun, and pumping barbiturates directly into the stomachs of cats via an inserted catheter. With cocaine alone, over five hundred experiments are still performed every year, some on monkeys strapped into restraining chairs, others on rats, whose nervous system so closely resembles ours that they make, ostensibly, reasonable subjects for the study of addiction. Almost all animal addiction experiments have focused on, and concluded with, the notion that certain substances are irresistible, the proof being the animal's choice to self-administer the neurotoxin to the point of death. However, Bruce Alexander and coinvestigators Robert Coambs and Patricia Hadaway, in 1981, decided to challenge the central premise of addiction as illustrated by classic animal experiments. Their hypothesis: strapping a monkey into a seat for days on end, and giving it a button to push for relief, says nothing about the power of drugs and everything about the power of restraints—social, physical, and psychological. Their idea was to test the animals in a truly benevolent environment, and to see whether addiction was still the inevitable result. If it was, then drugs deserved to be demonized. If it wasn't, then perhaps, the researchers suggested, the problem was not as much chemical as cultural.

I know a junkie. Emma is her name. At sixty-three years old, she is a science dean at a small New England college, and even when she's not in her office, she's stylishly dressed, today in linen pants and a scarf the color of merlot. A few months ago, something bad happened to the bones in Emma's back. The vertebrae, which snap together like Legos, began to loosen and slip. To ease the pressure, she went under the knife and came up to consciousness with a surgical seam and one brown bottle of OxyContin, the medicinal disks releasing her to a place without pain.

Opium, called in olden days the Sacred Anchor of Life, the Plant of Joy, Milk of Paradise, written about by classic Greek physicians as curing "chronic headache, epilepsy, apoplexy, tightness of breath, colic, lilac poison, hardness of the spleen stone, the troubles to which women are subject, melancholy and all pestilence." Opium, a strange substance harvested from the leggy poppy plant with its testicular pod full of seed; in nineteenth-century England, nursing women used to brew the poppy plant's seeds, drink the tea, and quiet their fitful infants. Opium, possibly the precursor to Ritalin, the first psychotropic, sold in the streets of smoky London as "Infant's Quietness" and "Mrs. Winslow's Soothing Syrup

Emma Lowry, however, has a different view of the drug. Surgery cured the bad bones in her back but left her with "a terrible dependence. I never much thought about drugs, never much cared for them one way or the other, but I'll tell you, I'll never look at a poppy plant and think it's pretty—never, ever again," she says when I visit her in her home, a solar-paneled contemporary with high white walls. Today, Emma is reading a book by George Eliot, talking on the phone to her staff about hiring procedures, and in between that, telling me her tale. She doesn't need to tell me really. I can see it, in the way, after two hours without a dose, her body begins to quiver; I watch her ease two tablets from the bottle, place them on the pad of her tongue. She could, it seems, no more refuse these pills than a plant could deny the sun it tilts toward.

Hers is a common, undisputed story. Our predecessors may have thought opium an elixir, but we know better, we with our needles gone blunt from sharing, our collective nasal cavities collapsing. We know drugs are addictive. If you mainline heroin long enough, you will develop a taste for it. If you smoke crack cocaine, you will be rushed and rocked and later feel the need for more. We think these things because the media and the medical establishment have repeatedly told us it is so, their proof in PET scans showing brains bright red with craving.

And yet, in the end, even proof itself is a cultural construct. Bruce Alexander, Ph.D., a psychologist who lives in Vancouver, British Columbia, will tell you this. He has spent his life studying the nature of addiction and has come to the conclusion that it does not reside in the pharmacology of a drug at all, but in the complex weave of unsupportive societies. According to Alexander, there is no such thing as a chemical that *causes* addiction, as, say, anthrax causes pulmonary distress. In Alexander's schema, addiction is not a fact, but a narrative, and one quite poorly plotted. Therefore, he very much doubts the stories of the Emma Lowrys, or the AA converts, or the research by E. M. Jellineck, who was the first physician to dub alcoholism a disease in the 1960s, and the later research by James Olds and Peter Milner, who found that animals in cages will choose cocaine over food until they starve to death, boned rodents. Instead, Alexander has two stark claims: (1) there is really nothing "inherently addictive" about any drugs, and (2) repeated exposures to even the most enticing drugs do not usually lead to problems.

"The vast majority of people," Alexander says, "will use even the most addictive substances, and will use them perhaps repeatedly, but there is NO inexorable progression to hell."

History may prove him right. Prior to the temperance movement, when opium was legal, addiction levels remained at a steady one percent of the population. Despite the Emma Lowrys of the world, Alexander can recite studies that support his view like some musicians play scales, in full command of their keyboards—the study, for

instance, done fifteen years ago, that showed the vast majority of hos-
pitalized patients exposed to consistently high doses of morphine
were able to come off without a problem once their pain had
resolved, and the Ontario household survey, which showed that
ninety-five percent of Ontarians who use cocaine do so less than
once per month. In a 1974 San Francisco study that followed
twenty-seven regular cocaine users over an eleven-year period, all
respondents remained gainfully employed; only one, during the
decade, had turned into a compulsive imbiber. Eleven of the respondents reported they had used their addictive drug daily at some
point, but were no longer doing so. Seven of those eleven had
reduced their consumption from seven to three grams. Alexander is
especially fond of citing the Vietnam War as a natural experiment in
drug addiction; ninety percent of the men who became "addicted" to
heroin on the war fields stopped using once they hit home turf,
stopped simply and quietly, never to go back to compulsive use. And
then there's the excellent crack cocaine survey: a 1990 study of
young Americans which showed that 5.1 percent of them had used
crack once in their life, but only 0.4 percent had used it the month of
the interview, and less than 0.05 percent had used it twenty or more
days in the month of the interview. "Therefore," crows Alexander to
me, "it would seem the most addictive drug on earth causes persistent
addiction in no more than one user in one hundred."

We could go on. There are still more studies to prove his points,
and Alexander likes to sound them. In fact, he likes to rant and rave.
He speaks in a soft voice tinged with a bit of British, I think, but
there is something compulsive in his talk, his eyes wide and sort of
startled behind their oval glasses, his folded hands tightening to prove
a point. "Do you use any drugs yourself?" I ask him, because he
sometimes seems a little tilted. He says, "With special friends, I use
acid. I don't use it regularly, but it has provided me with the opportunity for profound self-understanding." He pauses. I'm waiting.
"Once," he says, "I took some LSD and felt my head was in a
dragon's mouth, and when I looked down, my lower body was in

another beast's mouth and I thought, 'Okay, I'll just lie down and die.' So that's what I did. My heart seemed to stop beating. I knew not to fight the beasts. As soon as I stopped resisting, the monsters turned into a yellow bed of flowers, and I floated away. Since then I have not feared my mortality."

"How long ago was that?" I ask him.

"Twenty-five years ago or so," he says.

Well, I think that's a pretty good advertisement for acid. Not only does it break you into Buddhism faster than you can crack the easiest koan, but it keeps you there without, apparently, much follow-up.

I eye him, warily. As a psychologist I have worked in substance abuse facilities, and I have seen firsthand the powerful chemistry of craving. I'd like to dismiss Alexander as a pure propagandist, except there is this problematic, delightful, fascinating fact: Alexander has facts, in the form of his own ingenious experiments, to prove his theories and substantiate the studies he so likes to quote. You can resist him, or you can come with him, here and here and here, to the oddest places, where your assumptions die down and in their place, an open field—strange sorts of flowers, all of them unexpected.

BRUCE ALEXANDER WAS raised in "a red, white, and blue" household. His father, an army officer and later an engineer for GE, spent the last years of his life insisting he be called Colonel Alexander. At nineteen years of age, Alexander, whose early photographs show a heartbreakingly handsome man, married a heartbreakingly beautiful woman, and together they moved to a tiny town called Oxford, Ohio. Oxford was often cold, and the Ohio River made a dull gray cut through the tasseled cornfields. The marriage went cold quickly. Alexander was studying psychology as an undergraduate at Miami University when he saw Harry Harlow's famous monkey tapes. "I thought, 'Here is a man who is studying the nature of love, and I am unlucky in love, so I should seek this man as my mentor.'" Which he did. He wrote Harlow a letter and was invited to Madison to study for his master's and doctoral degrees. Alexander went, fully expecting to learn something, or everything, about the ties that bind.

He traveled, then, across the land, exchanging one cold state for an even colder one, although he had no idea at the time. He arrived at Harlow's lab to be immediately assigned to the maternal deprivation experiments, recording how many times a day a motherless mother monkey bit or otherwise abused her young. He watched the monkeys, but he watched still more carefully Harlow himself. "He was a terrible drunk," says Alexander. "He was always, always intoxicated. I thought, what would propel a man to so absent himself from the world? I thought about that a lot. I came to Harlow's lab wanting to study love, but I wound up contemplating addiction."

The Vietnam War broke out. Alexander, now divorced, left his wife and two toddlers for Canada, because "I became radicalized. I could not live in this country anymore." Across the border, he signed on as an assistant professor at Simon Fraser University, and as chance would have it, the psychology department assigned him to teach a course in heroin addiction, something he knew little about. He did an internship himself at a substance abuse clinic in Vancouver, and it was there he first began to consider addiction in ways distinctly non-pharmacological. "I especially remember this one patient. He had a Christmastime job as Santa Claus in a mall. He couldn't do his job unless he was high on heroin. He would shoot up, climb into that red Santa Claus costume, put on those black plastic boots, and smile for six hours straight. I began to consider then that the current theories of substance abuse were wrong; that people used, not because they HAD to pharmacologically, but because the substance was one valid way of adapting to difficult circumstances."

This thinking violated the theories back then and continues to go against the theories of today, despite the frequent nods contemporary researchers make to the importance of "complex factors." Read enough contemporary conventional substance abuse literature, and you'll note that it all starts out with an acknowledgment that environment plays a role, and then it slides lickety-split into the inevitable lockstep electrical and chemical cascades that overtake the human brain, the Harlow heart. Back in the 1950s, there was a lot of very compelling research into the physiological mechanisms of addiction, and that research dominated the day, and today as well. In 1954, at McGill University, two young psychologists, James Olds and Peter Milner, were the first to discover the fact that a white lab rat will monomaniacally press a lever to receive electrical brain stimulation in what was thought to be "the reward center." In several famous variations of the original Olds and Milner experiment, scientists such as M. A. Bozarth and R. A. Wise hooked the animals up to self-injecting catheters and let them get high as kites while they slowly starved to death. These demonstrations ended, quite literally, in bones, bones, delicate lattice work, white piping, whiskers. In still another set of experiments, the white lab rats would receive an opiate bolus if they were willing to cross an electrical field that delivered severe shocks to their padded paws. Now, a brief digression into the anatomy of the paw. Despite its leathery feel, its cracked and calloused appearance, an animal paw has nearly as many nerve endings as the head of a penis; it is sensation packed in pink. And yet, the rodents crossed the charged field, flinching, squealing, and then collapsed on the other side, sucking up their drug through a straw.

Well, this was compelling evidence for the pharmacological power of certain substances, was it not? This was compelling evidence that addiction is a physiological inevitability. After all, you could replicate these experiments in monkeys, and there were human correlates everywhere, drifting down our inner-city streets, rummaging in our trash. Alexander, however, read the research and was not convinced. He followed Olds and Milner's work. The two psychologists were getting quite famous; in fact, perhaps they should not be this story's subplot, but its main meat, Olds and Milner; Alexander was virtually unknown. Olds and Milner decided they wanted to locate the brain's "pleasure centers" and hypothesized that they existed in the subreticular formation. They split a rodent skull or two, implanted tiny electrodes here and there on a brain no bigger than a bean, appending the electrodes first with dental glue and later, for stability, with tiny jeweler screws, and then stepped back to see what would happen. Here's what happened: The rats appeared to love the small cortical sizzles. An electrode placed just the tiniest bit to the right caused the animal to become incredibly docile; a little bit to the left and it practically panted in pleasure; a little down and it licked its genitals until they were awash in gloss; upward and the appetite expanded expansively. Olds and Milner hypothesized that throughout the brain there are hot spots of pleasure, and they proved this by showing that when the rats could self-stimulate by pressing a lever that delivered a pulse to their exposed brains, they would do so up to six thousand times an hour if the electrode was embedded just right.

"Just right," it turns out, was in what's called the median forebrain bundle. That, Olds proudly proclaimed, was the pleasure center. I myself went to see this bundle, because, well, pleasure's hard to resist. A friend of mine who works in a rat lab introduced me to another friend who works in a rat lab, and I watched a "sacrificed" animal's meninges being peeled back to reveal the coils and rumples of cognition, volition, and there, a few skeins and gray strands, the weave of pleasure, surprisingly monotone.

Alexander, meanwhile, was counseling his heroin abusers, most of them dirt poor and disaffected. Why, Alexander wondered, if the pleasure center is so easily stimulated by pharmacological agents, if we are so easily taken over, then why do only a portion of users become addicts? Certainly all of us are in possession of the delicious but sadly plain-looking median forebrain bundle. Alexander knew what the rest of the researchers were forgetting, back then, in the 1960s and 1970s, when many magazines featured the newly found country of pleasure on its cover, the brain aloft, on a blue stem. Alexander knew that physiological "facts" exist in complex sets of emotional and social circumstances; pharmacology is linked to luck and weather, coincidence and pay raises, white beards and plastic presents. He knew these things, but he had no proof. He wanted proof.

Groups of psychologists and pharmacologists began to hypothesize about the nature of drug addiction, based on the pleasure center findings. Drugs, perhaps, are like chemical electrodes. They excite that dormant median forebrain bundle, causing it to crave more and more, the same way scratching a bug bite only ignites the itch.

That's the simple explanation. But it's not very specific or scientific. On a pharmacological level, researchers began to claim an interesting story. We have in our heads a little pharmacology factory. We have endorphins, which are exactly like opiates, the body's natural pain killers; we have dopamine; we have serotonin—we all know about that—a drug of calm and reason, and, left to its own devices, the body just manufactures these little vials of goodness, in moderate amounts, to get us through. However, when we start importing from foreign countries, taking, say, Mexican dope into our balanced blood or Chilean crack still smoking in its bowl, then our body thinks, "Okay, let's take a break." We stop producing our own natural drugs and come to rely on an external source, a kind of mixed-up foreign economic policy that leaves us depleted in the end, without internal resources. In other words, our body adapts to the synthetic input by ceasing its own private production. This is called, in fancy terms, "the neuroadaptive model," and it poses, once again, that drugs inevitably throw off our homeostatic systems and make it so we must cross distant borders.

"But," says Alexander, "let's take the dopamine depletion hypothesis. You use cocaine enough and your brain stops producing dopamine, so you have to take more cocaine, which excites dopamine production. Let's start with that hypothesis. There's no hard evidence that the dopamine depletion causes people to crave more cocaine." I decide to call in a conservative, the former assistant drug czar, a Yale man, Herb Kleber. "Of course there's evidence," he says to me. "Have you seen the PET studies? There's definitely dopamine depletion in a cocaine user's brain and that depletion is strongly associated with increased craving."

Yes? No? Maybe? In no other segment of psychology do you get, perhaps, such conflicting answers than in drug studies, where politics and science do not so much inform as infuse each other.

"Look," says Joe Dumit, a professor of psychology at MIT. "PET studies can be unreliable. It's easy to create images that look like they're showing a great change, but those images can be misleading. Who knows?" Dumit sighs. Studying the brain all day sounds hard. It's an endless, hopeless exercise in trying to use the self to see beyond the self. Just give me a glass of wine.

ALEXANDER WANTED PROOF. He was living in Vancouver, a beautiful city edged with sea. He observed other scientists' junkie rats. They had, in some cases, catheters inserted into their raw shaved backs, their cages cramped and dirty. Maybe here was proof, its bare beginnings. Alexander thought, "If I lived like that in a cage, I'd get as high as possible too." What would happen, he wondered, if he removed the cage or, in other words, altered the cultural constraints? Would the inevitable physiological fact of addiction stay the same in happier surroundings? Alexander wondered this to himself and smiled. He has an incredibly sweet smile, two dents of dimples on either side of his face, a nick in his chin like some strange being touched him way back when, in the womb. He smiled and thought, "Rat park." And then he began to build it.

Instead of a small cramped cage, Alexander and coinvestigators Robert Coambs and Patricia Hadaway constructed a two-hundred-square-foot housing colony for their white Wister lab rats. Into this space, which they heated just right, they put down delicious cedar shavings and all manner of bright balls and wheels and tin cans. They made sure, as this was to be a co-ed colony, that there was ample space for mating, special space for birthing, room to roam for the toothy males, warm nests for the lactating females. Then, Alexander, Coambs, and Hadaway painted the walls of the rats' Ritz Carlton in jeweled greens and saffrons. They painted deciduous trees, mountains ribboned with roads and studded with tiny trees, creeks flowing over smooth stones. They cared little for the actual environmental accuracy of the backdrop. Jungles gave way to evergreens; snow melted into sand.

Alexander, Coambs, and Hadaway devised a few different experimental conditions for the rats. One they called the Seduction. This condition is predicated on the fact that rats have a sweet tooth and are rarely, if ever known, to turn down dessert. In the Seduction condition, the investigators put sixteen lab rats into the fancy rat park and kept another sixteen in the standard laboratory cages, where space was cramped and isolation extreme. Because plain morphine is bitter, and rats hate bitterness, the researchers gave both sets of rats morphine-laced water sprinkled with sucrose, at first just a little sucrose, but as the days progressed, more and more, until the drink was a veritable daiquiri of sugary delight, delivering supposedly irresistible opioids in an irresistible liquid. To both sets of rats, they also gave plain old tap water, which must have looked so gray and filmy, next to the stocked and glowing bottles.

Here's what they found: The cramped and isolated caged rats loved the morphine-laced water right from its subtle, sugary start, slurping it up and, I imagine, falling down dazed, their pink eyes stoned, their miniscule wizened feet waving slowly in the airy air. The rat-park residents, however, resisted drinking the narcotic solution, no matter how sweet the researchers made it. While they did occasionally imbibe (females more than males), they consistently showed a preference for the straight H_2O, and when the two groups were compared, the caged isolated rats drank up to sixteen times more than the park residents, clearly a finding of statistical significance. Highly interesting is the fact that when the researchers added Naloxone to the morphine-laced water in the rat park, the rat-park rats reversed their aversion to the narcotic water and drank it. Naloxone is a substance that negates the effects of opioids but spares the sugary taste of the conduit. This rather stunning finding shows, perhaps most clearly of all, how rats, when in a "friendly" place, will actually avoid anything, heroin included, that interrupts their normal social behaviors. The rats liked the sweetened water, so long as they *didn't* get stoned. At least in rodents, opiates are actually, in favorable situations, distinctly undesirable, which is a far cry from our understanding of them as inherently tempting.

We think these results are socially as well as statistically significant. If rats in a reasonably normal environment consistently resist opiate drugs, then the "natural affinity" idea is wrong, an overgeneralization of experiments on isolated animals.

These findings are compatible with the new "coping" interpretation of human opiate addiction if one keeps in mind that rats are by nature extremely gregarious, active, curious animals. Solitary confinement causes extraordinary psychic distress in human beings and is likely to be just as stressful to other sociable species, and therefore to elicit extreme forms of coping behavior such as the use of powerful analgesics and tranquilizers, in this case morphine.

It may also be that socially housed rats resist morphine because it is such a powerful anesthetic and tranquilizer. As such, it interferes with a rat's (or a person's) ability to play, eat, mate and engage in other behaviors which make life rewarding.

The Seduction experiment showed that there is, in fact, nothing inherently, inexorably seducing about opiates, and as such it stood as a real challenge to the temperance mentality, which rose to prominence in this country as prohibition laws came into effect and which, in one way or another, weaves and has woven through so much of addiction research. In 1873, a journalist observing a temperance rally wrote, "Then the ladies, joined by the spectators, sang, 'Praise God from whom all blessings flow,' while liquors were rolled into the street. Of the women around, some were crying, a few alternately singing and returning thanks . . ." You can see that quote as the barely visible fuel behind Olds and Milner's work, behind the current drug wars and the scientists who support them, and behind the naysayers, like Alexander, who have done some ingenious things to refute a superstition so entrenched we don't even know we hold it.

———

THE EXPERIMENT, HOWEVER, was not complete. Alexander, Coambs, and Hadaway successfully showed that rats will resist even the most irresistibly delivered drug if it interferes with the alternatively gratifying opportunities available to them. However, the research team had another question, and this one had to do with addiction already in progress. They had tried to start an addiction in the fancy rat residences, pretty unsuccessfully. The opposition, however, could easily say, "Fine. Give a rat Nautilus equipment and sex twenty-four hours a day and it won't get high. In the real world, people are more vulnerable, and they may begin to use at a bad point in their lives, and once they've started an addictive pursuit, they cannot stop. The withdrawal is so painful, it in and of itself guarantees continued use." So to test this assumption, the researchers again took two sets of rats and kept one set in their cages. The other set they moved to rat park. Over the next fifty-seven days, which is a good long time in heroin time, they made junkies out of each and every rodent, giving them no liquid to drink except the morphine-laced water. "Long enough," writes Alexander, "to produce tolerance and physical dependence."

They then again provided both groups with both plain and morphine water. Predictably, the caged group continued to partake in the morphine; the rat-park group, *even when already* addicted, however, did not choose the morphine solution regularly and in fact decreased their morphine use, despite withdrawal. The implications: addictions in progress are not inexorable. As drug researcher Stanton Peele points out, everyone seems to agree that nicotine is even more highly addictive than heroin, and yet ninety percent of people who start smoking quit on their own, without any "program" or "sponsor" or "professional help." But what about withdrawal? Alexander suggests that withdrawal may not be the force we think it is. "Rats in rat park showed what looked to be some minor withdrawal signs, twitching, what have you, but there were none of the mythic seizures and sweats you so often hear about." Well, maybe not for rats, but surely for humans, as we have seen it before our very own eyes. Retorts Alexander, "The vast majority of people who experience heroin withdrawal have something like a common cold. That's it." His point, borne out by his rat-park findings: while withdrawal is real, it is not necessarily the force our media has described, what with the flagrant flus and deep tissue miseries. And more importantly, withdrawal does not consign the user to repeated use, if the rats are any example. Alexander says, "I think withdrawal, like drugs themselves, is consistently overplayed; it's part of the narrative people have heard about drugs, and so continue to tell; it's the paradigm by which drug users interpret what may be in fact only discomfort, not agony. Certainly the rats did not appear to be in agony. Neither were the Vietnam vets or the scores of others who start, go through withdrawal, and then stop."

Alexander's research suggests that addictions are in fact quite subject to free will. Rats and humans pick up the proverbial pipe and then put it back down, no problem. And when they don't put it back down, it's not because there's something inherently irresistible about the substance, but because the particular set of circumstances the mammal finds itself in offers no better alternatives than such destructive snacking. Addiction in Alexander's world is a life-style strategy, and like all human-constructed strategies, it's malleable to education, diversion, opportunity. It's a choice.

Alexander remembers rat park well, even though he's sixty-two now and he did the experiment over twenty-five years ago. He remembers addicting his animals and then watching, waiting, to see what would happen. "We talked about it all the time, over dinner, on weekends. My kids came up and met the rats, did some data collection. It was of course tremendously exciting to see all the commonly held notions about addiction so challenged by the rats. I've had only one good idea in my life," Alexander says, "and that was it. But one good idea, who can complain about that?"

I don't hear wistfulness in his voice when he utters this statement, but maybe something ever so slightly disappointed, even though he denies it. The fact is, while the rat-park study is extremely significant in its findings, and poses relevant challenges to ourselves collectively and individually, the fact is, no one paid much attention, then or now. "We wrote up the findings," Alexander says. "We wanted them to be published in *Science* and *Nature*. That's where they should have gone. But the papers were rejected. Again and again. It was disappointing." At last a well-respected but smaller journal, *Pharmacology, Biochemistry, and Behavior*, published the rat-park findings. "It's a good journal," Alexander says, "it has as much credibility as you could ask for, but it's not as widely read. It's, it's pharmacology."

ALEXANDER'S CAREER, with its psychosocial slant, remained modest, while in the meantime, biological paradigms rose to prominence, spinning off still more scientific studies. In the 1970s a Stanford researcher, Avram Goldstein, discovered the body's natural opiates—endorphins—and speculated that heroin abusers were deficent in this endogenous substance. He hypothesized that injecting addicts with endorphins would eliminate their cravings; the strategy failed completely, but it didn't matter. It got good press because it was a biologically based explanation in a culture with a taste for just such explanatory models—models of molecules, models that eschew or even ignore the issues Alexander cares most about: race, class, the nuanced circumstances of our multilayered lives.

Alexander is angry sometimes. He accuses the biomedical establishment of suppressing important scientific information about the complexity of drugtaking for political purposes. After all, if rat park's findings were given their due, we would have to clean up our inner-city projects and change our policies, funding education over medicalization. Alexander's critics, however, accuse him of distorting information in hopes of inflaming a public debate, and being the star at its center. This according to drug czar Kleber, who is proud of his Yale education and disdainful of any research "north of the Connecticut River." According to Kleber's Ivy League compass, rat park happened in the scholarly equivalent of the tundra, which may be why the drug czar says, "When I first heard of that Vancouver experiment, I thought it was ingenious. Now I think it has all sorts of methodological flaws."

"Like what?" I ask him.

"I can't remember," he says.

"Alexander says you say addiction is pretty much inevitable, that exposure leads to addiction."

Kleber says, "That's ridiculous! I never said that and I don't think that."

"If you don't think that," I say, "then why aren't you for legalization?"

"Caffeine," he says. "How many people are addicted to caffeine in this country?"

"A lot," I say.

"Roughly twenty-five million," he says, "and how many are addicted to nicotine? Roughly fifty-five million. And how many are addicted to heroin? Two million. The more people exposed to a drug, the more become addicted. Nicotine is easy to get, so we're swarming with addicts. If heroin were easy to get, the number of addictions would dangerously, dangerously rise."

And yet, Alexander claims that addiction levels remained steady before temperance, at merely one percent. He also says that saying availability leads to addiction is like saying food leads to obesity, which clearly it doesn't in the vast majority of cases.

Kleber continues. "Now," he says, "how long would it take you to get a glass of beer?"

"A minute," I say, thinking about the mason-green bottles we have cold in the fridge.

"And how long would it take you to get a cigarette?" he asks.

"Twenty minutes," I say, picturing the convenience store several blocks away.

"Right," he says. "And how long," he says, his voice dropping, "would it take you to get cocaine?"

Thank god we're on the phone during this conversation, because my face goes red and my eyes, I feel them flinch. The fact is, I could get cocaine or its chemical equivalent in three seconds flat, along with various hallucinogenic plants my chemistry-loving husband has found advertised on the Internet. We're a family of pharmacophiles.

"How long?" he repeats, and is it my imagination, or do I hear something a little threatening in the drug czar's voice now, like he suspects?

"A long time," I say, too quickly. "Hours. Weeks."

"So you see my point," he says. "Availability increases exposure, exposure increases addiction."

And yet, here I am, as exposed as anyone could possibly be; we have access to poppy straw tea, magic molecules, prescribed hydromorphone, tiny white disks, and none of it interests me. I have occasionally wondered why it is that I have no desire to try the bountiful mind-altering drugs in my midst, while my husband, who has chronic pain, likes to partake. I often worry about my husband, who not infrequently sits down with a cup of tea and two hydromorphone tablets and sips until his pupils turn tiny. I have said to him, "You'll soon be hooked, if you aren't already," and he has said to me, being a rat-park fan himself, "You know the REAL research, Lauren. I'm in a colony, not in a cage."

IN THE MEANTIME, there are the actual addicts, who care not a whit for the theories or the politics, because they are simply suffering in their skins and want relief. There is, for instance, Emma Lowry, whose own body tells a tale it is difficult to ignore. While she, like my husband, lives in the human equivalent of rat park, she seems unable to extricate herself from the soft sway of her medicines. Every time she tries to cut down her dose, "Awful things happen. My stomach goes into spasm." The next time I visit her, she seems desperate. "No one told me this stuff was THIS dangerous," she says. She has taken to using an exacto knife to shave off tiny crescents from the pill, making it minutely smaller each time she swallows—a slowly diminishing dot—in the hopes of easing herself from her hook. At the same time, an OxyContin scare is rippling through our country. The *New York Times Magazine* writes on its cover "OXYCONTIN" and everywhere frightened pharmacists are putting up signs, "No OxyContin here," in the hopes of diverting break-ins.

It is not hard to find evidence that goes against rat park's conclusions. Wealthy people, with all their needs met, are often substance abusers, and there is compelling evidence that shows the brain's significant alteration when consistently exposed to opioids or cocaine, an alteration that very well might make free will irrelevant. Alexander, of course, has an answer to these objections: the rich are as caged by social strife as any of us; the PET scans of altered brains prove only correlation, not causation. You can listen to Alexander's counterarguments to his critics, but listening does nothing to dispel the undeniable reality that despite what Alexander showed way back when, in his painted rodent dreamland, the experiment has done little to alter the way we collectively think about substances and thus, to some degree, experience them. Therefore, what makes the experiment great? Kleber says, "The experiment's not great." Alexander himself says, "Rat park's not famous. Why would you include it? It has a small cult following, but that's it." True, rat park may not be big; neither is Sherwood Anderson's *Winesburg, Ohio* or Richard Seltzer's essay, "Lessons of a Knife." Those works, however, are little gems that resonate in ways subtle but strong. More importantly, they became the unacknowledged models from which more recognized literature was spun; so it is with Alexander's rats. His experiments were in part responsible for the famous surveys, cited earlier in this chapter, which showed how unlikely addiction is in the human population. His experiments in part led to intensive studies of cancer patients on morphine, and the fascinating research that is now being done on the bio-psycho-social differences between using morphine for pain, where it rarely leads to addiction (Emma excluded, of course), and using it for pleasure, where it supposedly more often leads to trouble. Most importantly, his experiments were in part responsible for an interesting string of work that followed the effects of environment on human physiology. In 1996, research conducted in Iran showed that women living in single-family housing units had significantly higher fertility rates than women living in multifamily units, meaning fertility goes down as crowding goes up. Studies of prisons have shown that as density increases, so too do problems like suicide, homicide, and illness. Humans in small spaces perform far worse on tests of problem solving than do their counterparts in more capacious settings.

THE DECIDEDLY LUKEWARM reception rat park got may have disappointed Alexander, but not for long. Unlike his teacher, Harlow, Alexander does not appear prone to depression or substance abuse, although he does mention, quite a few times, that he has been unlucky in love. That lack of luck, however, didn't seem to get in the way of his continued, rather vivacious explorations into the question at hand. Rat park went the way of a midlist book, and he just kept on thinking, planning, joining. He joined the board for the Portland Hotel, a downtown Vancouver establishment where HIV-positive addicts can come for clean needles, a warm room, and a way to die in dignity. He studied China's old opium dens, where the walls had a fine white scrim of powder clinging to their craggy surface. He began to read Plato, "the first psychologist," even as Simon Fraser University withdrew his funding based on rat park's publicity failure. Eventually, the university, in conjunction with animal rights activists, who found the rat lab's ventilation system inadequate, shut the whole thing down, only to reopen it months later as a student counseling service—without a ventilation system upgrade. "It wasn't okay for the rats," Alexander says, "but for humans it was fine."

He speaks without bitterness, though. Instead, labless and ratless, Alexander turned toward history, funneling himself back into the portholes of the past, looking to long-lost cultures for still more clues as to how addiction does and doesn't happen. He was interested to find that there have been many times in human history when addiction was practically nil: the Canadian Indians, for instance, prior to assimilation, had a negligible addiction rate, as did our very own British brothers before the upheavals of the Industrial Revolution, when people farmed and lived off the land and watched the moon, that medicinal disk in the sky. Alexander found that addiction rates seem to grow not as drug availability increases, but as human disloca-tion, the inevitable result of a free-market society, becomes common-place. His theory: a free-market society treats its people as products, to be uprooted, moved, altered, according to economic need. "At the end of the 20th century, for rich and poor alike, jobs disappear on short notice, communities are weak and unstable, people routinely change families, occupation, technical skills, languages, nationalities, software and ideologies as their lives progress. Prices and incomes are no more stable than social life. Even the continued viability of crucial economic systems is in question. For rich and poor alike, dislocation plays havoc with the delicate interpenetrations of people, society, the physical world and spiritual values that are needed to sustain psy-chosocial integration." In the absence of these things, says Alexander, we, like rats in cages, turn to substitutes, not because the substitutes are alluring in and of themselves, but because our circumstances are deficient, we without our gods.

In the final analysis then, Alexander the renegade is really a tradi-tionalist in tie-dye. Years of radical inquiry have led him to this con-servative conclusion: what matters are the ties that bind, love, affection, and the daily rhythms that rise from these—friendship, family, a small plot to work. Weekends he spends on his small island farm, writing in the early mornings, structuring a simple life. Maybe here is where he and his opponent, Kleber, can come together. Alexander believes that difficult circumstances lead to addiction; Kleber believes it is exposure to fixed pharmacological properties. But in the end these different scientists are asking for similar things— that the web of social structure be beautiful and meaningful, that families replace gangs, that tradition provide direction in a wasted culture. Writes Kleber, "Our policies should aim to reduce drug use and addiction to a marginal phenomenon. . . . At its best America strives to give all its citizens the chance to develop their talents." Says Alexander, "When we provide our children with heritage and beliefs that bring shape to culture, we reduce the likelihood of psychopathology." In the end it comes down to dignity, and both men believe in it.

I WISH I could wend my way to a solid ending, but in the study of solid substances, everything is, finally, as wavy as an opioid dream. According to "findings," Emma Lowry, because she took opiates for pain and not for pleasure, should not be addicted, but she is. According to "findings," my husband, who has consistent exposure, should be addicted, and he isn't. Kleber claims addiction rates rise with exposure, and he has the figures to show it; Alexander says if that were true, poppy-growing cultures would be addicted cultures, and they're not. Who knows what the facts are here.

In the end, then, I decide to see for myself. Sample size: one. Hypothesis: none. I'm in a cage or a colony, I'm not sure which. My house is large, my life good, my human interactions rich and robust, but I'm a free-market gal, as dislocated as any in this new millennium, where I have no religion, no extended family, no god. What I do: I take my husband's hydromorphone pills. I decide I'll take them for fifty-seven days, like Alexander's rats, and then see what happens when I try to stop.

I swallow two. I swallow three. Sure enough, I get high. I get happy. The air feels silky, and when I see a seagull in the Target parking lot, I think it's the most beautiful bird ever, sugar-white and winged.

Three days go by. Four. I'm feeling fine. I have weeks of regular nightly opiate use, of mooning at the moon and thinking everything both silly and sweet. During the days, I watch myself. Am I looking forward to my nightly elixir? Am I CRAVING it? I watch for signs of craving just like early in my pregnancy I watched for cramps that might signal a miscarriage: there, a little something, oh my god, it's happening—did I feel that? Was it a twinge? But there was no blood then, and there's none now. My stomach starts to hurt. For me, the morphine is like a difficult dessert, unpleasant to get down, fun to actually digest, but altogether unremarkable. I'd rather have dinner with a friend than sentimentalize a seagull, in the end. And, after fourteen days, when I stop abruptly, I am a little cranky and stuffy in my nose, but who knows, my kid's got the flu.

What this little experiment shows me is (pick one):

(a) There in fact is nothing inherently addictive about morphine, and the physiological substrates of withdrawal are overplayed.
(b) As Kleber might say, I lack the deficient gene that would increase my vulnerability to addiction.
(c) Because I did not proceed to injection, where the high is higher and the median forebrain bundle more intensively stimulated, I wasn't really at any risk anyway.
(d) I do live in a colony, not a cage.
(e) No one knows.

Pick one, or none. I myself have really no idea. I'm tired now. And my cortical pleasure centers will call me away from this interpretive task long before I even get close to comprehension; I will be called back to my regular life, where my husband occasionally needs painkillers, where my house leaks on the left side but is warm and familiar, where my child toddles, and the snow falls like latticework outside my window—my world, imperfect, but good enough from where I stand now, apart from it, Kleber here, Alexander there, myself in the midst of their maze.

IN THE END, I want to see rat park for myself. I want to lie in it and feel its space, smell the pungent cedar shavings, crispy in my fingers. I'd like to feel I'm in a land, a time, as honest as the Indians before they were assimilated, a land, maybe, that has my hand prints in it, that grows because I tended it, erect ears of corn splitting their seams. So I go. Alexander has saved the wooden plywood walls, rat park's backdrop, where the coniferous trees brush the skin of a perfect sky. There are clouds here, pink streaked and white, and a river burbles as it runs toward some sea beyond the backdrop. Imagine living in a place like this, or its human equivalent, a kind of perpetual California without any fault lines, where food sources never diminish, where there are no predators, where the smell is always like the secret insides of your great-grandmother's wood-lined chest. Alexander calls rat park a normal environment: he says, "We suspect that the normal environment provided by our colony allowed the rats enough species-specific gratifying behavior so morphine was irrelevant." But when you see the preserved pieces of the experiment, the painted plywood, when you consider the abundant food, the readily available exercise equipment, the river in its plush streaks of silver, "normal environment" does not come to mind. What comes to mind is "perfect environment," of which I feel sure there are none in the labless worlds we live in. Here may be one of Alexander's biggest methodological flaws. He created heaven and found—no surprise—that in it we are happy. But where is there heaven on earth? Does rat park truly reflect "real life," possible life, or does it in fact only confirm that addiction is only avoidable in a world of utter myth, which is not, never has been, and never will be the human world, we with our dented genes and buildings.

In the end, Alexander—the man unlucky in love, the man married and divorced two times, the man who has just now, at sixtysomething, settled down with his third spouse—in the end this man is a romantic. He believes rat park is possible in our world, that we can construct a culture full of gentle give-and-take. Who knows, maybe he's right. The romantic view of the world, which holds that we are able to actualize our potent selves if only given the chance, is as powerful and persuasive a stance as its opposite, the classical view, my view, rooted in skepticism, even cynicism: life is hard; everywhere you turn there are flaws; every colony you enter is really a cage, and if you squint hard enough, you'll be able to make out the bars around your body. That's my view, but I can't, and certainly don't want, to prove it.

BACK AT HOME, I receive a phone call from Emma Lowry, who tells me that she's finally "off" those "damn drugs." She says she'll never use painkillers again. I know if I call Alexander up and tell him Emma's story, he'll begin to rant and rave. He'll find all sorts of smart reasons as to why it doesn't contradict his data: maybe she was still in the cage of pain and wasn't quite admitting it; maybe her happy home was really dimmed with an unacknowledged depression; maybe her husband has never been so supportive; maybe she works too hard. He would say what he's said to me so many times before: "I have never met a person, Lauren, never, in my thirty years of searching, who had adequate internal and external resources and who was an addict. Never. Find me one and I'll throw out all my beliefs."

I won't call up Alexander and tell him about Emma. Nor will I call up Kleber and tell him about my husband, and how he, exposed and immersed, seems to have sidestepped major drug problems. I don't want to hear the inevitable diatribes that come from both sides of the question. The real drug war may not exist in our streets, but in our academies, where scientists hiss and search, compulsively, intoxicated by the questions they are pursuing. And what, finally, are these questions? What does the fierce debate about addiction really stand for? It doesn't stand for itself, that's clear. Addiction is really, it seems, about questions of chemistry and its intersection with free will, responsibility and its relationship to compulsion, deficit and how we can creatively compensate or not.

I head upstairs to my study. It is night now and the little painted lamp on my end table glows, infusing the shade in tones of yellow and gold. The walls here are also warm, painted halo-yellow, hung with prints of plums and peaches on sketched stems. I love my study. I love how the cat, fat and furry, sleeps curled on the daybed, almost groaning as he purrs in pleasure. The cat is a new addition to our household. We took him in because we have mice, many mice, scurrying under our floorboards, hanging off the coils in the back of the fridge. Even now, with the cat, I can hear them chirping in the heating duct, a new litter I suppose, their naked heads, the smell of milk. Mice. I can hear them when I sleep, infiltrators, gymnasts, they prance and birth and scratch. They chew tiny holes in the Ritz Cracker boxes, so the spoils of comfort spill out. Mice. I hope they're happy here.

8

Lost in the Mall

THE FALSE MEMORY EXPERIMENT

Memories are the footprints we leave in our lives; without them we look back and see just a blank stretch of snow, or someone else's signature entirely. If there is anything that makes us, as a species, feel some kind of continuous authenticity, it is our memory. Plato believed in a form of absolute, or ideal memory, a sphere one could reach where all of one's past would appear to be perfectly preserved. Freud waffled on the subject, sometimes claiming memory a mishmash of dream and fact, but just as often claiming it as movie, rerun, the film scrolled in some section of the brain recoverable through free association. Our notions of memory are largely based on these two men's ideas: Freud and Plato, by no means bad company to keep. Psychologist Elizabeth Loftus, however, decided to challenge the field's great fathers. Her hunch? Memory is as slippery as a stream, as unreliable as a rat. One of the field's most innovative female experimental psychologists, Loftus invented a rather alarming and philosophically profound experiment designed to test the text of our rememberances so as to determine whether to call them fictions or to call them facts. Her results caused outrage.

First she studied stop signs, beards, barns, and knives. "Wasn't that traffic signal yellow?" she might ask her subjects, and sure enough, once she had implanted the possibility, her subjects remembered yellow when the reality was red. She showed movies in her lab—a shot-gunned face, a masked man on an empty street—and when she asked questions like, "Do you recall that man had a beard?" most recalled a beard, but the man was really masked. "Only the flimsiest curtain separates reality from imagination," experimental psychologist and University of Washington professor Elizabeth Loftus says, and she has powerfully proved it in her prize-winning experiments on how memory gets contaminated by the subtlest suggestion. Tell someone he saw a blue barn and he'll make the barn blue, the brain bleeding its facts, our world a watercolor painting, the kind my child makes, loose soupy pictures that might be this or might be that: all cloud.

Well before she became famous—or infamous, depending on where you cast your vote—Loftus's findings on memory distortion were clearly commodifiable. In the 1970s and 1980s she provided assistance to defense attorneys eager to prove to juries that eyewitness accounts are not the same as camcorders. "I've helped a lot of people," she says. Some of those people: the Hillside Strangler, the Menendez brothers, Oliver North, Ted Bundy. "Ted Bundy?" I ask, when she tells this to me. Loftus laughs. "This was before we knew he was *Bundy*. He hadn't been accused of murder yet."

"How can you be so confident the people you're representing are really innocent?" I ask. She doesn't directly answer. She says, "In court, I go by the evidence. . . . Outside of court, I'm human and entitled to my human feelings." What, I wonder, are her human feelings about the letter from a child-abuse survivor who wrote, "Let me tell you what false memory syndrome does to people like me, as if you care. It makes us into liars. False memory syndrome is so much more chic than child abuse. . . . But there are children who tonight while you sleep are being raped, and beaten. These children may never tell because 'no one will believe them.'" "*Plenty* of people will believe them," says Loftus. Pshaw! She has a raucous laugh and a voice with a bit of wheedle in it. She is strange, I think, a little loose inside. She veers between the professional and the personal with an alarming alacrity. "The results of our experiment showed that twenty-five percent of our respondents, which is a statistically significant minority, were subject to . . ."—sentences like that and then a sudden swerve, a brief beat of silence and, "Did I tell you about my valentine?" Today is February 14. She's just received a card from her ex-husband, whom she refers to as her "was-band," Geoff. "You know what I love about you?" Loftus reads from the card. "All your Freudian slips." Loftus laughs. "I still love my was-band," she says. "Too bad he remarried such a twit."

In 1990 something big happened to Loftus. Most lives cannot be defined by particular turning points. Most lives build incrementally, a series of sedimentations that over time yield a shape we can see, if at all, only by the very end. Not so for Loftus. In 1990, a lawyer, Doug Horngrad, called her to testify in a particularly troubling case. Horngrad's client was a sixty-three-year-old man, George Franklin, whose beautiful red-headed daughter Eileen claimed she remembered, twenty or so years after the fact, that her father raped and murdered her best friend. It's a long gruesome story of stones and skulls, perfect for Loftus, the diva of drama. She jumped on it. "Totally forgetting that you witnessed something that traumatic, and then suddenly recalling it whole decades after the fact? Burying every detail and then having it float flashbulb into your mind, every inch intact, I don't think so," says Loftus. Loftus does not dispute the fact that trauma happens ("of course children are hurt at the hands of others"), only that it can be severed completely from consciousness, stored unmarred in an anterior capsule, like some sunken treasure chest that one day opens to reveal its green mineral stones, its chunks of bright ore. When it comes to memory, Loftus says, the shine fades fast. She has observed firsthand how recollections can be contaminated; her early experiments had shown her how it always decays with time. Now this man, George Franklin, was about to be convicted based on nothing but his grown girl's remembrances, excavated at the hands of some new-age therapist who practiced all sorts of suggestion. Suggestion! That's Loftus's personal hobgoblin. People are just so suggestible, their skin more like shift barely covering bone and muscle; anything can come through. It's scary.

So, Loftus went to testify on behalf of George Franklin, went to tell the jury Eileen's memory could not be counted on as accurate, not because of Eileen, per se, but because of the mechanics of memory itself, the way it rusts in the rain. In one of the most publicized recovered memory cases of the decade, Loftus stood before the court and told of a mind that blends fact with fiction as a part of its normal course; she told how her subjects in the lab made red signs yellow, put barns in places where they never were, recalled black beards on bald chins. Eileen spoke of *seeing* the stone her father used to crush the skull of her best friend Susan, seeing the ring flash in the sunlight, seeing again, in her mind's eye, a bit of blood, a bit of blue, and Loftus said, "Untrue. All these details Eileen later read about in newspaper reports." The jury didn't buy it, didn't buy Loftus, that is, and she went home defeated. She claims it was this event that shaped her future work. Franklin was convicted of raping and murdering his daughter's best friend more than two decades after the fact, and Loftus felt a chill. "My mission in life," she says to me, "my mission since then has and always will be to help the falsely accused. I realized that talking about barns and stop signs and yield signs wasn't going to cut it as evidence, especially in the new climate, where recovered memory therapy was all the rage, and everyone believed in the reality of repression. I realized I was going to have to prove not that it's possible to *distort* a memory, which god knows I've proven, but that it's possible to plant *an entirely false memory in a person.*" Loftus says these words with glee—trick or treat, it's always trick, the little goblin. She has a Ph.D. from Stanford. She's a math whiz. She has a genius for putting her finger right on the pulse of popular culture, pollinating it with the spores of her beliefs. And listen, many of her beliefs are good. Some are maybe not so good. In the end, she's probably just like the rest of us, only amplified, a blend of intelligence and blindness, with many soft spots.

IT WAS 1990 when Loftus testified in the Franklin trial, disputing the validity of Eileen's repressed memory. Only a few years earlier, Ellen Bass and Laura Davis had published their phenomenally successful book *The Courage to Heal: A Guide for Women Survivors of Child Sexual Abuse*, which, much to Loftus's disgust, announced, "If you think you were abused, . . . then you were." Other therapists were instructing their traumatically repressed patients to "let the imagination run wild." Around this time, the courts began peeling back the statute of limitations for sex abuse crimes; instead of five years from the time of occurrence, charges could be pressed five years from the moment of memory retrieval, which meant that hundreds upon thousands of elderly parents were now being accused by their therapized daughters. "There were accusations of satanic cults," says Loftus, "And never, ever, has the FBI found a single piece of evidence to support this stuff."

A convergence of factors. The Bass and Davis book. The Franklin trial. But mostly letters pouring in from across the country from parents who had seen her defend George Franklin, and who were pleading with her for help. Couples wrote about children accusing them of grotesque satanic abuses beyond any believability—accusations Gothic and seemingly absurd, accusations that destroyed families and devastated mothers and fathers, who swore their innocence.

"My home became a one-way relay station for these people," says Loftus, "and my phone bills were hundreds of dollars each month, and I knew I couldn't help them unless I could scientifically prove that the mind not only distorts real memories but can create totally false ones. I wanted to prove experimentally that this was possible. But how? There are all these ethical issues—god, what with human ethics committees you can't get ANYTHING by anymore. You try one tiny harmless psychological experiment on a person and it's like you're a doctor leaving syphilis untreated." She chuckles. "The best thing to do would be to plant a memory of sexual abuse," she says, "but that's not ethical, so I thought and thought about how to come up with an experimental situation that touched on trauma but did not traumatize. It took me a long time. I went through so many different scenarios."

"Like what?" I ask her.

"Oh god," she says, "I can't remember now."

And then it came to her, how she could do it, experimentally implant false memories without violating ethical guidelines. Loftus and her students came up with Lost in the Mall, a Don Dellilo–type trick that captures our national as well as individual absurdities.

THE EXPERIMENT HAD many phases. In some pretest versions, Lofts had university students attempt to implant false memories in their siblings over Thanksgiving vacation, tape the sessions, and then present them to her after the holiday. These, although part of the pilot, proved to be some of the richest demonstrations of fact buckling under fiction's weight. In the formal experiment, she recruited, with her assistant Jacqueline Pickrell, twenty-four individuals. Loftus prepared for each subject a small booklet containing three written accounts of real childhood memories provided by a subject's family member, and one false written account of being lost in the mall. The constructed stories, done with family members who agreed to help in the hoax, were each one paragraph long. Subjects came to the lab, read the memory booklets, and were instructed to elaborate on them with their own recollections, and if they had none, to simply write, "I don't remember this."

What surprised Loftus most about the results of her experiment were not the statistically significant figures, but the narrative detail that accompanied some of the false memories. "The detail people confabulate and then believe in just astounds me," Loftus says, but her

voice is not astounded—it's delighted, like she has come to the core
of fairy tales, peeled back the brain to find where myths are made. In
one pretest, for instance, Chris, who had been convinced by his older
brother Jim that he had been lost in a shopping mall at age five,
recounted the false episode with flourish and feeling. Just two days
after the memory implantation, Chris reported, "That day I was so
scared I would never see my family again. I knew that I was in trouble." By day three Chris was recalling conversations with mom: "I
remember mom telling me never to do that again." A few weeks later
Chris, entirely unsuspecting, returned to the lab with the small memory seed now in hothouse bloom, colorful, scentful, absolutely
authentically inauthentic, a perfect plastic pearl: "I was with you guys
for a second and I think I went over to look at the toy store, the Kay
Bee toy and uh, we got lost, and I was looking around and I thought,
'uh oh, I'm in trouble now.' You know. And then I . . . I thought I was
never going to see my family again. I was really scared you know. And
then this old man, he was wearing blue flannel, came up to me . . . he
was kind of old. He was kind of bald on top . . . he had a ring of gray
hair. He had glasses." Amazing. None of the details had been provided in the tiny suggested seed; apparently our minds abhor blank
spots, are existentially unprepared for emptiness. We fill in.

Loftus's work reveals example after example of this kind of confabulation. In another pilot study, an Asian girl confabulated an entire
Kmart, the terry-cloth feel of the towels, the long white wincing
lights, the lurch of the slippery aisles as she ran to find her grand-
mother. In the formal experiment, twenty-five percent of the subjects suddenly remembered being lost in a mall and, when debriefed,
expressed surprise, or even shock, at the deception.

"LOST IN THE MALL," says psychiatrist Judith Herman, founder of
Victims of Violence and author of *Father-Daughter Incest,* "is cute. It's
a cute experiment that tells us exactly the opposite of what Loftus
thinks she's telling us. Loftus thinks she's telling us that peoples'

memories can't be relied upon, but look at her data. Seventy-five percent of her subjects did not confabulate. They were reliable."

Bessel van der Kolk, another psychiatrist who specializes in trauma, is even more forthcoming. "I hate Elizabeth Loftus," he says. "I can't even bear to hear the name."

Loftus knows her reputation in some circles. It doesn't seem to bother her. This may be because she's so passionate about her science that the politics simply cease to exist, or it may be because she knows, like any good self-promoter, that no publicity is bad publicity and bad publicity is better than no publicity. When I ask her about Herman's comment, the seventy-five-percent nonconfabulators and the implication that, therefore, most survivors are telling the truth, she snorts. "I think twenty-five percent is a VERY significant minority," she says. "Furthermore, Lost in the Mall became a springboard for other false memory experiments that got as much as a fifty percent or even higher confabulation rate." Loftus goes on to tell me what some of those other experiments were: the "impossible memory experiment," where subjects were induced to believe they recalled the first few days of their infancies; the spilling-the-punch-at-the-wedding experiment, where people dredged up fictional memories of a white dress, a crystal bowl flying from their hands, a pink, seeping stain; their fault. "The best false memory planter in this country," Loftus says, "is Steve Porter, formerly from University of British Columbia. You should see that guy." After Loftus's Lost in the Mall experiment, Porter was able to convince roughly fifty percent of his subjects that they'd survived a vicious animal attack in childhood. "And of course," says Loftus, "it never happened."

LOFTUS PUBLISHED HER Lost in the Mall findings in 1993 in the *American Psychologist*. The mood in this country was exuberant. Everywhere walls were coming down. Mikhail Gorbachev announced the disintegration of the Soviet Union. Berlin integrated. In this country, scores of people were identifying their own iron curtains, their own split selves, and pushing pieces together. What we wanted was wholeness, a united world, a single self, no more covert constructions. The international media went to work reporting astounding events, the USSR morphing into Russia, a suddenly accessible land where reindeer lived and the sun set in a Siberia where the grass was the color of corn, the color of rust. Not so far away, in our own country we had our own, typically schmaltzy and solipsistic version of this going on: Miss America stepped forward and claimed she'd recovered netherworlds of frosted memories in the basement of her brain and, having lured them to the surface with a silver hook, was on her way to becoming complete. "I split into a day child who smiled and giggled and a night child who lay awake in a fetal position, only to be pried apart by my father." Thanks to the fishing expedition that her therapy was, Miss America, however, was finally coming together.

So too for Roseanne Barr, whose caustic iron curtain came straight down when she confessed on the cover of *People* magazine, "I Am an Incest Survivor." Roseanne claimed she had multiple personalities, but she was integrating, along with many other people, mostly women, some men, whose voices joined the jubilance, and the terror. So popular was the idea of recovered memories that *Time* and *Newsweek* reported on them, and a Pulitzer prize–winning novel, Jane Smiley's *A Thousand Acres*, described them.

It was into this climate that Loftus published her study. It was a climate of outrage and healing, pink scars and tender intimate tissues; it was the time of a certain story. And Loftus challenged it, saying, in effect, that a lot of people can be induced to believe false things at someone else's suggestion. Who is to say these so-called survivors weren't being induced at the hands of their therapists, especially those who actively practiced suggestion? After she published her article on Lost in the Mall, Loftus went on record saying she disbelieved a number of abuse narratives; they were concoctions, same as her subjects'. She then went one step further and challenged the whole Freudian notion of repression. According to Loftus, there is absolutely no substantial evidence that repression as a psychological or neural mechanism exists. Loftus instead posits that the rising of repressed memories is really a concatenation of fantasy, fear, innuendo, and news, with wisps of truth woven in. There are two kinds of truths, Loftus says, "Story truth and happening-truth. . . . As we put meat and muscle on the bare bones of the happening truth, we can get caught up, captured if you will, with the notion of our own stories. We become confused about where the happening truth leaves off and the story truth begins." As to why someone would concoct such a gruesome tale, Loftus says, "The real facts are sometimes so subtle as to defy language. A person can't find the words to talk about banal hurts that nevertheless have a searing significance, so they substitute an obvious plot. Other times a person concocts a story that they believe with every cell in their bodies because it provides them with an identity: survivor."

Now, no one particularly likes to have the dominant paradigm challenged, but to do it when the stars at the story's centers are victims, and when one of the story's main themes is the destructiveness of denial, to do it then takes courage, which Loftus clearly has. A long, long time ago, Darwin held back his theories because he feared religious reprisal; many scholars accuse Freud of abandoning his original theories regarding the origins of hysteria because he knew they wouldn't fit well with the sexual and social mores of Victorian Vienna. Never for a second did Loftus consider doing this. "I couldn't wait to get my ideas out there," she says. Part of her courage surely comes from a compulsion toward controversy. Part of her courage surely comes from a deeper place, but what it is I do not know.

"After I published my findings, people did the meanest things," Loftus says. "I've had to have body guards. People threatened to sue programs that were inviting me as their speaker; they wrote letters of complaints to Washington's governor; the clinical psychology students at the university practically hissed when I walked by. My students and I endured a lot of abuse," she says, "but you know what? We didn't repress any of it."

LOFTUS FREQUENTLY WALKS around campus with only one ear-
ring on, because she has her other ear pressed to the receiver of her
phone so many hours of the day. She sleeps little, and when she does,
she dreams of work, statistics splattered across her mind, high-flying
planes, lectures with no notes. She is utterly focused, constantly
fueled. Therefore, the criticisms did nothing to stop her—not the
woman who yelled "whore" in a hallway a few years back. Instead,
Loftus just plundered on, accruing enemies and frequent-flier miles
and fans and fame at a rather astounding clip. Outside her office,
accused parents were posting love letters and supposed survivors
were sending hate mail; inside, Loftus just worked on. After she suc-
ceeded in implanting false memories of surviving a traumatic event,
she began to wonder, would it be possible to implant false memories
of perpetrating an event? Before she could construct an experiment
to test this, an astounding case came forward.

Olympia, Washington, a place where the trees are always green,
where the fields are softly mounded. A church, a Christian man
whose name was Paul. Paul Ingram. He was forty-one years old and
had two daughters. These two daughters one day remembered, during a religious retreat where sins were called forth and darkness dis-
pelled, that they had been horrifically abused by their father. Their
father, Paul, was questioned by detectives, held for hours in a
cramped room, a tape recorder whirring: did you do it, did you do it?
The detectives asked, leaning forward, so close Paul could probably
feel the soft blast of breath on his face. He was a middle-aged man,
this Paul, frightened of Satan's wily ways, and the detectives were saying things like, "You did it. Your daughters wouldn't lie." Day turned
into night turned into day—sleeplessness, coffee, questions—remember, try to picture it. Paul tried. He said, "Jesus, O Jesus, O Jesus,
Merciful Jesus help me," crying and clutching the table. And then,
after days of drilling interrogation, of vivid scenes the detectives
sketched when he supposedly fondled his daughters' breasts, he said
he remembered. He said it haltingly at first. "Sweet Jesus, oh sweet
Jesus," he kept calling out and then he said it was coming clearer.

Right there in that room this man Paul Ingram first confessed to raping both his daughters, and then he went on, he just went on. He
recalled rapes and gang bangs and an entire decade-long participation
in a Satanic cult—it became real to him—the chanting, the things he
did. He wept. He was imprisoned.

Loftus, of course, when she heard about this case, and the kind of
questioning Ingram underwent, well, Loftus raised one eyebrow,
smelled something fishy, and thought about it. She got in touch with
her friend and cult expert Richard Ofshe, who trundled down to see
Paul in his jail cell. Ofshe, like Loftus, is an expert in suggestibility,
and like Loftus, he has a passion for revealing the fictions that many
facts are. So Ofshe went to see Ingram, and he told him that one of
his sons and one of his daughters had accused Paul of forcing them to
have sex with each other while Paul watched. Ingram's eyes went
wide. Oh. Oh. Ingram said what he always said, in the very beginning, "I guess I don't remember that." "Try to think about the scene,
try to see it happening," Ofshe said. He told Ingram to return to his
jail cell and try "praying on" the scene. And then Ofshe went away.

When he came back a day later (note how similar this structure is
to Loftus's Lost in the Mall experiment, planting the memory, waiting twenty-four to forty-eight hours), Ingram had composed an
entire confession about an event that Ofshe had completely concocted. He wrote that yes, he had forced his daughter and son to have
sex in front of him, and he wrote about it in graphic detail, the pink,
the pleasure, the horror. Ofshe and Loftus presented this as evidence
to the court that Ingram was being led down the primrose path of
presuppositions, that he was so malleable as to confess to anything.
And indeed, later on when they told Ingram the story was false, he
recanted all the other supposed memories, but it was too late for
him—he was behind bars, where he has stayed for too many years,
guilty of one thing for sure: a graphic imagination.

Loftus learned from the Ingram case that the tendency toward
invention is strong and all encompassing. It is a tendency so strong it
overrides self-preservation. We don't only concoct stories that make

us look innocent; no, we concoct stories at all costs, because we need to, because we have to. So powerful is the urge to have a socially sanctioned narrative that we will adopt one even if it means we are the villain at its center.

Meanwhile, Loftus herself was sleeping less and less. Her work acquired a kind of frenetic energy. Much of what she drew our attention to was valid and balanced. She wrote in one article, "False memories can be created by a small suggestion from a trusted family member, by hearing someone lie, by suggestion from a psychologist . . . of course, the fact that false memories can be planted tells us nothing about whether a given memory of child sexual abuse is false or not, nor does it tell us how one might distinguish the real cases from the false ones. The findings on the malleability of memory do, however, raise questions about the wisdom of certain recommendations being promoted in self help books . . . and by some therapists themselves." That's nothing if not nuanced. But then, not long after, in another article, Loftus writes, "We live in a strange and precarious time that resembles at its heart the hysteria and superstitious fervor of the witch trials." She took rifle lessons and to this day keeps the firing instruction sheets and targets posted above her desk. In 1996, when *Psychology Today* interviewed her, she burst into tears twice within the first twenty minutes, labile, lubricated, theatrical, still whip smart, talking about the blurry boundaries between fact and fiction while she herself lived in another blurry boundary, between conviction and compulsion, passion and hyperbole. "The witch hunts," she said, but the analogy is wrong, and provides us with perhaps a more accurate window into Loftus's stretched psyche than into our own times, for the witch hunts were predicated on utter nonsense, and the abuse scandals were predicated on something all too real, which Loftus seemed to forget: Women are abused. Memories do matter.

Talking to her, feeling her high-flying energy, the zeal that burns up the center of her life, you have to wonder, *why.* You are forced to ask the very kind of question Loftus most abhors: *did something bad happen to her?* For she herself seems driven by dissociated demons, and so I ask.

What happened to you?

Turns out, a lot. Loftus grew up with a cold father who taught her nothing about love but everything about angles. A mathematician, he showed her the beauty of the triangle's strong tip, the circumference of the circle, the rigorous mission of calculus. Her mother was softer, more dramatic, prone to deep depressions. Loftus tells all this to me with little feeling. "I have no feelings about this right now," she says, "but when I'm in the right space I could cry." I somehow don't believe her; she seems so far from real tears, from the original griefs, so immersed in the operas of others. Loftus recalls her father taking her out to see a play, and in the car, coming home at night, the moon hanging above them like a stopwatch, tick tick, her father saying to her, "You know, there's something wrong with your mother. She'll never be well again."

Her father was right. When Loftus was fourteen, her mother drowned in the family swimming pool. She was found floating face down in the deep end, in the summer. The sun was just coming up, the sky a mess of reds and bruise. Loftus recalls the shock, the siren, an oxygen mask clamped over her mouth as she screamed, "Mother mother mother," hysteria. That is a kind of drowning. "I loved her," Loftus says. "Was it suicide?" I ask. She says, "My father thinks so. Every year when I go home for Christmas, my brothers and I think about it, but we'll never know," she says. Then she says, "It doesn't matter."

"What doesn't matter?" I ask.

"Whether it was or it wasn't," she says. "It doesn't matter because it's all going to be okay." Then I hear nothing on the line but some static.

"You there?" I say.

"Oh I'm here," she says. "Tomorrow I'm going to Chicago, some guy on death row, I'm gonna save him. I gotta testify. Thank god I have my work," she says.

"You've always had your work," I say.

"Without it," she says, "where would I be?"

IN LOFTUS'S UNIVERSITY of Washington office, she has a picture of herself standing with a Supreme Court justice, and next to it, a picture of Demi Moore's body on top of which Loftus has perched a photograph of her own head. "I wish I had thinner thighs," she tells me. Maybe the odd combination of loopiness with gravity has contributed to her success. She is certainly accessible; by the end of the interview, I know not only Loftus's shoe size but her bra size too. "Can we keep that out of the chapter," she asks; we can. She has, perhaps, of any psychologist this century, crossed the line between the professional and the public. She's been on *Oprah, Sally Jesse Raphael.* She's published in *Glamour* on the one hand and in journals with names like *Psychology and Its Neural Substrates* on the other. It's clear why some people, alleged victims and their accusers, would feel so strongly about her, but how or why has she managed to become so known in certain fields? What is the resonance in her message?

Loftus is talking about so much more than memory. She's talking about authenticity and whether, as human beings, we have it. She's pointed out to the public—in a way no postmodern scholar ever could—how pastiche are our pasts, how all of us are artists whose images have only the vaguest relationship to reality. She has tossed us into an existential abyss, and we don't like it here. She has made us all Alzheimer's patients, long before our brains have begun to atrophy, for in Loftus's world, memory decays, its traces so far from indelible; as soon as an event hits the hippocampus, it begins its dissolution.

Loftus's view of memory and its incredibly fragile structure runs counter to deeply held notions and neurological beliefs. We have interpreted Freud's work on repression to mean that we hold pieces of our pasts in clear capsules and can access them—our lives!—with enough verbal maneuvering. Loftus says no: what we access is half-dream, half-construct, entirely unreliable. Thus, with one swoop of her hand, this psychologist has driven a stake through Father Freud's heart. We don't like that, our father. Sometime soon after Freud, a researcher by the name of Wilder Penfield found what appeared to be the material substrates of Freud's repression. He split the skulls of epileptic patients and, before taking out the damaged tissue, moved a charged probe around on their bare brain tissue while the patients were conscious. Penfield found that when he touched certain areas in a person's brain, all these memories seemed to float back, crisp and clear—memories of a child crying by a stone wall, memories of a mother, memories drenched in yellow; it lived in us, our whole lives. Most of us don't know Penfield's work, but it has made its way into our culture, his charged probe, the secret drawers deep in the brain where yellow and mothers live. Of Penfield, Loftus says, "Let's look at the data. Only three percent of his patients actually had these memories when the probe touched their brain, and we have no idea if they were real memories or dream fragments." True. Boom. There goes Penfield; he's on the floor with Father Freud.

After Lost in the Mall and its rather astounding results, and after the follow-up experiments by other researchers, who were able to implant such extreme memories as being attacked by vicious animals, Loftus began to tackle the whole notion of repression. She already suspected that many repressed memories were probably false memories suggested by therapists and self-help books, and from there it was an easy leap to question whether repression really existed at all, as a psychological or neurological phenomenon. Was there any real proof of repression? she wondered. In our culture, this is like asking if there's any real proof of the sun. It's up there, you can see it, it singes your skin. But I can't see repression, Loftus said. Show me. No one could.

She went on a hunt then. Perhaps repression was repressed somewhere, and she could dig it from its dirt and examine its mechanisms. She examined hundreds of papers on the subject, but not one of them presented real evidence that people can completely forget a trauma, store it in human RAM, and then call it back up on cue years later. There's no indisputable neurological evidence of this, no repression coffer that has ever been definitely identified in the brain. But more than that, her studies of trauma showed just the opposite of what the dominant cultural story said. What Loftus found was that most trauma survivors obsessively remember what happened to them. There are, for instance, no cases of Holocaust victims just forgetting they were in concentration camps, or plane-crash victims just forgetting when the jet went down, only to recall it on their eighty-fifth birthday, when they take the Concorde to France.

While that may be true, and Loftus eagerly cites this as evidence, she overlooks the fact that these traumas are different from sexual abuse traumas, which are shrouded in secrecy, erased as the acts are performed. Says Loftus when I throw this her way, "If secrecy is the ingredient of repression, then why aren't all sexual abuse acts repressed? They're almost all secret."

"What kind of evidence would you need in order to believe in repression?" I ask.

"Corroboration," she says. "It's so simple."

But simple it is not. Says Judith Herman, "Lauren, as a psychologist you should know. There's plenty, PLENTY of evidence that repression is possible. Look at Charcot, Janet." And indeed Daniel Schachter, a memory researcher at Harvard, cites one case in which a forty-year-old man, bothered by an intrusive mental image of himself at ten years old surrounded by assaultive boys, was eventually able to uncover a traumatic memory regarding this incident and sexual abuse. The event was then corroborated by a cousin, who had been present during the abuse. So there's one example; it can happen. However, Schachter also writes, ". . . there is as yet little or no scientifically credible evidence that people who have suffered years of violent or horrific abuse after the years of infancy and early childhood can immediately and indefinitely forget about the abuse."

WHEN LOFTUS WAS young, she kept a diary. It was a small red vinyl-covered book with pages lined in pale blue. She knew her mother sometimes read it, so she devised an ingenious strategy for preserving her privacy. She would write one acceptable story on the actual diary page, and if there was something really personal, she would write it on a separate page, append it with a paperclip, and then, if she felt her mother was on the prowl, she would hide the paper-clipped pages. These paper-clipped pages Loftus called her "removable truths."

Right from the beginning then, Loftus lived in a world that was shape shifting and relentlessly narrative. Right from the beginning she suspected history was construction, and this in the 1950s, before "postmodern" had landed on anyone's lips. Precocious. Prescient.

Her critics, however, resist the trope of removable truths, especially as they apply to trauma. Says Bessel van der Kolk, "Loftus may have shown us that kids in a lab can think they were lost in a mall, but this cannot be applied to traumatic memory. Traumatic memory is encoded in the brain entirely differently."

Van der Kolk, a handsome Dutch psychiatrist who lives in Boston's South End, on a fairy-tale street of cobblestones and gas lamps, a street that seems stuck in time, believes "the body keeps the score." His street has preserved its history; so too does the brain. Van der Kolk's theory of trauma and memory goes something like this: When a traumatic event happens to a person, it is frequently so overwhelming that it cannot be comprehended by the normal narrative means. So the memory of the event gets stored in the nonnarrative parts of the brain, the somatosensory cortex, where it exists as muscle aches, keen but nameless surges of panic, serrated flashbacks that burst and then dissolve before the mind can say what it saw. The job of healing, according to van der Kolk, is to somehow elevate the nonnarrative trauma into the storytelling circuits of the brain, so the spell can be broken by speech and then woven into the larger tapestry of the person's life story, where it can take up residence as one event among many, blending in, integrated.

Loftus claims van der Kolk has no real evidence of this theory, although van der Kolk, in his writings, cites brain imaging studies and anecdotal evidence. Loftus calls anecdotal evidence "anecdata." And even, she might say, if van der Kolk's lyrical theory of splits and mergers were correct, it still wouldn't support the idea of repression per se. Sure, the person may have physiological responses to cues that bring back the trauma. Sure they may have panic attacks and muscle stiffness and all the rest. But just because the body contains traces of horror doesn't mean the mind has completely forgotten it. Ask shell-shocked soldiers if they forget their battles? Ask rape victims if they forget the man in the greasy alleyway? The body keeps the score, Loftus might say, but that doesn't mean the mind has taken time off.

Judith Herman cites as evidence for the theory that traumatic memory is reliable, and that it is emblazed in the brain, certain lab experiments with rats. When rats learned a task in a state of high stress, it was difficult, if not impossible, for them to subsequently extinguish their behaviors. "This is an animal analogue, if you will, of the 'indelible imprint' of traumatic events on memory." What Loftus says to this, "And they accuse me of generalizing from college students to trauma victims. They're generalizing from a rat!"

Loftus began a broad survey of other studies regarding traumatic memory and its reliability. She cites one study of children who had witnessed a sniper attack on their school. Immediately after the shooting, children reported where they were and what they were seeing. A week or so after the shooting, however, the children's memories had faded or become distorted, and they gave reports that differed from their original ones. A little girl, for instance, who had been in the schoolyard at the time of the shooting, later reported she had been outside the playground fence. Her memory seemed far from emblazed; within seven days it was already going the way of decay. Colleagues of Loftus's studied memories of the *Challenger* explosion. The day after the explosion Ulrich Neisser of Emory University asked people where they were when they saw the space shuttle blow up. They took down specific accounts from witnesses. "I was standing in front of a phone booth." "I was frying an egg in my kitchen, the radio on the windowsill." And then Neisser some time later followed up on these accounts they did the day after the explosion. Very few of the respondents gave the same account they did the day after the explosion. Their memories had shifted considerably, so the egg morphed into meatloaf morphed into the beach, and the phone booth, Dali-like, melted and stretched its shape so it was a museum. When subjects were shown their original accounts, written fresh in the wake of disaster, they could not believe them. They felt certain of their current description, which illuminates the tenuous connection between feeling sure and being right. The false memories were saturated with subjective veracity, so fictions felt like facts in a topsy-turvy world.

WHEN THE *CHALLENGER*   blew up, I was with my sister in the Tufts University cafeteria. We were eating tuna-fish sandwiches, lettuce with scalloped edges peeking out between the tan crusts. Outside the huge plate-glass windows, the trees branched dendritically, bare and black against the shiny sky. I have always remembered this, but now I'm not so sure. I'm not so sure of anything. Maybe I was in my mother's living room, with the yellow brocaded furniture and the coarse raspy rug, watching on the television the two-tailed plume of vapor in the darkness. But no, I think. That's not quite right. It was raining that day, was it not? And my big-chested Irish boyfriend and I were drinking beer at the Black Rose pub, or was that later, at night? The spaceship was always falling, whenever we turned on that TV; what I remember are the jubilant faces of the crowd, tipped toward the patriotic sky, and then the sucking-in sound, the Oh. Oh, and the ship breaking up, fluffy pieces of it drifting down, the bodies invisible, already gone.

"Where were you when the *Challenger* blew up?" I ask Loftus.

"I was in my office, alone," she says, and I picture her there. And then I picture her alone in her home, her spacious West Coast home, the ties from her ex-husband still in the closet, as though he might someday return. "He left because I couldn't stop working," she says. "He wanted to take vacations and lead a normal life. My idea of fun is to sit in front of my computer and try to figure things out."

Loftus has no husband, and she has no children, which she says she regrets. "By the time we tried, it was too late," she says. "I was thirty-six. Every month, a little spot of blood on my underwear."

I picture her alone in her office or alone in her home, alone, most of all, in her field of inquiry, while another woman, Christa McAuliffe falls through the sky. I have to wonder, if a man were asking Loftus's questions, would he be so questioned? But in truth, I don't think its gender that occasionally undermines her credibility. It's not that she's falling through some sky, radically alone, where a woman shouldn't be. It's the fact that when all is said and done, Loftus does not seem quite in control. She does not appear to be steering her ship. She blurts out odd comments, has targets from a rifle practice affixed to her office wall; but at the same time she does brilliant memory experiments while comparing herself to Schindler. She calls me up, then slams down the phone, and then calls back sheepishly: "God that was rude." No explanation, so strange. "I just," she says, "I just have this NEED to reunite families fractured by false memory accusations; I just want to reunite people," Loftus says, this motherless girl, who, twenty years after a divorce, still keeps her wasband's belongings in a cradle in her living room. "This NEED," she says to me, "reunions," she says to me, but she appears to have little consciousness that the need is evidence of what she's trying so hard to disprove. There is something split off in Loftus, unresolved, damped down, working its way out sideways. She is the survivor who questions the validity of survivorship. That's one way out of a bind.

But listen, Loftus has given us many gifts. Her singular free fall has yielded absolutely significant insights that we can't dismiss. Where were you when the *Challenger* blew up? Do you remember this? Do you remember that? What Loftus has shown us is how high we fly, how far the ground—we are weightless.

"What grounds you?" I ask her. "If you can't trust memory, what can you rely upon." I'm thinking of how Dostoyevsky claimed that a few good memories were all one needed to find faith in the world. But after you've lived in Loftus-land for awhile, it's hard to know where to place your faith. "Do you have a religion?" I ask her.

"What do you have?" I ask her, but what I really mean is: what do any of us have then? What?

Loftus doesn't answer me. Instead she says, "I wrote a letter to my mother a few days ago." She shows it to me.

Dear Mother,
It's Sunday, it's raining, it's dreary outside. I woke up this morning with a sense of dread. You've been gone for forty years. . . . I'd like to tell you some of the things I've done in the past four decades. Recently I gave a speech about my research on memory at a conference in Chicago. It was a National Conference On Wrongful Death convictions and The Death Penalty. While there, I watched twenty six men and two women, all wrongly convicted former death row inmates, weep and hug each other. . . . My work has brought me into contact with people suffering a terrible injustice. . . .

When I'm not working on the research or teaching my classes, I spend time on the cases of the falsely accused. Of course, I'm not sure that someone I'm helping is being falsely accused rather than rightly, but the idea that the accusations could well be wrong consumes me. . . . I feel compelled to help and almost guilty if I let up for a minute.

Why am I such a work-a-holic? Does it give me a way to escape from painful thoughts? Does it help me feel an importance that is and was otherwise missing from my life. . . . Me now: busy with work, and I don't have much time to think about what is missing. A family love and closeness. That's what I miss. That's what I miss about you.

Love forever,

Beth

In the end, then, Loftus does not give me an answer about what she has, rather what she has not. In the end, there is this flash of insight and one woman's plain pain. Maybe that's all any of us have, just plain pain. No solid memories, but real regrets, regrets as substantial as stones—we can count on those. We can, like Loftus, pile those stones one on top of the other, standing skyward, stretching out toward something.

9

Memory Inc.

ERIC KANDEL'S SEA SLUG
EXPERIMENT

In the 1980s, Elizabeth Loftus based many of her claims on the "fact" that there were no neural mechanisms for repression. In this chapter, however, we will meet one of Loftus's challengers, Eric Kandel, who performed a series of experiments that have given long-outmoded Freudian concepts a new lift. Kandel originally aspired to become a psychoanalyst; he recalls its golden days of intellectual vibrancy, but he became enamored, eventually, with the biology of the brain. Kandel set out on a journey to discover the actual workings of memory, its intricate cellular mechanisms. Kandel, now seventy-three, is the oldest scientist in this collection, but he is practicing in the youngest way; his techniques and areas of inquiry define the field's future and, at the same time, stake a solid claim for a radically reductive approach to the human mind.

PART ONE

It was 1953. The day of the surgery was hot, still, the sky a blue–white shimmer above Hartford. The young man, Henry, had severe epilepsy, with fits so frequent they had just about ruined his life. Henry spent his time seizing and dreaming of life before epilepsy, when his hand had been steady enough to shoot rifles in the woods. His father was appalled by his son's disease. His mother tried to hold him as he foamed into frenzies. Drugs did not work. Exercise did not work. Prayer did not work. Then Dr. Scoville, of Hartford Hospital, offered the family an experimental cure. They said yes.

Henry and his family didn't know Dr. Scoville. They did not know, for instance, that he was fond of the lobotomy, having performed well over three hundred, going into area mental hospitals with his hand-cranked drill and moving from patient to patient until he'd done every one. Scoville was unusually handsome—anyone could see that—and the family may have sensed his upper-class heritage, but surely they were not aware that their surgeon-to-be was considered by some to be recklessly audacious. In his free time Scoville liked to race red Jaguars on Connecticut's open highways, pursued by the police. He liked to spend money, and his wife tells of how, in an attempt to woo her, he leapt onto the running board of a moving Chevrolet. "He is an innovator, never willing to accept the status quo. Behind a façade of wild activity, driven by an insatiable ego, he seeks better ways of doing things," one colleague wrote of him in the *Journal of Surgical Neurology*.

And it was to this man that Henry was giving his head. He had no idea. Dr. Scoville had an idea. He suspected Henry's seizures might be kindling deep in the wetlands of the temporal lobes, a little spark quickly catching flame in a supposedly toss-away part of the brain: the hippocampus. Scoville offered to excise Henry's hippocampus. He had done this operation before on several patients with epilepsy, and it seemed to cure them. He told this to Henry. What he didn't tell Henry was that all the prior patients had been severely psychotic before the surgery, and so there was no way of assessing what sort of damage the procedure may have done.

In those days, not much was known about the biology of the brain. One psychiatrist observed that his psychotic patient seemed to calm down while riding a bumpy train; from there on in, the treatment consisted of shaking the poor man for greater and greater time lengths. Other doctors believed malaria might cure schizophrenia. Based on a series of experiments by Karl Lashley, scientists believed that there were no specific locales linked to memory in the brain. Lashley, in 1929, removed different portions of live rat brains and found that no one excised portion had any more effect on memory than any other excised portion. Memory, concluded Lashley—memory, thought Scoville—was diffuse, without locale, scattered like widely sown seed over the whole rind of the cortex.

Based on this last assumption, Scoville had no hesitation about removing Henry's hippocampus. The operating room was cool. Henry lay awake on the steel table. Because there are no nerves in the brain, such surgery was performed with the patient completely conscious, only a local anesthetic to numb the skin of the scalp. Swoosh went the shot of lidocaine. A moment later Henry must have seen Scoville coming at him with his hand-cranked drill, and then two holes were bored above each of his open eyes, and into these holes Scoville inserted a small spatula, with which he jacked up Henry's frontal lobes.

The operating room was quiet. Nurse, hand me this. Nurse, hand me that. But otherwise, no sound. Scoville was looking into Henry. He was looking under the hood of Henry's brain, and how beautiful it was beneath the cortical coral reef, in the brain's interior capsules, where pyramidal cells are shaped like hyacinth, in complex cones, where neurons are tiny but dense. Into this nether region Scoville now inserted a silver straw. Scoville slowly threaded the silver straw deep into Henry's pulsing brain, and then—there—he suctioned out the pink-gray seahorse shape on either side, the entire hippocampus now gone. Inside Henry's head, a great gap appeared, a ragged hole where once something had lived.

What did Henry feel as Scoville sucked out his hippocampus? He was, after all, wide awake, thoroughly alert, and the hippocampus, although no one knew it at the time, is the seat of many of our mem-

ories. Did Henry feel his past leave him in a single suck? Did he feel
the entrance of forgetfulness, like a cold thing coming in, or was it
more a sensation of sliding: your lover, your qualms, the cats calling
beneath the porch in the summer—all dropping down into nothing?

In the days following the surgery, it became clear that Henry was
having far fewer fits. It also became clear that he had lost the ability
to form any memories. A nurse introduced herself, left, and five minutes later, Henry had not the faintest idea who she was. He did recognize his mother, but anyone he met or anything he learned from
the day of surgery onward he couldn't retain. Fifty years later, Henry
is still that way. He lives now, a very old man, in a nursing home near
MIT. His mother died in the 1960s, and every time Henry hears this
news, he cries afresh, believing he is hearing it for the first time. He
thinks Truman is still president. In his nursing home, he can form no
new relationships, cannot retain the shape of a face or the sound of a
voice: face and voice, the essential components of comfort. Henry,
now known in the medical literature as H.M., has no comfort.

A few weeks after Henry's surgery, when his mental confusion
did not clear up, Dr. Scoville realized he had inadvertently ampu-
tated the mill of memory, as well as the seizure's starting point. He
may have been frightened, then. He may have felt bad. But what
likely struck him the most was the scientific import of his wayward
operation, for it showed that Karl Lashley was wrong. Wrong!
Memory was not a scattering of sites, impossible to locate, as Lashley
had written and scientists of the day had subsequently believed.
Obviously, the hippocampus was the royal seat of remembering, for
without it, Henry was consigned to a stretch of the palest present.
Scoville published his findings from this grand but botched experiment. He had touched the tissue of memory, which was not spiritual
or mythical in its essence. Memory was flesh. It could be pinpointed,
like a country on a map. There. There lives your past. There lives
your future. In the seahorse. Beneath the cortical coral reef. In one
man's silver straw.

PART TWO

Brenda Milner may be the person who has come to know H.M. better than anyone else. She recalls the case, how she heard with horror what Scoville had done and then wanted to see it for herself. Back then, in 1957, when Scoville first published his findings, Milner was studying memory with Wilder Penfield, the famed physician who touched his epileptic patients' bare brains with an electric probe, observed whether touch, or smell, or vision was stimulated, and then tacked onto the actual region a piece of paper stating what the region was responsible for. This is how early brain mapping happened, with Post-it notes.

Milner may have been ready to go out on her own. She may have been tired of the paper trail. She says that when she heard about Henry, she grabbed a few memory tests and hopped on the first train. She had seen memory loss before, but H.M. offered her the chance to study the purest form of amnesia ever known to humankind.

Brenda Milner wanted to know exactly what mental functions H.M. had lost, but more importantly, she wanted to know what mental functions H.M. had been spared. For instance, while he couldn't recall a conversation held five minutes prior, he could still walk, and walking is a kind of memory, is it not? H.M. did not know, upon getting up in the morning, that he was supposed to brush his teeth, but once a toothbrush was placed in his hand, his hand took over. Perhaps this is similar to what musicians experience when they are deep in a song, their hands taking over, rhythm pouring through their fingers, as though each one is tipped with its own tiny brain, separate from the main calyx.

Over years of tests and observation, Brenda Milner was able to show a few important things about the mechanics of memory, with H.M. as her proof. Yes, the hippocampus is clearly essential for memory of explicit, autobiographical detail—one might call it the core of consciousness itself—but there is another memory system located in a whole other place in the brain, and this Milner called procedural memory, or unconscious memory. Even if, and when, we lose our ability to recall names and faces, we may still know how to ride a bike, or smoke a cigarette. H.M. couldn't tell you how old he was, or recognize his face in a mirror, but if you brought him back to his old Hartford neighborhood, he would wend his way through the streets, walk up the steps to his old house, knock on the door of a past he could find few words for. Henry was living proof that Freud's unconscious had an actual neural basis. But how those neurons worked, no one knew.

Milner drew her understanding about the neural substrates of memory, not by observing those substrates, but by watching their manifestations in an intact organism, a whole human being, Henry. This was her singular gift to psychology, the long-term study of H.M. and the resulting knowledge that memory operates on at least two levels. Since Milner, in part inspired by Milner, scientists have discovered multiple separate memory systems in our brains: there is procedural memory, which is mostly the unconscious memory for motor skills; semantic memory, whereby we retain facts; declarative memory, whereby we know who we are. There are even, some scientists suggest, separate memory engines for separate categories, our knowledge of fruits in one neural stream, our knowledge of vegetables in another, cats here, dogs there, so all our world, it seems, lives crunched up in cortical containers.

PART THREE

Eric Kandel is not at all afraid to hide the fact that he is a reductionist, that for him science is lived in a series of disassembled parts, not the intact organism. For Kandel, the secrets of memory lie in the study of how nerve cells talk to their neighbors.

Kandel started out training to become a psychoanalyst, but in his fourth year of medical school he heard about the H.M. case and it made an impression on him. He subsequently decided to do a post-doctoral fellowship at the National Institutes of Health (NIH) in Bethesda, where he took intracellular recordings of the hippocampus of a cat. "I was good at it," says Kandel, who is now in his seventies. "I didn't realize how good I'd be at lab work."

Kandel was born in Vienna. His father owned a toy store, and so, on the one hand, he had access to a childhood full of color. But then, in 1938, Hitler's army marched in. Kandel recalls Kristellnacht, all that glass, and later the toothbrushes the Jews were forced to use to scrub the streets.

One has to wonder: What role does the Holocaust play in Kandel's lifelong dedication to the cellular study of memory? Kandel says, "Sometimes I feel I have not faced things fully enough. I can tell you everything that happened to me, but I have no affect surrounding these events. By the grace of god I could have ended up at Dachau and I can talk about it, but I can't feel the fear."

In 1939 Kandel emigrated to the United States. He grew up in New York, while, fifty miles away from him, in Connecticut, H.M., just about his age, was negotiating a whole different kind of childhood. Kandel turned out to be unusually bright. He went to Harvard. Despite the childhood trauma, his brain expanded, growing ever more dense with new knowledge. H.M., on the other hand, was just experiencing his first seizure; he was dropping out of school as Kandel was rising through its ranks, H.M.'s brain aflame in all the wrong ways. The two had never talked, of course, but their lives would intersect in space, someplace above our heads, above our flesh, where we meet and touch and might not ever know.

At Harvard Kandel was captivated by psychoanalysis, but once he entered the neuroscience lab in medical school, his focus shifted. "Actually," says Kandel, "I never really thought psychoanalysis and neuroscience were incompatible. Freud, after all, was a neurologist. Psychoanalysis primarily concerns itself with memory, and my work is trying to illuminate memory mechanisms. I think one will ultimately be able to show the neural bases for many psychoanalytical principles."

Kandel is charming. He wears a bright-red bow tie, and sus-penders. He is interested in joining the disparate fields of psycho-analysis and neuroscience, but that is really a secondary pursuit for him. His primary pursuit started over forty years ago, in that NIH lab, where, in an attempt to elucidate the biology of memory, he studied nerve cells in the hippocampus. The hippocampus, however, is hard to work with. It has millions of neurons, and thousands of them can fit inside this o. It would take Kandel years to trace such tiny, complex architecture. He needed another model. "In the 1950s and 1960s, many biologists and most psychologists believed that learning was the one area of biology in which the use of simple ani-mal models . . . was least likely to succeed. . . . It was my belief, how-ever, that concerns about the use of a simple experimental system to study learning were misplaced. If elementary forms of learning are common to all animals with an evolved nervous system, there must be conserved features in the mechanisms of learning at the cell and molecular level that can be studied effectively even in simple inverte-brate animals."

With this belief, Kandel did an extensive search for a suitable experimental animal, and settled on slugs, specifically the giant marine snail aplysia. Aplysia has only twenty thousand neurons, many of them visible to the eye. Here would be an animal at once simpler to study, but still relevant to human beings because, as Kandel says, our nervous systems are the same, straight down the food chain. "I needed a radically reductionist approach to the problem of mind," Kandel says. So he settled on aplysia, purple, gelatinous, leaving behind a pale trace of wetness on the palm.

THIS IS WHAT Kandel did. He trained his sea slugs. He touched their goopy bodies—their siphons—with an electric probe, and the sea slug's gill withdrew. Kandel, along with several of his colleagues, soon discovered that this simple reflex could be modified by three different forms of learning: habituation, sensitization, and classical

conditioning. Of course Skinner and Pavlov had discovered somewhat similar things, but what they called "learning theory" in the
beginning of the century, Kandel was calling "memory" at the century's end. Same problem. Different packaging. But packaging is
important; it influences how we see and question the contents
within. In framing the pursuit as a problem, in part, of memory,
Kandel cleared the way for an all-out investigation into how we hold
our histories, and this was perhaps the core question of a post-
Holocaust world.

Kandel also went one critical step further than Skinner in his
study of pigeons or Milner in her study of H.M. Kandel observed
what actually happened to the sea slug's neurons as they learned—
remembered—a new task. Many scientists from as far back as the
eighteenth century had hypothesized about what happened to neurons when memory formed, but no one had as yet ever demonstrated
a thing. In 1894 Santiago Ramón y Cajal proposed a theory of memory storage according to which memory is stored in the growth of
new neural connections. Alexander Forbes proposed that memory is
stored by a self-reexciting chain of neurons. Donald Hebb later
championed this theory, but that's all these were: theories. Until
Kandel, no one had translated intuitive belief into physical proof.

So, Kandel trained his sea slugs, and he watched. He measured. He
conditioned the slug to withdraw its gill whenever it was touched,
and as he did this, he actually observed, with a microscope and a
recording device, aplysia's neurons change. He discovered that the
links between the neurons, called synapses, grew stronger by passing
electrochemical signals that reinforced the relationship. He watched
two neurons, one sensory, the other motor, pass stronger impulses to
each other as behavior became engraved.

Therefore, the use-it-or-lose-it credo is correct. Every time you
practice a task, you further burn into your brain the webwork of
neurons responsible for carrying out that task; the more you rehearse
a memory, telling it to yourself over and over, the stronger and
smoother the electrochemical conversation between those particular

synapses in your skull. I know this to be true. We have in our house a small piano. My fingers at first were clumsy on the keys. Now though, a few weeks later, having played every day, I feel a linked loop de loop in my brain. I feel how the grooves up there give grease to my fingers so they can trot smoothly over the notes, just one simple song. But by playing that piano, I jostled at least two noncommunicating neurons into a relationship, and this, in the end, is what memory depends on—relationship—our brains are relentlessly relational, yes, it's one big match.com in there, strangers contacting strangers, finding their well-worn ways to each other's doors.

KANDEL WAS ONE of the first to actually provide a molecular model of primitive memory. Now he had another question. How, he wondered, did the brain convert short-term into long-term memory? Perhaps he thought of H.M. The fact that H.M. was able to remember the face of his mother even without a hippocampus suggests that the hippocampus is the binding site where memories go, to be wrapped up in ribbon and then transferred to a long-term storage bin elsewhere in the cortex. H.M.'s mother's face was obviously processed and bound in the hippocampus long before the surgery, and then archived where no knife could reach.

Volumes of impressions, noises, feelings, interactions happen to us every day, and if we retained it all, we'd be in a sea of mental clutter. Instead what we usually recall are general impressions of our past: for me it's my grandfather's house, its cedar smell, the dense white sky of so many winters that it becomes unclear whether I am recalling the sky, or my memory of the sky. But then there are those few memories from the past that stand distinctive, even if incorrect. I remember walking in the field one winter morning and coming upon a huge hole in the ground, and when I looked down into it, I saw a man's hat floating on the water. I remember the time I mixed two vials from my chemistry set together, and created a small but impressive explosion. I remember my mother telling me Dr. King had been shot, and I thought she meant my pediatrician, whose name was also Dr. King. I remember very well our neighbors, the seven children who were burned to death in a nighttime fire, the stench of smoke that hung in our house for weeks.

The question: What process in my brain allowed those memories to exit their short-term status, get twined up in the hippocampus, and then stored for my perusal on this paper right now? Kandel believed there was a mechanism that allowed for the conversion of short term to long term, and, as is typical of him, he went at it like a kamikaze reductionist, this time using not the simple sea slug, but a snippet of it. He cored aplysia and put just two of its preserved neurons in broth.

He then manipulated the neurons so that they "talked" to one another, so that neuron 1 grew synaptic connections with neuron 2. This was the mechanics of memory in its most minimalist form. Kandel then showed that by blocking a tiny molecule deep in nerve cell 1, a molecule called cAMP-response element binding protein (CREB), he could disrupt the conversation. With CREB blocked, the events associated with long-term memory formation—protein synthesis, the growth of new synapses—did not occur.

What, exactly, is CREB? It's a molecule that dwells in the nucleus of a brain cell, and its purpose is to switch on the genes needed to produce the proteins that groove permanent connections between the cells. That's the simple scientific answer. The metaphorical answer: CREB is a cell's own Velcro; when it's "on," your mother's voice and your first ballet recital stick to the circuits of cells for years; when it's "off," you can still recall things, but it's brief, that phone number just sliding from your mind. Or we can try it another way. Short-term memories, perhaps, are a little like crushes, with a single surge of chemistry that fades fast; long-term memories are more like marriages, bound together, even trapped together, so you cannot get a new point of view. CREB—so physiologically fixed, so metaphorically malleable, Velcro, glue, snap, sex—CREB is as lyrically potent as it is scientifically significant. It gives us a way to grasp ourselves.

CREB was a finding that made a real splash in psychology. It was a finding that allowed psychologists, and others, their first glimpse at the makings of permanent memory. It also raised, for the first time, the possibility that we could manipulate our minds at a level of specificity previously unheard of. Tim Tully, a forty-two-year-old researcher at that time, heard about Kandel's CREB and got excited. Tully genetically rigged his fruit flies so they were born with the ability to have massive amounts of CREB switched on, and, sure enough, he had created insect geniuses, drosophila with photographic memories. They could learn a fruit-fly task in one training session, as opposed to normal fruit flies, who had to have about ten practice rounds before they recalled whatever trick they were being taught. Tully and Kandel entered into a competition then—aplysia versus drosophila, the slug against the fly—and within years Kandel created CREB-enhanced sea slugs who could recall—what? I can't imagine—the swirls on a neighboring seashell, the colors of a coral reef, or something far more prosaic, a paired association, food in a corner of the cage.

Along with CREB, Kandel also discovered CREB repressor, a molecule that caused mice to almost instantly forget whatever new tasks they had learned. Kandel realized the implications. In 1997 he joined up with Harvard molecular biologist Walter Gilbert, the venture capitalist Jonathan Fleming, and the neuroscientist Axel Unterbeck, and together they founded a company called Memory Pharmaceuticals, which, today, as I write, trying to keep all the details of this complex story in my aging brain, today, right now, Memory Pharmaceuticals is closing in on a new class of drugs that promise to revise our notions of age, of time, turning us all, perhaps, into mini Prousts, borne aloft on the simple scent of cinnamon, or tea, or the sudden bakery smell pouring through those doors.

I ONCE READ, or wrote, I can't recall now, a story about a woman who decides to forget. This woman lives alone in a house with roses on the wallpaper, and she has been unlucky in love, and she is old, and so, one day, she decides to just forget the roses on the wallpaper. After that, she decides to forget the coffee cup she's holding, and then the hand that holds it, and then the legs that move her through the lonely world, and as she forgets each piece of herself, she gets smaller and smaller, sitting there in her kitchen, she is shaved away, and she forgets her face, her eyes, until at last there is nothing but her heart left, and then she forgets that too, and so she floats, unconscious and free and utterly unhuman.

The tale points to the centrality of memory in our sense of what it means to be alive. We hear it all the time: Memory makes us who we are. Those who forget the past are condemned to repeat it. Memory is narrative, giving continuity and meaning to our existences. We are, if not obsessed with memory, at least deeply concerned with it. This may be because it's a force of such metaphysical and molecular import. It may also be, however, that we are living in a time that has elevated memory to a unique status; everywhere we go, we see memory. Our computers hold much of our memories, and so become extensions of our brains. By the year 2110, half the population will be over the age of fifty, and because those people—me and you—are living longer, greater and greater percentages will fall behind the haze of dementia, or straight into the swamp of Alzheimer's. Improved screening devices mean that many of us now know we have Alzheimer's in its earliest stages, and so we will watch our own brain waning.

Kandel's company, Memory Pharmaceuticals, knows this. The company, some forty minutes from the New York State Psychiatric Institute, is located off the Garden State Parkway in Montvale, New Jersey. Inside there are twisty corridors, rats and cats in cages, husked brains hung up on strings, sickle-shaped slices of animal cortices suspended in rich broth, closely monitored by Unterbeck's team of twenty drug-discovery scientists. The company's goal: to find a chemical compound that will help the disembodied neurons in the petri dish, and then the embodied neurons in the human head, to form stronger, longer-lasting connections. The hope: to enhance

CREB pharmacologically, so that we may emerge from the haze of age-related memory loss, our senses newly sharp.

Kandel believes his drugs, which Memory Pharmaceuticals has started to develop, will be available to the public in ten years. The compound being developed is actually not targeted at Alzheimer's patients; it is, instead, for you and me, the bulk of the baby boomers who can't recall the location of the car keys, or that tip-of-the-tongue word. The actual drug on trial is called Phosphodiesterase-4, and, so far, when given to very grizzled mice, it yanked them into youth again, those old octogenarians running mazes as efficiently as any rodent youngster.

"The little red pill," Kandel calls it.

Of all the twentieth century's psychological experiments, none have yielded an actual treatment that is poised for such huge impact when it hits.

Already, even before its release, it is mired in ethical issues. A drug, Kandel says, for normal, age-related memory impairment. Well, according to some scientists, age-related memory impairment begins at twenty, so should we pass these crimson capsules around in our children's junior year of college? Maybe we should give them to our teenagers prior to taking the SAT, or even during the inevitable Kaplan preparatory course. Will certain companies require that the employees use the drugs, or will employees feel they have to in order to keep pace with the imbiber in cubicle 4? These are the obvious ethical questions. Less obvious: What happens if this drug, by helping us consolidate and store memory, also somehow loosens the lids of our archives, so our past comes pouring over us, a kind of nostalgic incontinence that carries with it the oh so specific memory you did-n't even know you had of your aunt in a tide pool, of the humidifier in the hallway in your house, its dial with every number etched, illu-minated, the smell of your father's neck, the swooshing sound of sprinklers underground, the key in the corner, the dust on the long-ago ledge? Who's to say? The drugs that are meant to propel us invigorated into the future might trap us in a past so detailed and descriptive we cannot concentrate on where we are.

There are a million potential problems with memory-enhancing drugs. Ramp up CREB and god knows what will happen to our hold on the present as well as the past. Even if the past doesn't come pouring back, might not such a drug make every aspect of the present so unforgettable that we are kicking around in mental clutter? There's a reason, after all, why our brains are capable of forgetting. There's an evolutionary imperative. We toss out the detritus and keep what we need in order to survive, in a high-tech world, on the Pliocene plains.

I wonder if anyone has ever considered the benefits of memory loss. While I'm sure this shows my gross naiveté, I've never considered Alzheimer's, once the patient has crossed the line into its fluid world, to be as horrible as it's portrayed. Our memories, after all, are bulky noisy things that keep us trapped in the past or fretting about the future. We are so busy remembering backward or projecting forward (and thinking forward is a kind of memory, for whatever expectations you project are based on what you have learned) that we rarely dwell in the present. We probably have little idea of what the actual pure present feels like—right now—untainted by our sense of time. Animals probably have an idea, and they seem a happy lot, and late-stage Alzheimer's patients may have an idea—in fact, in David Shenk's excellent book, *The Forgetting*, he quotes an Alzheimer's patient: "I didn't know I could see such serenity in this disease, but I have; life is very beautiful as the curtain slowly closes." Perhaps H.M. felt something similar, somewhere. For H.M., every single time he tasted a strawberry, it was the first time. Everytime he saw snow, it was brand new snow falling from the sky. Every time he was touched, it was the first touch, the original touch; come here.

KANDEL MUST KNOW about the dangers associated with too much memory, and, conversely, the human brain's need to forget. One of

the most famous patients in the literature of neurology was a twenty-
one-year-old man, treated by A. L. Luria. S., at twenty years old, had
such vivid recall you could present him with four columns of numbers, and after only a moment's glance, he could recite them all back
to you. Luria tested S. for years, and maybe most amazing was that
even after much time had passed S. could remember every single column; he could remember the precise arrangements of words on a
page; twenty years later he still knew every story word for word in
every newspaper printed in his province.

S., however, had serious problems. He was unable to glean meaning from anything he read. Show him *The Odyssey* and he could
recite the thousand-page tome back to you after six minutes of staring, but he had no idea what it meant. People baffled him because he
was unable to read facial expressions. So caught up was he in the
miniscule mechanics of a mouth moving that he couldn't step back
and see—was that a smile or a smirk? S. couldn't for the life of him
imagine how he might solve the problem. He never did solve it. S.
lived, dull-witted and aimless, crippled by his keen capacities.

And then, there are the less florid examples of people's need to
forget. The Vietnam vet, for instance, who obsessively replays the
trauma in his brain. The child raped in her own canopied bed. The
boy, just nine, hearing the crack of glass and seeing his father dragged
off under a midnight moon, perhaps never to return. We want to
remember, but perhaps for Kandel, and us all, we have an equally
strong need to forget.

Kandel might well deny any personal motivations for his work in
memory-suppressing drugs, a concoction that Memory Pharmaceuticals is also investigating. He might say he is motivated simply by
a love of scholarship, the raw thrill of discovery, but one wonders.
When Kandel discovered CREB, he also discovered its opposite. He
discovered that the normal human brain has built within it mechanisms that allow for forgetting. Essential to these mechanisms is an
enzyme called calcineurin. Kandel and his team, in 1998, overex-
pressed the gene responsible for calcineurin production in rats and

found, sure enough, the rats had Teflon-coated cortexes; everything slipped off. Fears were forgotton.

Could Memory Pharmaceuticals, or one of its rivals, make such a drug for humans? Tim Tully already has one in the works. If marketed, the drug could be used within twenty-four hours of a trauma, and it would delete your memory of the trauma, along with whatever else happened that day. Such a drug could be used for survivors of terrible events, terrorist bombings, plane crashes, vicious personal attacks. Such a drug would effectively obliterate the diagnosis of post-traumatic stress disorder; post-trauma would be a pill, a pharmacological capsule of water from the river Lethe, where old souls in Hades go to erase their pasts.

Kandel might like the idea of a drug for forgetting, and on the one hand this makes sense, given how his difficult past is always there and not there, present but "lacking in affect." Does he see potential ethical problems with such a drug? Does he see it could be used in survivors of the next genocide, as a tool of political silencing, given to the girl in her bed before her father rapes her? Yes, Kandel surely sees these things. Which may be one reason why, while he has discovered the molecular-chemical processes involved in forgetting, he and Axel Unterbeck, Memory Pharmaceuticals' CSO, are not actively pursing the compound.

In the end, it seems, Kandel in the end is casting his lot with the power and importance of memory. On the day I see him, a sunny spring day, light streaming into his multiwindowed office, on this day Kandel is working on his own memoirs. "You see this," he says, waving a sheaf of papers at me, "these are my memoirs, I'm beginning them. I want to set it all down for my children, before it's too late."

He sets the sheaf of papers on the coffee table between us. I'd like to lift the pages up and have a look, but I know I'm not welcome to them.

Kandel's eyes flick away from the manuscript, over toward the windows in his office. "I was six inches from Dachau," he says, "and that's one reason why I like to squeeze everything I can out of life."

Kandel then tells me he's going to Austria in a few months, that he's organizing a conference there. I assume it will be a scientific conference, but when I ask, he says no. "Austria," he says, "has never faced its past, which the other European countries did. I'm going to Austria to do a conference to help the country recall what happened," and I picture him then, with a syringe, injecting into Austria the CREB-enhancer drug, so all those mucked-up brains are jostled back to Kristellnacht. Kandel started out his career wondering how a single neuron remembers, and he is finishing it wondering how to help a whole country form new neural pathways, a national set of synapses. His twentieth-century canvases have been at once miniscule and mammoth, the approach undoubtedly reductive, but yielding insights so much more than the sum of their separate parts.

A FEW DAYS after visiting with Kandel, I go to Kendall Square, where MIT sits amidst coffee shops and bookstores. I'm here to use the library, but instead of turning right and heading out onto Memorial Drive, where the entrance is, I turn left and walk down the narrow side streets and alleys of this campus. I've lived in Boston my whole life, but I've never been back here, in the bowels of science, where students hurry past me, cellphones clutched in their hands. I don't know where I'm going, just walking, the springtime air with its faint smell of soap a pleasure to breathe, the magnolia trees in bloom, their flowers big as artichokes, I pick one. I think of Kandel's little red pill and wonder if soon we will be able to undo not only aging, but death itself, a purple pill for that, would we want it? If we knew we could live to see our children's children's children's children's children, would we say yes? And in saying yes, would we not lose what it means to be human, birth and death bracketing back our memories, giving our lives some shape? What, exactly, is our shape as we accept and fund and finally imbibe whatever enhancers we can? Kandel is taking us to new cognitive heights, but at some point we may find ourselves spinning in space, with no tether.

Now, up ahead of me, I see a very old man leaning on a nurse, taking in some sun on the sidewalk. Next to them is a building with tinted doors. I squint. The building says, "Clinic for Neurological Disorders." Is not H.M. housed near here? I wonder if that could be him even as I know it's not. I go closer, parsing my way down the sidewalk. The old man has bland, boiled eyes, and just above them, I imagine Scoville's holes. H.M. He lost his own personal history even as he took up permanent residence in the larger literature of an ever expanding field. It seems a poor trade-off, terribly unfair, and then I know, when I see that old man standing there, that I would rather have my memories than see things anew each time, than over and over again bite into fruit, the enjoyment sucked back into blackness before it can leave the faintest residue. Let us leave residues, stains, pictures, prints. Let us take Kandel's medicine, if it comes to us, and return to people who have lost them their lives, pulling them out of the gap of forgetting that is in wait for us all, if we live long enough.

But no drug, of this I am sure, no drug will be able to stave off senility indefinitely. We may be postmodern, but we are not, in fact, posthuman. No science, in any field, has yet to deliver us from our own flesh. Eventually, the lights go out. We go back, into blackness.

Now, the old man and his nurse begin to shuffle toward the building, going into the tinted-glass entrance. After they've left, I stand by the doors, looking in, but all I see is my own face reflected back to me, and I am disturbed. It must be something about the glass, its wavers or tints, but there I am, looking terribly tired, my face full of holes, eyes sunken in, and on my forehead, strange spots, what are they? Freckles, moles bleeding out of their borders, or reflections of my aged neurons suspended in a cortical sea, the synapses shrinking, shrinking, even as I think.

10

Chipped

THIS CENTURY'S MOST RADICAL
MIND CURES

Practitioners of current-day psychosurgeries—lobotomies, leucotomies, and cingulotomies—insist the procedures are not experimental; their claim raises questions as to how the term at hand should be defined. If one defines an experimental procedure as one lacking institutional acceptance, then psychosurgery indeed is not experimental; insurance carriers cover it. However, as this chapter explores, lobotomy, or its off-shoot, cingulotomy, is performed with as much guesswork as actual knowledge, is rooted far more in opinion than fact, and is always an unpredictable journey into the grayest matter. Psychosurgery's long history, and ironically its dark reputation, illuminate perhaps most powerfully the central ethical questions raised by experimental psychology throughout the twentieth century, while at the same time laying the groundwork for the field's future excavations into the tactile minds of human beings.

PART ONE

His head is on a stamp, in Portugal. This seems appropriate for the father of lobotomy—that every day thousands of mouths tongue him to tackiness, flip him backward into cavernous bins, his cortex run through sorters and slicers, buried beneath mountains of white, only to emerge days later at its destination, this head, his head, still stuck on, scored with dark lines, a date pressed in like a brand.

António Egas Moniz, the man on the stamp and the winner of the Nobel Prize in 1949 for his discovery of psychosurgery, was born at the turn of last century, in a small coastal fishing village miles from Lisbon. Little is known of his mother or the circumstances of his birth, but we can imagine he came out head first, the midwife placing her hands on either side of his still-soft skull and pulling him like a rooted vegetable from the red earth. Moniz's father was landed gentry, and his childhood home was large, with a chapel on the second floor, a tiny flame burning on a silver platter.

Moniz did not live with his mother, and, it turns out, he did not live with his father for long. He spent his youth in the next town over, with an uncle named Abadelde, who was a priest and wore the frock and collar. Strangely, Abadelde failed to convey to Moniz the expected priestly things, the image of Christ on a cross, a humble life where the poor shall inherit. Abadelde was a man infused with a sense of Portugal's glorious past, the blood, the battlefields, the dream-blue seas on which white sails walked like apparitions; he read to the boy, the finest literature, so Moniz could recite epic poems before he started school, could translate passages of Latin, his own brain like a blade, honed and shined in his uncle's hands.

He went to college, of course—such a boy would have no choice—and in his senior year he decided to study medicine. The winter that year was chilly in Lisbon, and the peacocks at the palace died. Moniz developed gout in his hands, so all his joints swelled red and tender, his fingers curling up into claws. He never fully recovered from the gout, and years later, when he did his lobotomies, he had to have help holding the knife, his assistant making the critical cuts while Moniz looked on, instructing from the sidelines as his patients, completely awake, could hear his words, words like, "Cut the nerve tract. Go deeper into the left lobe. Are you feeling anything strange, Mrs. M.? Make a fist for me, please. Okay, next side, drill in."

But that was yet to come. In the late 1800s Moniz was just a young man at Coimbra College with hurting hands and a desperate desire to somehow make his mark in the vast field of neurology. When the acute gout passed, he packed his bags and took a train to Paris, where he studied with Pierre Marie and Jules Dejerine, former students of Charcot. Moniz roamed the wards of Salpetriere and watched people foam and faint and tremble; it must have amazed him, how utterly strange people can be, how very sick their souls, and it seemed obvious to him that there was no schism between mind and matter. From the very beginning he saw mental illness as utterly organic, the product of a tangled neural net.

Back in Portugal, he wondered how one might visualize the brain. This all-important organ lay out of reach, encased in a cage of bone. Surely, if one could see the brain, one might be able to see the illnesses affecting it. Perhaps there were tumors, burst blood vessels. He experimented, then, with dyes and cadavers. Since the seventeenth century, scientists had been trying to use dyes to illuminate the microscopic or the merely obfuscated. There had been saffron dyes, dyes made of crushed crocus, silver nitrate dyes that glossed the veins of a leaf's body, but no one had yet seen into the skull of a human. Before Moniz actually altered the human brain, his ambition was just to view it.

And that is what he did. He developed a dye that could be injected straight into the neck's blood vessels, spreading upward to illuminate, with the aid of an x-ray machine, the previously hidden branches of vessels and lobes. With this invention, Moniz made it possible to locate tumors and fault lines; he made it possible to see sickness in the pulsing human head.

But success came at a price. Says Elliot Valenstein, "Think about it. Who would have had the hubris to inject bromide into the carotid arteries of live human beings? Who would have dared to have done that? I'm sure many people had thought of it before, but a man like Moniz, who let his ambitions get the better of him, he's the one who actually did it."

First into cadavers, then into people he plucked from his own thriving neurology practice; he shot the patients up and one of them died, the brain aflame, backlit blue and silver.

Moniz claimed he was "tormented" by the death.

Nevertheless, he went ahead, shooting up patient after patient. He called his technique angiography, and it became widely used and still is today, albeit with more technological sophistication. Angiography is an indispensable diagnostic tool. Moniz strode into the landscape of people's lives and took things he shouldn't have—which is why he's not liked—but he left, he always left, some useful things behind. The father of psychosurgery, you can hate him but chances are, in many ways, he could have helped your head.

A CHILD DEVELOPS vision first, grasp second. We have to see what it is we want to hold. So it was with Moniz. First he saw the brain, and then with his gout-swollen hands, he wanted to touch it, to try to change it. This was in the 1920s and 1930s when there were few available treatments for mental patients except institutionalization, some living out their whole lives raving and sweat stained. Moniz knew this, as up to one third of the patients in his thriving neurology practice were psychiatrically impaired. Doctors had already tried inducing hypoglycemic comas, cooling cures, removal of teeth and colons, injections of malaria; it's strange. On the one hand we have Freud, who was rising to prominence in Vienna, putting forth a scheme of human mind that relied entirely on history, and at nearly the very same time we had Moniz, who believed that the only cure was a somatic cure. The recent debates over chemistry versus history, drugs versus talk, are not recent at all. We are just repeating the same old schisms, with not necessarily much more or less insight.

In 1935, at the age of sixty-one, Moniz went to London for a neurology conference. It was held in a grand hall, with very French-looking busts of alabaster, a marble floor, a grand ceiling sporting medallions leafed with gold. Many important men were there, in

dark suits and whale-bone buttons, eyeglasses on chains, all conven-
ing to hear the latest reports in experimental studies. One lecturer
talked about burning the motor strip in the cortex of a dog; another
proclaimed he had severed the auditory cortex in a monkey. Then
came a pair of researchers, Carlyle Jacobson and John Fulton, who
described a female primate named Becky with a very bad attitude.
She was always screaming and pissing on things and turning over her
food and water dish in a frenzy. Finally these researchers put Becky to
sleep, lifted up the lid of her head, did a snip snip to the fibers connecting the frontal lobes to the limbic system, and upon awakening,
the animal was supposedly transformed. She was quiet and peaceful.
Her intelligence appeared to be intact, as she could do all the monkey tests, but whatever snarl had caused the chaos was gone. It was
cure by subtraction, removing something instead of setting it straight.
Moniz heard the Becky lecture, the chimp gone gracious, and he
thought of his own patients back in Portugal, the ones in the ward,
the ones in his clinic who couldn't stop shaking, and he was bold. He
stood up, there in that lecture hall, beneath the gold-leafed medallions and chandeliers, he stood up and said out loud, so all could
hear, "Why would it not be feasible to relieve anxiety states in man
by surgical means?"

History has it that everyone was startled, if not shocked by Moniz's
suggestion, the men maybe blinking and swiveling to see just who
had spoken. The room grew quiet. Was the silence because even science has its taboos, a place beyond which one may not travel? Or was
the silence because most men in that room had already thought of
traveling there, and were hearing in Moniz's words not the shock of
trespass but of recognition? After all, these doctors knew, as do we,
that the history of science has been the history of one incursion
more seemingly inappropriate than the next. In our time we have
those who want to clone whole humans, this desire springing in part
from the procedures that preceded it—in vitro fertilization, assisted
hatching, single-sperm injections, test tubes sprouting deiced life.
Like cloning, lobotomy was attached to a chain of prior interven-

tions. Autopsies, once prohibited by religion, eventually became acceptable, and so the human viscera was opened, the heart held in a hand. Evermore daring experiments were performed on dogs and pigs, their parts strewn about, and then live humans with electrodes at their skulls, their bodies flipping and twitching. Treatment had been one steady progression into the skin, beyond the skin, and the men at the conference understood this. We understand this. Maybe Moniz was the only one daring to utter what many have secretly whispered—*Let me go there. Let my knife excise a piece of his hurting head.* It made intuitive sense, even before Jacobson and Fulton's chimpanzee lecture. Do not those in psychic pain bow their heads and rub their temples, as though to erase those fiery frontal lobes?

Moniz traveled by train back to Portugal. He took a slow walk through some of the city's wards, where he regularly did rounds. The patients were foaming and filthy, and when distress overtook them, they were plunged into wooden tubs of ice. Moniz knew about these terrible tubs, and the wet rubber suits, and the ropes for restraint. In the 1930s, if you were admitted to a mental hospital, chances are you would stay there for an average of seven years, compared to today, where you'll stay for three days if you're lucky. The halls were packed with Dante-esque figures writhing in their rings of hell, people who prayed to aliens and felt angels sleeping in their stomachs. The patients may have looked up, seen Moniz strolling, his round shiny face and navy blue suit. He was here to help them, was he not? They didn't know that before he had entered the wards, just as soon as he had stepped off his train, he had gone straight to the morgue and ordered up three cadavers. Using a pen, Moniz had "practiced" his technique, stabbing it into the cadaver's cortex until he got the right angle and depth. There. Like that.

The first patient is known to history as Mrs. M. She was sixty-three years old. She was severely depressed and anxious. She had paranoid ideas, believing the police were trying to poison her. Before her hospitalization she had secretly been practicing prostitution in her apartment until other residents forced her to stop. Mrs. M. was miserable in the deep damp manner of the melancholic. Sometimes, she could not stop shaking. She had been in the ward for a total of four and a half years.

The night before the surgery her hair was cut and her scalp cleaned with alcohol. Of what was she thinking? How was this procedure explained to her? Did she grasp its experimental nature? Did she care, after so much pain? That night, the last night of life with an intact brain, she went to sleep in the narrow ward bed, and Moniz, he stayed up in his palatial house, the windows ablaze, the sea a dark inked line outside.

"On the eve of my first attempt, my justified anxiety and all fears at the moment were swept aside in the hopes of obtaining favorable results. If we could suppress certain psychological complexes by destroying cell-connecting groups . . . this would be a great step forward, making a fundamental contribution to our knowledge of the organic basis of psychic functions."

Indeed Moniz did have a theory regarding why lobotomy would work. He had heard about it working on Becky, the female chimp, but he was going on more than that. Moniz believed that insanity was a series of thoughts that were literally physiologically fixed in the brain's nerve fibers. The fixations were fossilized in the fibers connecting the forebrain to the thalamus, and if Moniz could cut those fibers, he could free a person of noxious ideas and feelings. As it turns out, Moniz's theoretical scheme is probably far too simplistic, but it is prescient of Kandel, who proved that memory and its attendant affect reside in a neural net. Kandel says, "Moniz made some contributions."

So did Mrs. M., of course, whose contribution was her poorly behaved buckling brain. On November 11, 1935, she was transferred from the Manicome Bombarda Asylum to the neurology service of the Santa Maria hospital, where he was waiting.

The first lobotomy was not actually done by blade. Mrs. M. lay down on a table, whereupon her shaved scalp was swabbed with novocaine and two pen point–sized holes were drilled on either side of her skull, into which Moniz and his assistant Lima inserted an alcohol-filled syringe. Moniz believed an injection of alcohol would be a safe and effective method for destroying nerve tissue. He pushed the plunger down.

Five hours after surgery, Moniz recorded the following conversation with his convalescing patient:

"Where is your house?"

"Calcada of Desterio."

"How many fingers?"

"Five." She responded with slight hesitation.

"How old are you?"

Long hesitation. She was not precise.

"What hospital is this?"

She did not respond.

"Do you prefer milk or bouillon?"

"I prefer milk."

Her answers certainly didn't indicate significant spectacular improvement; if anything, they indicated some cognitive decline, but Moniz wasn't worried. He knew that a period of confusion following brain surgery is normal. He had the patient transferred to a room, where she spiked a small fever, after which she was transferred back to the asylum. Two months later, one of the asylum's psychiatrists made the following evaluation of Mrs. M.:

The patient behaved normally. She is very calm, anxiety is not apparent. Mimicry still a little exaggerated. Good orientation. Conscience, intelligence, and behavior intact. Mood slightly sad, but somewhat justified because of her concern about her future. Fair appreciation of her previous pathological state; appreciation of her situation is appropriate.

There are no new pathological ideas or other symptoms and for the most part previous paranoid ideas are primarily gone. That is to say, after the treatment the patient's anxiety and restlessness had

declined rapidly with a concomitant marked attenuation of paranoid features.

Clearly a success.

Except—no one knows what happened to Mrs. M. because
Moniz's work suffers from poor follow-up. What became of her brain
as it floated with its neural cords cut? Did her improvement continue? Did she relapse? Where is her voice in this tale? We don't
know. The cords have been cut.

After Mrs. M., Moniz proceeded to find more patients. He chose
patients based on availability, not diagnosis, and he has been criticized
for this. He used humans as guinea pigs and conducted his experiment without the double-blind procedure. However, how *could* he
have created a double-blind experiment? There is no way to give one
group of patients a sham lobotomy, another group a real one. And as
for the patients themselves, it's true, they were used as guinea pigs.
But then there's this: many of them were in a rapid state of decline,
heading toward an inevitable deterioration. That by no means makes
the patients less human, but it does alter the cost-benefit ratio. Moniz
was probably thinking, *This could really help these people who have nothing left to try, and if it doesn't help, it surely won't make them worse. They are
as bad off as can be.* Moniz writes, "I recognized that the method could
be harmless, and capable of benefiting the insane."

So he went ahead, plucking patients wherever he could, drilling
them, filling the bulbs of their heads with cold clear alcohol, and then
checking their vital signs as the ether burned through intelligent tissue. Afterward, several scarred and barren places on the brain, like
land looks as it is seen from an airplane following a forest fire.

Moniz, in his initial experiment, subjected twenty patients to the
procedure, first using alcohol and then switching to a leucotome, a
bladed instrument that sliced sideways, cutting neural connections,
damaging tissue. He saw some remarkable things. Moniz saw patients
seized with a lifetime of anxiety grow calm; he saw delusional ideas
dwindle; patients who had spent years in the asylum now returned

home, some of them even to work. He performed a lobotomy on a thirty-six-year-old woman who, during a voyage to the Belgian Congo, threw her clothes overboard the ship and, in a deep depression, swallowed sulfuric acid. After the procedure the family found her "in excellent condition. Just as she was before the psychosis." The patient herself said, a few days after her surgery, "It's over now. I want to go back to live with my daughters."

Of the twenty original cases, Moniz claimed a complete cure for seven of them, a partial cure for another seven, and six who were unhelped. Altogether then, supposedly seventy percent of the patients had some significant remission of long-standing intractable mental illness with no reported long-term problematic side effects. Scholars of psychosurgery dispute these numbers, claiming that lack of long-term follow-up skewed the early results in a far too favorable direction. They also claim that the fact that IQ scores tended to rise postoperatively means very little, because the IQ test is not at all sensitive to the types of brain damage inflicted by lobotomy. These claims undoubtedly have merit. Nevertheless, the bald brute story of Moniz and the surgeons who followed in his footsteps contains within it numerous patients who experienced either significant relief or much improved behavior, and this data, if we are to believe it, demands we reconsider or renarrate the story of psychosurgery as a possibly good enough cure for some patients in the context of a time without Thorazine or Prozac.

MONIZ PUBLISHED HIS findings in 1937 in the *American Journal of Psychiatry*, and so it was that lobotomy made its way to the United States. Two surgeons, Walter Freeman and James Watts, went to work on this side of the sea. Freeman and Watts developed a technique called the transorbital lobotomy, where they entered the brain with a sharply pointed instrument just above the eyeball, forcing the point through the bony orbit into the brain's quadrants. The essential difference between the Watts-Freeman transorbital procedure and

Moniz's prefrontal procedure is the method of access. Moniz went in at the hairline. The American surgeons went straight for the softest door, inserting their knives up and under the open eyes, and then cutting what they could.

As horrifying as this procedure sounds, Freeman and Watts had findings similar to Moniz's when they restricted their operation only to patients suffering from anxiety and depression. Freeman recounts one woman from Topeka, Kansas, who suffered from severe agitation and chose the operation over institutionalization. As with Mrs. M., she had her hair cut the night before, weeping as the curls came off, and then the next morning she was delivered, her head as bald as an infant's bottom, pink and waiting, slit. Freeman and Watts went in and then sewed up her scalp, and the woman, lying on the table, reported, with a sense of awe, that all her terror was now gone.

> Freeman: Are you happy?
> Patient: Yes.
> Freeman: Do you remember being upset when you came here?
> Patient: Yes, I was quite upset, wasn't I?
> Freeman: What was it all about?
> Patient: I don't know. I seem to have forgotten. It doesn't seem important now.

Freeman wrote that the results were extraordinary. "Judgment and insight are apparently not diminished, and the ability to enjoy external events is certainly increased." Altogether, in their initial spree, the two surgeons performed five more operations within the next six weeks and found that in all of the patients, who shared "a substratum, a common denominator of worry, apprehension, insomnia, nervous tension, there was a lifting of the mesh of anxiety."

And then, of course, there were the downsides. Seizures. Deaths. Burst blood vessels. A blade lost in the brain. Postsurgical infections. Relapses. Incontinence. Moniz writes of one woman who, four days after the surgery, shouted obscenities and sang; other patients became childlike, clutching teddy bears and following directions meekly. Freeman wrote, "Lobotomy patients may make good citizens," a chilling comment but not in its essence different from the criticisms levied at the psychiatric drugs we imbibe today. One of the myriad central questions was, did lobotomy lead to a loss of some "vital spark"? Most patients in fact did not clutch at teddy bears and shout obscenities after the surgery, or if they did so, it was only for a while. But here's what wasn't for a while: many lobotomy patients were just a tad bit flatter after their skulls were sewn up, a slight and subtle shift, as though the patients were not really themselves, but Xerox copies, in black and white, the quirks and curves comprising their character irreproducible.

However, there is something to be said for flattening, and the spark, if it burns too brightly, can singe the skin. One lobotomized psychiatrist was able, after surgery, to run his own psychiatric clinic. Another built an extremely profitable business and flew his own plane. So who's to say? What makes lobotomy great is not necessarily what it did or didn't do, but how, in its extremity, it forces us to question medical ethics: What constitutes informed consent? Is it ethical to substitute one form of organic brain dysfunction for another? Can doctors ever justify harming apparently healthy human tissue? Is there some inherent sanctity to the human brain? Will surgeons soon, if they have not already, become the long arm of the law? It is ironic that the operation feared to remove the soul, the spark, forces us to ask the questions that bring us right to the burning place, where we must weigh what we're willing to lose, and tussle with the complexity of cure.

The press, never known for its complexity, caught on to the new procedure and promoted it. In 1948 the *New York Times* ran this headline:

Surgery used on the soul-sick; relief of obsessions
is reported. New Brain technique is said to have aided
65% of the mentally ill persons on who it was tried as a last
resort, but some leading neurologists are highly skeptical of it.

Harper's in 1941 reported the technique as revolutionary. The *Saturday Evening Post* touted it as well. Then appeared patient testimonials, not at all unlike the testimonials we have today, meant half as advertisement, half as meditation. One such patient, by the name of Harry Dannecker, wrote an article in the 1945 *Coronet Magazine* entitled "Psychosurgery Cured Me." He describes himself before the lobotomy as hopelessly suicidal, with nothing left to live for, and after the lobotomy, as having emerged "from that terrible underworld of the sick mind." Harry Dannecker lifted his head up and marched into the auto mechanics business, where he reported significant success. In his article he writes, "My purpose . . . is a simple one: it may give heart and courage to readers who have afflictions such as I had, or who have friends with similar miserable obsessions."

WHY, THEN, HAVE we persisted in narrating lobotomy as purely evil? Its downsides are evident: a seizure rate sometimes as high as thirty percent, and its American evangelizer, Freeman, a tilted cortical cowboy riding high with his knife, not bothering to sterilize his instruments or even drape the patient before the ten-minute procedure in which he ripped out cords. Freeman did a lot to give lobotomy its bad name; like the doctors of today who prescribe our newest antidepressants for just about any ill, Freeman was indiscriminate in his choice of patients, even as he appeared to care for those he cut, sending them Christmas cards every year, traveling across the country in his van to check on their progress.

Despite the poor outcomes reported here, despite Freeman's myopic and zealous view of the knife as cure-all, there is still no question that this surgery helped numbers of people. A congressional committee formed in the 1970s to investigate psychosurgery, with a plan to outlaw it, found, much to their surprise, that psychosurgery is a legitimate procedure that "can be of significant therapeutic value in the treatment of certain disorders or in the relief of certain symptoms." The committee went further and stated psychosurgery was "a potentially beneficial therapy." Elliot Valenstein, one of the sharpest critics of the lobotomy, writes that "following a lobotomy, many agitated and anxious patients did experience a striking relief from their most troublesome symptoms. In the best cases this led to a normalization of behavior."

Why, then, has lobotomy been preserved in the dust bins of history, told as a long dark tale in the development of somatic treatments, a dangerous digression? Perhaps we need to see lobotomy like this because, well, because of our brains. We may be wired to prefer a neat scheme of black and white over one with gray. And perhaps we never quite grow out of the puerile belief that if this object is bad, then that object must be good. We take pleasure in polarization, the way things on opposite ends of a single axis become clear and seemingly definitely defined. Therefore, in order to justify the general benevolence of our psychiatric cures today, we underscore the barbarism of what they once were. Dark and light. We didn't know what we were doing back then, BUT WE DO NOW. We say this as we pop our Prozac pills, our Ritalin tablets, as we toy with our hormones, egging on our estrogen in the hopes of happiness. But how different, really, are our contemporary cures from their historical brethren? Lobotomy has been widely criticized for its lack of specificity. Surgeons drilled into the head, stuck in sharp things, snapped the tough tissue of dream and thought, and knew not what they were snapping. They had vague ideas, of course—something about the thalamus and the frontal lobes, emotion and intelligence—but they didn't understand what underbrush in the brain they were really clearing. Consider, however, Prozac today. It is a drug hailed for its supposed specificity, and we like that. It makes us feel we know what we are doing, shooting well-aimed missiles into our mind now, instead of some primitive plunge with a knife. The truth of the matter is, though, no one really knows where or how Prozac operates in the brain; no one understands its mechanisms. "Pharmacological specificity," says researcher Harold Sackheim, "is a myth." And like lobotomy, no one knows quite why Prozac cures. It is about as blunt a tool as any Moniz used. When doctors prescribe a Prozac pill, they are acting as did Moniz, blindly but in great faith, with a real desire to heal, and with at least as much wish as fact.

People also criticize lobotomy because it is irreversible. However, who's to say our current imbibement of psychiatric pills isn't doing grave indelible damage we have yet to unearth? Psychiatrist Joseph Glenmullen has given warning that Prozac use can cause Alzheimer-type plaques and tangles in the brain, which may be why so many imbibers complain they can't retain a thing, the placement of those car keys or even where the car is parked. It is also possible that our newest medications could, over the long haul, cause irreversible dyskinesias, so in twenty years this Prozac nation might be twitching its way through the forgetful days. We take them anyway, our pills, because we hurt, because we have to, and so too did the patients who lay down for a lobotomy. Did they lose their vital spark after the procedure? This has been, of all things, the most persistent public objection to the lobotomized patient; that in cutting into the frontal lobes, the portion of the brain that is biggest in humans and that shrinks as we move down the phylogenetic line, doctors were cutting into the core of the soul and afterwards: empty.

Whether or not this was the case is actually less interesting than the fact that we have the very same fears and criticisms of our contemporary cures. Throughout all of history, actually, whenever presented with an opportunity for psychic well-being, we have immediately feared losing the dividends of darkness. Rilke did not want to enter psychoanalysis because he was afraid he would get well and no longer have poetry to write. The central character in the play *Equus*, whose love for horses brings much meaning to his life, finally agrees to psychotherapy, only to find he's been talked straight out of his passion. In today's day and age there are novelists and windsurfers and mothers and businessmen who complain their nifty new pills are making them "less intense" or "less creative." When one looks at the persistence of the complaint in every type of psychiatric intervention, one starts to wonder whether it has less to do with the intervention at hand and more to do with our complex relationship to suffering, which we hate even as we believe it humanizes us. The lobotomy may or may not have removed a vital spark, but perhaps no more so, no less so than what we do to feel better today. As for whether or not that vital spark is integral to our humanity, ask Henry Danneker. Ask Mrs. M. I imagine them saying, as seriously ill as they were, "Who gives a rat's ass about vital spark? Just deliver me from my symptoms."

Extreme suffering snuffs out the spark. Or makes it irrelevant.

We wish to be delivered.

IN 1949, WHEN Moniz was awarded the Nobel Prize for his discovery of the lobotomy, the procedure popularized to the point where twenty thousand operations alone were performed in the United States, and the *Nation* wrote it was worrisome, how we were creating conglomerates of brain-damaged people as citizens of this country. By some estimates, a total of thirty-five thousand operations were performed in the United States between 1936 and 1978, with the highest frequency occurring in conjunction with the Nobel Prize, and a fast falling off occurring after 1950, when the first antipsychotic was discovered. Pharmacology and all the profits it spawned were born in the 1950s and that, along with a growing low rumble of public suspicion regarding the cure, led to lobotomy's fall from favor. A drug seemed so much better, less invasive, even though the side effects were obvious stupefaction, sweating, and acute motor restlessness. It seems we would rather enter the brain through our stomachs than do so directly, same as we would often rather talk around a terrible truth than touch it.

There were other factors as well. The nation was becoming increasingly suspicious of unregulated medical experimentation. Stanley Milgram's shock machine set off an ethical furor over what one may do to subjects, as did the Tuskegee experiment, where doctors denied some black men syphilitic treatment so they could observe the demise of their brains. Perhaps most important, the press caught on to pharmacology as the new new thing and began promoting it as it once did lobotomy, so the public had another cure that held within it all our hope and desperation.

By the 1970s, fewer than twenty lobotomies were being performed each year in this country, even as a small group of neurosurgeons continued to refine their techniques so that less and less of the brain was lesioned, resulting in fewer and fewer negative side effects. The 1950s and 1960s saw the development of stereotaxic instruments that made it possible to insert a small electrode that destroys very minute bits of targeted tissue, in contrast to the rather blind gropings of the blade. Surgeons also began focusing less on the frontal lobes, and more on the limbic system, otherwise known as "the emotional brain." They began targeting a particular part of the limbic system, the cingulate gyrus, an area supposedly responsible for mediating anxiety. It is important to note, however, that there appears to be very little agreement, then and now, as to what brain sites to slash, and this lack of agreement underscores psychosurgery's experimental nature. Different neurosurgeons appear to have favorite cortical targets, a bias that preexists the patients. Some, for instance, truly believe that an amygdalectomy—removal of the amygdala—works wonders, while others hold fast to the site of the cingulate gyrus and still others promote the caudate nucleus. A combination of lack of consensus in the field and its history of controversial characters has kept modern-day lobotomies, dressed up in different names, a last-ditch option for only the sickest among us, a procedure shrouded in secrecy, in shame.

PART TWO

Massachusetts General Hospital is located on Fruit Street in downtown Boston. Its high-tech buildings and gleaming glass doors are at odds with its neighborhood of cobble-stoned pathways and titled townhouses where bright flower boxes charm every window ledge. If you were to stand just a block away, in historic Beacon Hill, you would never know how close you are to one of the most technically proficient institutions in this country.

You cannot get psychosurgery easily in this country; in fact, it is outlawed in several states, including California and Oregon. The USSR, when it was the USSR, banned psychosurgery completely, as being out of keeping with its Pavlovian past. Patients who seek this cure have to look long and hard; they have to have exhausted every other treatment option, and prove it to the ethics committee before they can get any holes drilled in their heads.

Emily Este, from Brooklyn New York, has suffered depression all her life, and she was unable to get approved for a lobotomy by the Mass General Psychosurgery Ethics Committee because she had not tried enough rounds of electroconvulsive therapy. Charlie Newitz, on the other hand, from Austin, Texas, was approved. He had been through over thirty rounds of shock therapy and on more than twenty-three different psychiatric medications; he can name them, ticking them off on his fingers like little rhymes—Luvox, Celexa, Lamictal, Effexor, lithium, Depakote, Prozac, Risperdal, Haldol, Serzone, Zoloft, Remeron, Wellbutrin, Cytomel, Dexedrine, Imipramine, Parnate, Nortiptyline, Thorazine—Charlie names his meds, his own personal poem of one life, his life, lived in perpetual illness.

Charlie is a forty-year-old big bear of a man with the barest shadow of a mustache and dazed-looking eyes, eyes that seem cloudy from all the concoctions he and his psychiatrist have poured into the bottle of his body. When Charlie was twenty-two years old and working as a geological engineer in Texas, he developed, quite out of the blue, incapacitating obsessive compulsive disorder (OCD). The urge to count, check, and tap glutted his mind, held up his hands, so he could do nothing—not work, not love—he was frozen in repetitious rituals. "The suddenness of it was amazing," Charlie says. "I was okay, and then one day, I was not okay."

And so it went from there. This highly skilled engineer, a man who knew how to read the flat faces of rocks for the oil that might lie beneath them, became a recluse, hovering in his hot Dallas apartment, turning on one toe in circles.

Charlie feels he is one of the unlucky ones in that he didn't respond to any of the drugs his psychiatrist, Dr. Roberts, prescribed for him. In one way he's right, but in another way he's wrong. Charlie is unlucky, but he's not among the minority in his lack of response, despite what the industry would lead us to think. Psychopharmacologists and the drug companies that back them proudly proclaim that pharmacology is the brave new world of mental illness treatment, that pills the size of peas have fairy-tale power, that we can feel them through piles upon piles of confusion and clouds, that they can alter our sleep, pull us into alertness, turn us more sensitive or less sensitive, each capsule made by each company jam-packed with powders and proteins that elevate.

This is the message, and it's wrong, not only because it's obviously oversimplified. It's more deeply wrong than that. The statistics drug companies and many psychopharmacologists like to quote are that seventy percent of people who try medication will get better, and thirty percent won't, so don't worry, you have a good chance. If we look closer though, a different sort of story emerges. It's true that roughly seventy percent of people who take medication will respond, but in reality only thirty percent will respond robustly; the rest experience only minimum or moderate relief, and of the total patient population, some estimate that up to sixty percent will develop a drug tolerance that makes their medication eventually useless. So refigure. Of all the people taking pills, the vast majority of them either stay seriously sick, or get only somewhat better, and "somewhat better," when you're horribly hobbled to begin with, isn't much to celebrate. Pharmacology has helped, but not nearly enough. These statistics alone should make us wonder why we cannot be at once critical of psychosurgery, while at the same time respectful of its place in our contemporary canon.

Charlie Newitz and Dr. Roberts worked long and hard to get Charlie approved for psychosurgery at Mass General. Here is still another way in which the procedure differs markedly from Moniz's time: First, stereotaxic instruments make it possible to create deliberate lesions that avoid the destruction of peripheral brain tissue, thus minimizing the chances for unwanted side effects, and, second, no one is walking the ward halls anymore, plucking patients at random. At the end of the twentieth century, strict guidelines for psychosurgery were constructed by the National Committee for the Safety of Human Subjects, the sort of committee Freeman's and Moniz's medical communities sorely lacked.

ON DECEMBER 15, 1999, Charlie Newitz and his wife Sasha flew to Boston. Charlie met his neurosurgeon there and submitted to endless rounds of testing. Throughout, Sasha, a diminutive blond who speaks with a southern accent, looked scared. When Sasha married Charlie in her early twenties, he was symptom-free. Then one day, he was incapacitated; obsessive compulsive disorder can work like that, appearing swiftly on a seemingly clear life.

"I'm afraid," Sasha kept saying. "Will he be any dumber after the procedure?" she asked the doctors, in the halls, in the testing rooms, and then she says it to Charlie himself, while we are eating pizza in a Beacon Hill deli. "Honey," she says in her sweet southern voice, "honey, I just hope you're not dumber after this operation."

Charlie, who is lifting a wedge of pepperoni pie to his mouth, stops all movement. The pie hangs suspended, and then he places it slowly back on his plate, where Rorschach blots of grease have spread. "My greatest fear," he says slowly. He touches his temple. "My greatest fear for some reason isn't about being dumb." He looks at Sasha, at me, the reporter he's let in to this intimate time in his life. "My greatest fear about the psychosurgery is that afterwards, I'll be incontinent. I've read that sometimes happens. I just don't want to be whizzing all over myself," he says. He looks toward his wife, smiles, takes her hand. "Or whizzing on you either," he tells her. Sasha laughs.

The next morning dawns clear and cold. The sun is the color of orange sherbet in the sky. The cobblestones of Beacon Hill have on them a dangerous skim of ice that cracks with your weight; down you go. We—Sasha, Charlie, and I—meet in a courtyard where, from an ancient-looking brick building, someone is playing a bugle, the sound terribly clear and full of portent. "Do you hear that?" Charlie asks.

We make our way down the hill, taking little mincing steps. Despite all the facts and figures I've read by now, I too find it hard to believe Charlie won't be left a little dull-witted by this procedure. I too think that here, right now, is a vital human named Charlie, but in a matter of mere hours, something substantial will have been sliced from his soul. This makes our descent down the hill almost mythic, full of meaning; earlier this century Freeman had written that psychosurgery does take something essential from the patient, but in the days and years following the procedure, a newer, mature self is born from the lobotomized lesions. Charlie's surgeon, has assured him that he will experience no intellectual or personality deficits; the procedure is so finely honed now, it targets only the problematic tissue. In any event, we slide down the ice. Bright daggers of ice hang from the eaves and drip.

At the hospital, Charlie is given his ID bracelet and then lies down. His head is shaved and swabbed with alcohol. Sasha starts to cry. "How many cuts are you going to make?" Charlie asks. "Two," the surgeon says. "No," says Charlie.

"No?" the surgeon says.

"No," Charlie repeats.

"I can't just make one," the surgeon says. "You won't get any symptom relief with one."

"I know that," says Charlie, and his eyes are wide and glistening. "I want symptom relief. I don't want one cut and I don't want two. I want three," he says, "at least."

ALTHOUGH DOCTORS TODAY are quick to point out the differences between cingulotomy and lobotomy, they in fact share significant similarities. Neither lobotomy nor cingulotomy involves cutting any obviously diseased tissue; they both cut apparently healthy pink-ish gray and white matter, turning the Hippocratic oath—do no harm—right on its head. Of course, sometimes harm leads to health, chemotherapy being a case in point, plastic surgery a still more subtle example, the nose sawed off and afterward, the bloodied patient's cri-sis of confidence cured.

There are important differences in the procedure though. In lobotomy, surgeons separate some of the cables connecting the frontal lobes to the thalamus. In cingulotomy, surgeons separate some of the nerve tracts from the frontal lobes to the cingulate gyrus, which is the place in our brain supposedly responsible for mediating anxiety. With these neural cords cut, anxious, obsessive messages sup-posedly can't get through; the phone line is down.

Suzanne Corkin, head of the psychology department at MIT, did one of the longest prospective studies of cingulotomy patients in the country and found it to be a procedure that did not mar nor-mal emotional reactions but did decrease some psychiatric symp-toms. In this country, scores of hopeless patients have been restored to sanity by the cingulotomy, which was born, of course, from its parent, Moniz. Unlike Moniz's lobotomy, however, there have been no deaths associated with the procedure; no blades are ever lost in the brain.

In the operating room, Charlie's head is placed in a steel halo to ensure he holds it absolutely still during the drilling. A high-tech imaging device reflects Charlie's brainwaves on a video screen. A doctor positions a drill right above Charlie's temples, and then it is in, slipping past the strangely yielding skin. And then, the needle stops. And then there is a slash sideways and the white line, a lesion, is made. This is the line that will lead to health, but to Charlie it is more like a minus sign or a frown, and it's monogrammed into the tissue. Another one is made. Charlie's eyes are wide open. The sur-geon moves the needle and Charlie's mouth starts twitching. His left hand leaps. "Sorry," the doctor says. "Can you blink your eyes?" "Can you count backwards from seven." "Almost done," the surgeon says. "Can you tell me your name?"

"I can't," says Charlie, lying braced on the table, his voice thick and slurred.

"You don't know your name?" the surgeon asks, looking worried.

"I can't . . . Charlie . . . you know," he says, "now my tongue's all numb."

IN 1997 *Discover* magazine ran an article titled "Lobotomy's Back." And while the author of that article clearly saw the trend as disturbing, it might actually be a welcome development in some instances. It might actually be that Moniz was on to something, that the dark digression was not psychosurgery, but psychopharmacology. We have never been able to create a drug that acts with the specificity of modern-day psychosurgery. No drug can go right to the one-millimeter target of tissue on the cingulate gyrus. Drugs are like oil spills; they leak everywhere, and washed up on shore are the slick black birds, the insomnia and sweats. Says neuroscientist Harold Sackheim, "Do you think sexual dysfunction is a result of Prozac's specificity? No, obviously the SSRIs are targeting other systems as well. On the other hand, an intervention that can target a very specific piece of tissue, without overloading the whole system, without causing massive brain dysfunction, which is what medication does, that's where the future of psychiatry is." Sackheim works at the New York State Psychiatric Institute, an old brick building in New York. Sackheim believes in the efficacy of modern psychosurgery; he also believes that when Moniz drilled the friable skull of old Mrs. M., he was creating a porthole through which much more than a singular cure could be conveyed. That surgical experiment lay the foundation for some of psychiatry's most promising future cures, and the cures aren't pills, anymore. The cures are cingulotomies—what Charlie is having—precise white lesions in an ancient brain system. And then more. Sackheim speaks of exciting and ominous new technologies:

transcranial magnetic stimulation wherein magnetic fields are held over the head in the hopes of recalibrating an out-of-balance brain; gamma knife surgery where radiation in the form of gamma rays is aimed at hot spots on the cortex; and finally, deep brain stimulation, which sounds almost spa-like, rub there. Deep brain stimulation has already been approved by the Food and Drug Administration for the treatment of Parkinson's disease, and Sackheim predicts that within the next few years it will be used for mental illnesses as well. This procedure requires the bilateral implantation of two tiny electrodes that stimulate specific brain locales, regions responsible for, say, obsessive worry, or rage, or compulsive behavior, or terrible melancholy. The theory, Sackheim explained to me when I visited him before Charlie's surgery, is that "we know the neural circuitry, the specific tissue, implicated in certain cognitive states. So we can do a PET scan, find that tissue, implant an electrode which by continuously stimulating the circuit effectively takes it off line."

As to the charge that psychosurgery and possibly its offshoots like deep brain stimulation harm healthy tissue, Sackheim is swift to retort, almost angrily: "Depression harms healthy brain tissue. There's ample evidence that depression and stress are neurotoxic, necrotic; depressed people's hippocampi are up to fifteen percent smaller than normal," says Sackheim, holding up his thumb and forefinger, showing me the smallest space between them, just enough to slide a knife.

Our cures are only as good as our courage.

CHARLIE'S SURGERY IS finished. He's wheeled back to his room with a big white bandage wrapped around his head. When his wife sees him, she says, "Honey, honey?" He makes terrible smacking sounds with his lips and puts his finger up his nose and then cracks up laughing. "Just kidding," he says. "I'm fine. I'd like some ice cream."

It appears his humor is still intact, and if humor is not at least part of the spark, I can't imagine what else is. Five days later he's back in

Texas. I wait awhile before I call him. When I do, he says, "The OCD is gone, and that's incredible."

"Gone," I say.

"Or at such a low level," he says, "that it's not bothersome."

Out there in Texas it is high and dry. Charlie's head is clear, the two tiny entry points closing over with the thinnest membrane of skin—does his wife touch him there? He is well, and he has, awfully or wonderfully, two more holes in his head that manage to be at once utterly high-tech and grossly primitive, two holes that point to the future even as they tether us to the past.

Charlie says, "The OCD's gone but I'm feeling a little low."

It's impossible to know whether he's low because he's lost the thing that both tortured and titillated him, or whether the surgery set off some depression, or whether he's just experiencing what Freud called the inevitable misery of normal life. He has no memory impairment from the surgery, and as is often the case, a recent battery of tests showed his IQ to be higher now than it was preoperatively.

"Are you glad you did it?" I ask.

"I would do it again in a second," he says. "It's remarkable. I have no more OCD. NO MORE OCD. If the depression doesn't go away, I'm going back. I want another lesion."

Good god! Doctor raise my dose. Doctor increase the cortical cuts. No matter what the facts show, no matter how persistently the information points to the possible efficacy of psychosurgery and the inefficacy of medication, there is still something holy about that three-pound wrinkled walnut with a sheen. It may be that as doctors enter it more and more directly and discretely, we'll become used to having holes in our head, and we'll show them like we do our other surgical scars—breast reduction, brain reduction, no difference. But I doubt this. Moniz gave us a way out of pharmacology; he gave us a procedure that led to a procedure that is leading now to a procedure as small and neat as a microchip, so thank you. Thank him. But he also gave us something else, I think. It has yet to be seen, but of all the twentieth century's great experiments, he gave us, I hypothesize, a

certain cherished reluctance that, while it will not stop us in our surgical journeys, will nevertheless prove to us again and again how we
believe the brain is sacred.

Conclusion

I began this book in search of Deborah Skinner, the mythologized daughter of the twentieth century's most radical neobehaviorist, who, it turns out, is alive and well. She remembers her father with fondness, and says her role in the air crib "experiment" was benign.

There are many things we don't know in regards to psychological experimentation, not the least of which is its effects on human subjects, who are its dubious beneficiaries. Without experiments such as Milgram's, or Rosenhan's, or Moniz's, we would be poorer in knowledge and in story, but who, in the end, can calculate the cost-benefit ratio and say with confidence what it is?

I wanted, when I came to the end of this book, to offer up an answer, a *conclusion*, but as oftentimes happens in experiments, which this book ultimately is, the data yields only new domains for further exploration. When I look back over these pages, I can see much rich material, but it all resists the kind of encapsulation that would allow me to pen a message for the future. Such a message, if I were even capable of conceptualizing one, would constitute a second book, occluding, perhaps, the one we have here. Therefore, I conclude, ultimately the message of this book is *this* book; the pattern must be discerned by the reader willing to dwell within the many viewpoints compressed between these covers.

I do notice, however, certain common threads haphazardly emerging from these chapters, a series of questions that inform and give density to many of these experiments. Over and over again arise issues of free will (Skinner, Alexander, Loftus, Moniz), conformity/obedience (Milgram, Darley and Latané, Festinger, Rosenhan), the perceptual inadequacy and inevitable imminence of the human condition (Rosenhan, Loftus, Kandel), and the ethics of experimentation itself on living beings (Harlow, Skinner, Milgram, Moniz). Even the most technically proficient experiments, like Kandel's, ultimately concern themselves not with the value-free questions we traditionally associate with "science," of which psychology insists it is a part, but with the kinds of ethical and existential questions we associate with philosophy.

In her deeply critical essay on psychology, Dorothy Braginsky writes, "The literature of the field of psychology is testimony to our failure to explore and investigate any meaningful problems in meaningful ways. Indeed, if all that remained of our society for anthropologists of the future were the psychology journals, they would have to conclude that we enjoyed near paradise. Although we have witnessed during this century some of the most enormous violent, social, political, economic and personal upheavals, the volumes of psychological research do not reflect upon or record these events."

Earlier in the century William James, in a letter to his brother Henry, expressed similar sentiments: "It is indeed strange to hear people talk triumphantly of 'the New Psychology' and write 'Histories of Psychology' when into the real elements and forces which the word covers not the first glimpse of clear insight exists. A string of raw facts, a little gossip and wrangle about opinions; a little classification and generalization on the mere descriptive level . . . but not a single law in the sense in which physics shows us laws, not a single proposition from which any consequence can be casually deduced." And in another letter to a poet, James writes, "The only

Psyche now recognized by science is a decapitated frog whose writhings express deeper truths than your weak-minded poets ever dreamed."

Braginsky and James have a point, although it should be just that, a point, not an eclipse of the entire question at hand. It is true that there is a kind of ridiculous reductiveness to certain psychological pursuits and formulations; it is true that the rise of logical positivism and its merging with psychology in the 1940s did a lot to pervert the kinds of conversations scholars in the field were able to have. Any ontological question had to be translated into a "formal mode of speech," where it became simply the issue of measurable relations between well-defined words. This sort of thing is tiring, and while it passes for thoroughness, it's often really just pickiness of the most obnoxious sort. And it is true that certain subspecialties of psychology were all too happy to study the timed reaction rates of the Wister rat ad nauseam, as though that is relevant to the grave issues we grapple with, in our human heads.

That said, however, Braginsky and James are not at all completely correct in their assessment of psychology's social irrelevance. Even a cursory glance at some of the prior century's leading experiments shows a series of setups clearly defined at tackling the deepest problems of living life in the particular time we live it—problems of cruelty, of genocide, of compassion, of love and how it happens; problems of memory and meaning, of justice, of autonomy. The experiments investigated these themes so persistently and imagistically that they are, indeed, almost fablistic; they certainly "prove" how experimental psychology and its supposedly sterile irrelevant labs not only reflect real life, but *are real life*. What we learn, perhaps, in the end is that what happens in the lab happens in the world, because the lab lives in the world and is undoubtedly as real, and therefore as relevant, as your breakfast table, or your bed. After all, many of Milgram's subjects claim that they were profoundly altered, and educated, by the revelations of that setup; Martin Seligman, one of Rosenhan's pseudopatients, wept when he told me the story of entering a mental hospital under false premise, the cruelty and also the kindness of what he found there. Thirty years later, Seligman, himself a famous psychologist, still recounts his role in the experiment as a vivid, life-altering event that taught him about the power of context and expectation in shaping experience.

And because, despite what its critics say, experimental psychology really is of the world, its questions are naturally raw, compelling, horrifying, funny. Why do we lack the moral center from which rebellion grows? Why do we fail to offer our immediate and global neighbors a helping hand? Why, time and again, do we abandon our own perceptions and capitulate to the dominant point of view? These are some of the dominant questions of twentieth-century experimental psychology, and they are interesting not only for their obvious relevance to the world, but also for their strange absence from psychotherapy, a subspecialty of psychology. At what point does experimental psychology and clinical psychology meet? Apparently at no point. I interviewed twelve licensed practicing psychologists— psychologists seeing patients, doing therapy—and none of them even *knew* most of these experiments, never mind used them in their work. Of course, there can be no coherent discipline when subspecialties fail to cross-pollinate each other; that's one problem. A bigger problem is how much is psychotherapy losing by failing to absorb the data, or demonstrations, yielded by its close cousin? Psychotherapy, as it evolved in the twentieth century, is all about *feeling good*, to its detriment I believe. Experimental psychology, on the other hand, with its relentless pursuit of ethical questions about obedience, conformity, is all about *doing good*, and when we do good, when we act with honor, we have a chance to experience dignity. If clinical psychologists, who have been trained to pass no judgment, or to hold the patient in "unconditional regard," instead dared to focus on their patients' moral lives, using information from Milgram, or Asch, or Rosenhan, or Loftus, they might finally offer what everyone really wants: a true chance at transcendence.

As for experimental psychology, even if we can't quite see what subdisciplines it has influenced, we can certainly see what disciplines it has been influenced by. Over and over again in writing this book, I asked myself, What is an experiment? Are these demonstrations or true scientific pursuits? What is science? Is psychology science? Is it fiction? Is it philosophy? That it is. Experimental psychology's insistence on asking the ethical and existential questions articulated by Augustine, by Kant, by Locke and Hume shows that its bloodline is here, in this tradition. Experimental psychology is in the end perhaps, a way of systematically asking philosophical questions that escape measurement just as you apply the tape to them.

Perhaps this is a shame. After all, psychology has had a great struggle to break with the humanities, to disentwine itself from the tentacles of philosophy, where for so long, in the 1800s, it was subsumed. The first psychologists were philosophers. For a long time no distinction was made between the two pursuits, and then one day, in the late 1800s, that man named Wilhelm Wundt said, *Enough of this!* He said, *You philosophers can sit around and think all you want, but I'm going to measure something, damn it.* He left his colleagues tugging at their beards, staring at the sky, while he, Wundt, started a lab with all sorts of instruments and began to measure the measurable things. Thus, psychology as a science was, supposedly, born.

It had birth defects right from the start. It never really breathed on its own, this conjoined psychology-science duo. If science is defined as the systematic pursuit of questions resulting in the revelation of universal laws, psychology has failed and failed again. Science depends on the ability to name, isolate, and temporalize phenomena, but how do you separate the thought from the thinker, or the idea from the current in which it flows? How do you survey a stream of thought itself? One can hold a body still, but a behavior? The nature of the field itself defies successful scientific exploration and experimentation, which hardly means we must dismiss the prior chapters, not at all. But the experiments, many of them anyway, may be best understood as kinetic philosophy, philosophy in action; the experiments may be at their most successful when they allow themselves, or we allow them, to yield us intuitive as opposed to quantifiable information. Milgram's work is a powerful piece of mysterious theater. Harlow shows us in our bones, in our lonely bodies, what loss looks like, and we know it to be true, whether we can quantify it or not. In fact, we need not derive a Harlovian law, for to do so would be bombastic, limiting love to a current set of equations. When psychology has tried to do this, it has sounded foolish, bloated, and insecure. We have no science here, and that may be good.

And yet, I do not mean to imply that there *can be* no science here. Some domains within the field—notably neuropsychology—clearly lend themselves to the techniques of chemistry, biology, and physics. It is clear to me that Kandel has something to measure, and that he is working with discrete phenomena that yield consensual agreement: *This is a sea slug. This is its neuron.* When I started this book, I thought I would find a natural narrative arc that would begin with experiments closely allied with the humanities and then would gradually, over time, move into experiments more and more akin to the natural sciences as the century progressed. However, it turns out that arc is nonexistent. There have always been at least two schools of experimental psychology, right from its bare beginnings: one school interested in somatic experiments (here we place Moniz, at the century's beginning, and Kandel, at the century's end), and another school more interested in describing social or cognitive phenomena. Our fascination with the neuron is nothing new; the decade of the brain has really been the century of the brain, tempered with other kinds of questions.

A question: as we move further into the twenty-first century, will experiments that are decidedly nonsomatic, like Milgram's or Rosenhan's or Festinger's, finally fall by the wayside? Will all experimental psychology occur at the level of the single synapse? Currently, the National Institutes of Mental Health reserves the vast bulk of its funding for somatic and neuropsychological experiments, and that, along with ethical guidelines and a litigious society, makes it unlikely we will ever see a Milgram, or even a Festinger, today. Too bad, I say, for there was an undeniable richness to the work, even as I recognize its problems.

Kandel believes that as this new century progresses, a biology of the mind will eventually eclipse all other subspecialties and the experiments they might spawn. He believes that we will find the neural substrates for everything, and, once we have, once psychologists have, well then, perhaps the field can finally free itself from its scientism to become truly scientific. As for myself, I await this day in great eagerness, because so much will be possible. If we know the neuronal basis of obedience, of love, of tragedy, of compulsion, then can we not fix it, radiate it, irrigate it, do something to it? My own head hurts, and I look forward to the cures brought on by new knowledge. On the other hand, my own head hurts, and there is something to be said not really for pain maybe, but for mystery. I'm not sure I want a psychology so smart it can tell me which action potential leads to what neurotransmitter that leads to the smile you see on my face. I'm not sure I want to know my parts, my Lego limbs, for then where are the questions? Bertrand Russell writes that our questions keep us human.

But of course, there will always be new questions, if only the question about having no questions and what that means, and here we are, back to philosophy again. It seems we can't escape. No matter how technologically proficient our newest experiments, we cannot escape the residue of mystery and murk, so we carry the residue with us. We seek out answers. We try this and that. We love and work. We kill and remember. We live our lives, each one a divine hypothesis.

Endnotes

CHAPTER ONE: OPENING SKINNER'S BOX

For the interview with Richard I. Evans, see his book *B. F. Skinner; the Man and His Ideas* (Dutton, New York, 1968), p. 54. *Time*, September 21, 1971, and the Gale On-Line Encyclopedia (Web address www.gale.com) are just two of the citations that list Skinner as being a highly influential psychologist. He was also referred to, again and again, in the many interviews I did regarding a whole range of experiments; he is clearly felt everywhere in the field of experimental psychology, from contemporary neurobiology to social psychology. Ayn Rand had a lot to say about Skinner, much of it negative, some of which can be found in her book *Philosophy, Who Needs It* (Macmillan, New York, 1981); I refer the reader specifically to p. 103. John Mills, *Control, a History of Behavioral Psychology* (New York University Press, New York, 1998), p. 123, is the source for the Winston Churchill quote applied to Skinner regarding mysteries wrapped in enigmas. Skinner's quotes about his own life were drawn largely from Daniel Bjork's thorough and thoughtful biography of Skinner, *B. F. Skinner, A Life* (Basic Books, New York, 1993); I specifically refer the reader to pp. 104, 152, 71, and 87. For an excellent, cogent description of Skinner's operant conditioning experiments, see Morton Hunt's *The Story of Psychology* (Doubleday, New York, 1993), p. 272, as well as Skinner's original papers, such as "Superstition in the Pigeon," *Journal of Experimental Psychology* 38 (1948), pp. 168–172. Skinner's daughter, Julie Vargas, provided me with access to the family archives and took the time to read sections of this chapter—specifically notes from our conversations and my descriptions of her father's work. *TV Guide*, October 17, 1971, published one review about *Beyond Freedom and Dignity* in which the reviewer compared Skinner's system to a dog obedience school. Jerome Kagan, of Harvard University, invited me to his office, regaled me with tales, and read over his portion of the chapter as well. All Jerome Kagan quotes come from direct face-to-face interviews with him. Quotes from Stephen Kosslyn and Bryan Porter also come from interviews. Kosslyn refers to interesting work being done on the basal ganglia and habit formation; for more specifics on this, I refer the reader to the work of Ann Graybiel, professor of brain and cognitive sciences and investigator at MIT's McGovern Institute for Brain Research (http://web.mit.edu/mcgovern). The Skinner boxes are no longer housed in the basement of William James Hall; they are now in a classroom on the first floor. The *Ladies' Home Journal* article that first mentioned "Baby in a Box" was from the October 1945 issue; citations from *Beyond Freedom and Dignity* (Alfred A. Knopf, New York, 1971) can be found on pp. 1, 19, 12, and 4.

CHAPTER TWO: OBSCURA

Quotes from Milgram's subjects are from the Yale University Archives, as well as Alan Elms's papers and books, specifically *Social Psychology and Social Relevance* (Little, Brown, Boston, 1972), p. 131. Milgram's interview with *Psychology Today* is also housed in the Yale archives, and can be found in the June 1974 issue, p. 72. Alexandra Milgram spent a long time with me on the telephone, and her recollections of her husband, his life, his work, and the specifics of his death were invaluable in preparing this chapter. The Yale University Archives contain much material regarding Milgram's mail orders and requests for the electrical gadgetry required of his experiment, in addition to an original sketch of his shock machine, scripts he intended for his A+ victim James McDonough to enact, and copies of the initial ads that went out asking for volunteers. Copies of these ads can also be found in many other publications, including Milgram's own *Obedience to Authority; An Experimental View* (Harper and Row, New York, 1974), and Ian Parker's "Obedience," in *Granta* 71 (Autumn, 2000). Lee Ross, professor of psychology at Stanford University, also provided me with interviews from which quotes are taken. Alan Elms's direct quotes are drawn from numerous interviews he was kind enough to give me, in addition to an extremely useful paper, "Personality Characteristics Associated with Obedience and Defiance toward Authoritative Control," *Journal of Experimental Research in Personality* (1966), pp. 282–289. Sharon Presely's dissertation, "Values and Attitudes of Political Resisters to Authority," has the dissertation publication number of AAt8212211. "Joshua Chaffin" is a pseudonym to protect the identity and privacy of this defiant Milgram subject. The *New York Times* article stating "65% in Test . . ." was cited in Parker's "Obedience," p. 114. B. Mixon's paper questioning the validity of Milgram's result is "When Is Obedience Obedience?" *Journal of Social Issues* 51, no. 3 (Fall 1995), p. 55. Edward E. Jones's rejection of Milgram's original obedience paper was cited in Parker's "Obedience"; other, similar objections can be found in the Yale archives from his National Science Foundation funders, who questioned whether the experiment went beyond demonstration and who also, initially, questioned its ethics. Daniel Jonah Goldhagen's quotes are from an interview. Diana Baumrind's 1964 article, "Some Thoughts on the Ethics of Research: After Reading Milgram's Behavioral Study of Obedience," *American Psychologist* 19 (1964), pp. 421–424, was the seminal paper that brought to light the putative ethical violations of this experiment. "Jacob Plumfield," is also a pseudonym to protect the identity and privacy of this obedient Milgram subject. David Karp's words are drawn from personal interviews. "In Defense of External Invalidity," by Douglas Mook, is in *American Psychologist* 38 (April 1983), pp. 379–387. Some of subjects' letters to Milgram, including the one from the conscientious objector, can be found in *Obedience to Authority*, p. 196. Harold Takooshian's quotes come from an interview. The chapter's final Stanley Milgram quotes again come from *Obedience to Authority*, pp. 196, 3, and 205.

CHAPTER THREE: ON BEING SANE IN INSANE PLACES

Jack Rosenhan's descriptions of his father and his childhood come from a personal interview. Martin Seligman's descriptions of his part in the pseudopatient experiment are drawn from interviews and email exchanges I had with him. Robert Spitzer's comments and reactions to the experiments are drawn from an interview and from his writings on the subject, "On Pseudoscience in Science, Logic in Remission and Psychiatric Diagnosis: A Critique of Rosenhan's 'On Being Sane in Insane Places,' " *Journal of Abnormal Psychology* 84, no. 5 (1975), pp. 442–452. The descriptions of Rosenhan's inpatient experience are drawn from his article "On Being Sane in Insane Places," *Science* 179 (January 1973); for the description of the nurse fixing her bra, patients being beaten, and other neglects and abuses, see p. 256 and 253; for examples of charts kept on pseudopatients, see p. 253; and for Rosenhan's quote, "clearly, the meaning ascribed . . . ," p. 253. The quote from the inpatients to Rosenhan and confederates can be found on p. 252 of the article, and the "writing behavior," on p. 253. Rosenthal and Jacobson's experiment with IQ and expectation was published in "Teacher's Expectancies: Determinates of Pupils IQ Gains," *Psychological Reports* 19 (1966), pp. 115–118. To locate discharge quotes of pseudopatients, see Rosenhan's article, p. 252. Florence Keller's words come from a personal interview. For the letters written in response to Rosenhan's article, see Paul R. Fleischman, "Letters: Psychiatric Diagnosis," *Science* 80 (April 1973); the reader can also find there the letter by Fred M. Hunter. The letter regarding the quart of blood is by J. Kety and is cited in Robert Spitzer's "More on Pseudoscience in Science and the Case for Psychiatric Diagnosis," *Archives of General Psychiatry* 33 (April 1976), pp. 459–470. Quote from Adolph Meyer is cited in Edward Short, *A*

History of Psychiatry: From the Era of the Asylum to the Age of Prozac (John Wiley and Sons, Inc., New York, 1997), p. 175.

CHAPTER FOUR: IN THE UNLIKELY EVENT OF A WATER LANDING

Transcripts and descriptions of the Kitty Genovese murder, as well as the letters from the *New York Times,* are drawn from A. M. Rosenthal's book, *Thirty-Eight Witnesses: The Kitty Genovese Case* (University of California, Berkeley, 1999); see pp. xix, xxi, 4, 43, 46, 40, and 41–42. Quote from Susan Mahler drawn from personal interview. Quotes from John Darley recalling the catalyst for the experiment are drawn from a personal interview. Quotes about the pre-recorded seizure, the experiment's meth-ods, the subjects' reactions, and the statistical results are from John Darley and Bibb Latané's paper, "Bystander Intervention in Emergencies: Diffusion of Responsibility," *Journal of Personality and Social Psychology* 8, no. 4 (1968), pp. 377–383. Quotes from Genovese witnesses who chose not to get involved are from Rosenthal's book, pp. 27, 32, and 34. "Oh my god! He stabbed me! Please help me," cited on www.crimelibrary.com/serial/killers/predators/kitty.genovese/3html?sec=2. Darley and Latané's interpretation of a bystander's inaction in their own experiment is from their above-mentioned article, pp. 381 and 382. All data from Darley and Latané's phase two, smoke experiment, is drawn from their paper "Group Inhibition of Bystander Intervention in Emergencies," *Journal of Personality and Social Psychology* 10, no. 3 (1968), pp. 215–221. David Phillip's studies into the Werther effect are cited in Robert Cialdini's book, *Influence, the Psychology of Persuasion* (William Morrow, New York, 1984), p. 146. The writings of Robert Cialdini are also drawn from this book, pp. 146–147 and 149–151. The effects of education as inoculation in the bystander effect are cited in A. Beaman, P. Barnes, B. Klentz, and B. Mcquirk's paper, "Increasing Helping Rates through Information Dissemination: Teaching Pays," *Personality and Social Psychology Bulletin* 4 (1979), pp. 406–411.

CHAPTER FIVE: QUIETING THE MIND

"The psychological opposition of irreconcilable ideas . . ." quote is from Leon Festinger, *A Theory of Cognitive Dissonance* (Stanford University Press, Palo Alto, Calif., 1957), p. 863. All quotes regarding the Marion Keech/prophecy experiment are taken from Leon Festinger, Henry W. Riecken, and Stanley Schacter's work, *When Prophecy Fails* (Harper and Row, New York, 1956); see pp. 56, 169, 175, and 182. Note that all names of subjects in this experiment are pseudonyms chosen by Festinger. The quote from Elliot Aronson is drawn from an interview with him. The lying-for-one-dollar-versus-twenty-dollars experiment is from L. Festinger and C. Carlsmith, "Cognitive Consequences of Forced Compliance," *Journal of Abnormal and Social Psychology* 58 (1959), pp. 203–210. The Induced Compliance

Paradigm is from E. Aronson and J. Mills, "The Effect of Severity of Initiation Rites on Group Liking," *Journal of Abnormal and Social Psychology* 59 (1959), pp. 177–181. Material regarding Linda and Audrey Santo is from personal interviews with Linda Santo and friends of the family, in addition to TV shows and numerous articles written on the subject. Festinger's quote "we spend our lives paying attention only to information consonant with our beliefs," is from "A Theory of Cognitive Dissonance," p. 361. V. S. Ramachandran's articles and books, specifically *Phantoms in the Brain* (William Morrow, New York, 1998), describe some of what could be considered the neural correlates to cognitive dissonance. As of this writing, Mathew Lieberman's work with East Asians and cognitive dissonance at UCLA is ongoing and unpublished; material comes from an interview. Festinger's speculations on Christianity as a form of cognitive dissonance can be found in *When Prophecy Fails*, pp. 24–25.

CHAPTER SIX: MONKEY LOVE

Much of the material regarding Harlow's life came from his biographer, Deborah Blum, who was kind enough to provide me with information, via personal interview, before she finished and published her own excellent volume on Harlow's life, *Love at Goon Park: Harry Harlow and the Science of Affection* (Perseus, Cambridge, Mass., 2002). Robert Israel, Harlow's son, also provided me with autobiographical writings, as did James Harlow, who described for me his father's drawings and imaginary land of Yazoo. Material regarding Harlow's testing of monkey intelligence is drawn from H. Harlow and J. Bromer, "A Test Apparatus for Monkeys," *Psychological Record* 2 (1938), pp. 434–436. The written quote regarding the human heart and breaking it comes from Deborah Blum's book, *The Monkey Wars* (Oxford University Press, New York, 1994), p. 82. The descriptions of wire and cloth mother monkeys are from H. Harlow, "The Nature of Love," *American Psychologist* 13 (1958), p. 3. The description of the primate reaction to separation comes from Clara Mears Harlow's volume of her husband's papers, *From Learning to Love: The Selected Papers of H. F. Harlow* (Praegar, New York, 1986). The quote "we were not surprised to discover that contact comfort was an important basic affectional love variable . . ." comes from Harlow, "The Nature of Love," p. 5, as does the quote "Man cannot live by milk alone." John Watson's quote is cited in Morton Hunt's *The Story of Psychology* (Anchor Books, New York, 1993), p. 259. The quote "love for the real mother and love for the surrogate mother appear to be very similar" is from "The Nature of Love," p. 20. The faceless-versus-masked-mother experiment is described in *From Learning To Love*. Robert Israel's words are from a personal interview. All quotes from Harlow's speech to the American Psychological Association are cited in Harlow, "The Nature of Love." Harlow's comments about wives and women's libbers are from a personal communication from Deborah Blum. Jonathan Harlow's description of his own work is from a personal interview. Descriptions of the effects of the cloth mother–raised monkeys' later pathologies are from *From Learning to Love*, p. 282. The description of the *New York Times* reporter and Harlow's response to him is from a personal interview with Deborah Blum. Len Rosenblum, one of Harlow's former students, also provided me, via an interview, with descriptions of some of the later experimental variations. Helen LeRoy's words are from a personal interview. The experiment with the "rape rack" appears in a 1966 paper, "The Maternal Behavior of Rhesus Monkeys Deprived of Mothering and Peer Associations in Infancy," reprinted in *From Learning to Love*. Roger Fouts's words are also from a personal interview, while William Mason's statements about animal experimentation as it relates to his own ethics are from Deborah Blum's *The Monkey Wars*, as is the interview with Stuart Zola-Morgan. Descriptions of "the well of despair" can be found in L. Joseph Stone, Henrietta T. Smith, and Lois B. Murphy's edition, *The Competent Infant; Research and Commentary* (Basic Books, New York, 1973).

CHAPTER SEVEN: RAT PARK

The physician Galen wrote extensively on opium, and his words regarding the substance as a means of curing "chronic headache," etc. can be found in his published *List of Medical Indications*, which I found cited on www.opites.net (accessed 1/3/2002). The names of opium, as "Mrs. Winslow's Soothing Syrup," etc., are also posted on that site, as well as in Bruce Alexander's book, *Peaceful Measures, Canada's Way out of the War on Drugs* (University of Toronto Press, Toronto, 1990). Alexander's two claims about the nature of addiction are from a personal interview as well as an unpublished manuscript, "Do Heroin and Cocaine Cause Addiction; The Interplay of Science and Conventional Wisdom," which can be accessed by contacting Alexander at the Department of Psychology, Simon Fraser University, Vancouver, Canada. That manuscript also cites the Ontario household survey and the 1974 San Francisco Study. Alexander's direct, conversational quotes are drawn from my personal interviews of him, as was the biographical information regarding his early life and his memories of Harlow's monkey lab. The information on the electric brain stimulation experiment and its relationship to pleasure centers is drawn from James Olds and Peter Milner's paper, "Positive Reinforcement Produced by Electrical Stimulation of Septal Area and Other Regions of the Rat Brain," *Journal of Comparative and Physiological Psychology* 47 (1954), pp. 419–422. The experiments involving animals hooked up to self-administering catheters were very common in the 1970s and 1980s; the one I cite here is from M. A. Bozarth and R. A. Wise, "Intracranial Self Administration of Morphine into the Ventral Tegmental Area in Rats," *Life Sciences* 28 (1981), pp. 551–555. Olds and Milner also published, in their 1954 paper cited above, that rats will self-administer pleasurable electrical pulses up to 6,000 times an hour. Herb Kleber's comments regarding PET studies and the rat park experiment in general are from a personal interview. Quote from Joe Dumit drawn from personal conversation. Rat park statistics are drawn from B. Alexander, B. Beyerstein, P. Hadaway, and R. B. Coambs's paper, "Effect of Early and Later Colony Housing on Oral Ingestion of Morphine in Rats," *Pharmacology, Biochemistry, and Behavior* 1 (1981), pp. 571–576. Naloxone is used to reverse the potentially lethal effects of a heroin overdose; it has also recently been discovered as an effective agent in treating autism. Some researchers theorize that autism, with its vacant stares and intensely inward behavior, is in part the result of a brain saturated in opiate-like substances called endorphins. A small percentage of children given naloxone show a reduction in rocking, chanting, and other repetitive behaviors. On naloxone these children are better able to interact with the world, and, most importantly, with those in their specific "colony," in far more socially appropriate ways. The quote "we think these results are socially as well as statistically significant . . . ," is cited in B. Alexander, P. Hadaway, and R. Coambs, "Rat Park Chronicle," in *Illicit Drugs in Canada*, edited by J. Blackwell and P. Erickson (Toronto University Press, Toronto, 1999), pp 65–66. Temperance quotes are cited from www.prohibition .history.ohio-state.edu/xeniah.html (accessed on 5/15/2003). The quote, "long enough to produce tolerance and physical dependence" is from "Rat Park Chronicle," p. 65. Information about percentages of smokers who quit is from Stanton Peele, *The Diseasing of America: Addiction Treatment out of Control* (Houghton Mifflin, Boston, 1989), p. 202. Avram Goldstein's research on endorphins is cited in Richard Restack, "The Brain Makes Its Own Tranquilizers," *Saturday Review*, March 5, 1977. Why opiates rarely lead to addiction when they are used for pain appears to be unclear. Neurophysiologists use diffuse phrases to describe the mechanisms underlying the hypothesis that opiates are less addictive when used for pain than pleasure. "There's just some sort of difference in the pain versus the pleasure systems in the brain," one researcher said to me. "On a neurocircuitry level, heroin interacts differently with pain than with pleasure." Answers like this, while obfuscatory, are also instructive. They serve as potent reminders about how little we know and how vastly nonspecific that knowledge is, despite the high gloss of drug company advertisements and the ease with which we engage in a kind of collective "neurospeak." Research into crowding and fertility in Iran is from A. Padyarfar, "The Effects of Multifamily Housing on Marital Infertility in Iran," *Social Biology* 42, no. 3/4 (1996), pp. 214–225. Prison studies regarding crowding are from G. McCain, V. C. Cox, and P. B. Paulus, "The Relationship between Illness Complaints and Degree of Crowding in a Prison Environment," *Environment and Behavior* 8 (1976), pp. 283–290. The study of humans and problem-solving abilities in small spaces is from G. W. Evans, "Behavioral and Psychological Consequences of Crowding in Humans," *Journal of Applied Social Psychology* 9 (1979) pp. 27–46. Alexander's thoughts on dislocation, free market societies, and addiction are drawn from his article "The Globalization of Addiction," *Addiction Research* 8, no. 6 (2000), pp. 501–526. Herb Kleber's quote is from "Clinical and Societal Implications of Drug Legalization," in *Substance Abuse*, edited by H. Kleber, J. Calafano Jr., and John C. Demers (William and Wilkins, Baltimore, 1981), p. 862.

CHAPTER EIGHT: LOST IN THE MALL

All quotations that are not identified as coming from Loftus's articles are from personal interviews. In addition, I relied on Jill Niemark's article, "The Diva of Disclosure: Memory Researcher Elizabeth Loftus," *Psychology Today* 29, no. 1 (1996), p. 48. In the interviews with Loftus we focused on her false memory experiments, with the result that the wider range of her work is not reflected in this chapter. Loftus has been instrumental in using her work on memory and its malleability to alter the legal system's appraisal of eyewitness accounts, and in June 2001 she was awarded the William James Fellow Award for scientific achievement. The award read, in part,

> Elizabeth Loftus is an example of the rare scientist who is instrumental in both advancing a scientific discipline and in using that discipline to make critical contributions to society. . . . Beginning in the mid 1970's, following acclaimed basic research on the workings of semantic memory, she waded into relatively uncharted waters, investigating how and under what circumstances complex memories change . . . her innovative yet highly rigorous research on this topic brought her renewed praise in the scientific community. At the same time, however, she realized the fundamental applications of her related findings to the legal system, particularly in understanding the circumstances under which a sincere eyewitness may have misidentified an innocent defendant. It is not hyperbole to say that in response to her ingenious laboratory work and her ubiquitous public presence, both the quality of basic memory research and the fairness of the criminal justice system have advanced substantially.

From the American Psychological Association William James Fellow Award presentation, on June 14, 2001. The quotes "if you think you were abused . . . then you were," and "let your imagination run wild," are cited in E. Loftus, "Creating False Memories," *Scientific American* 227, no. 3 (1997). Loftus has described for me, and provided me with, examples of the letters she received from parents who believed they were falsely accused; for more information on these types of correspondences, I refer the reader to the False Memory Foundation Web site (www.fmsfonline.org). Quotes from Chris, one of Loftus's pretest subjects, are from E. Loftus, "The Reality of Repressed Memories," *American Psychologist* 48 (1993), p. 18. The Asian girl who confabulated the Kmart story is cited in E. Loftus, "The Reality of Repressed Memories." Quotes from Judith Herman are drawn from a direct interview, as with quotes from Bessel van der Kolk. Marilyn Van Derber was the 1958 Miss America who, on May 8, 1991, delivered a public statement in a small college auditorium in Denver, Colorado, regarding her history of sexual abuse. Her comments were later reported in *The Rocky Mountain News*, May 11, 1991:6, and in *People*, June 10, 1991. Roseanne Barr's confession is from *People*, October 7, 1991. Jane Smiley's novel is *A Thousand Acres* (Ivy Paperbacks, New York, 1996). Given the plethora of incest reports, in the realms of both fiction and journalism at that time, there is an obvious question with no clear answer: *Why* was multiple personality disorder (MPD)—a consequence, many thought, of severe abuse—becoming so popular at the time that it did? What cultural forces led to MPD's popularity in the 1980s? A possible, if plain, hypothesis is that in the 1980s, managed care came into being. Under managed care guidelines, most mental disorders required medication and, concomitantly, a physician to prescribe them, with the exception of MPD, for which there was no agreed-upon drug treatment. Managed care, therefore, posed a real threat to the vast majority of mental health workers, who, because they are not M.D.'s, have no prescribing rights. Therefore, it may have been to much of the mental health profession's financial benefit to diagnose MPD, because otherwise, psychologists, social workers, and counselors had to refer their patients to physicians. The quote "story truth and happening truth . . ." comes from E. Loftus, *The Myth of Repressed Memory: False Memories and Allegations of Sexual Abuse* (St. Martin's Press, New York, 1994), pp. 38–39. Quotes from the Paul Ingram case are from Richard Ofshe and Ethan Watter's book, *Making Monsters: False Memories, Psychotherapy, and Sexual Hysteria* (Charles Scribner's, New York, 1994), pp. 169 and 172. Lawrence Wright, in his book *Remembering Satan* (Alfred A. Knopf, New York, 1994), has written a full account of the Ingram case as well. Elizabeth Loftus also writes about it in *The Myth of Repressed Memories*. The quote "false memories can be created by a small suggestion from a trusted family member . . . and by some therapists themselves" is from "The Reality of Repressed Memories," p.19. "We live in a strange and precarious time . . ." is from E. Loftus, "Remembering Dangerously," *Skeptical Inquirer* 19 (1995), p. 20. Schachter's words and ideas are from *Searching for Memory: The Brain, the Mind, and the Past* (Basic Books, New York, 1996), pp. 264–265, and a personal interview. Judith Herman's reference to rats and high stress is from Judith Herman, "Crime and Traumatic Memory," *Bulletin of American Psychiatry and Law* 23, no. 1 (1995), p. 8. The sniper study is from R. S. Pynoos and K. Nadar, "Children's Memory and Proximity to Violence," *Journal of the American Academy of Child and Adolescent Psychiatry* 28 (1989), pp. 236–241. The *Challenger* explosion study is from Michael D. Yapko's *Suggestions of Abuse* (Simon and Schuster, New

York, 1994), pp. 73–74. Loftus's letter to her mother comes from her own personal archives and is reprinted with her permission.

CHAPTER NINE: MEMORY INC.

Quotation from the *Journal of Surgical Neurology* cited in Philip J. Hilt, *Memory's Ghost: The Nature of Memory and the Strange Case of Mr. M* (Simon and Schuster, New York, 1995), p. 93. Kandel's quotes are from a face-to-face interview. Information regarding CREB is from "The Molecular Biology of Memory Storage: A Dialogue between Genes and Synapses," *Science* magazine, available at www.sciencemag.org/ cgi/content/full/294/5544/1030. Also instrumental in my thinking about Kandel is his paper "Biology and the Future of Psychoanalysis: A New Intellectual Framework for Psychiatry Revisited," *American Journal of Psychiatry* 156 (1999), pp. 505–524. Descriptions of the H.M. case and Dr. William Scoville are from Philip J. Hilt's *Memory's Ghost*. The quote from the Alzheimer's patient is from David Shenk's *The Forgetting: Alzheimer's, Portrait of an Epidemic* (Doubleday, New York, 2001). Suzanne Corkin's paper "H.M.'s Temporal Lobe Lesion; Findings from Magnetic Resonance Imagery," *Journal of Neuroscience* 17, no. 10 (1997), pp. 3964–3979, also provided information about H.M. and the effects of the surgery. An autobiographical account of Kandel's life and work can be found in *Les Priz Nobel*, 2000. Description of S. drawn from A. R. Luria, *The Mind of a Mnemonist: A Little Book About a Vast Memory* (Harvard University Press, Cambridge, Mass., 1968).

CHAPTER TEN: CHIPPED

All descriptions of Moniz's life story are drawn from Elliot Valenstein's excellent book, *Great and Desperate Cures: The Rise and Decline Of Psychosurgery and Other Radical Treatments for Mental Illness* (Basic Books, New York, 1986). Moniz's claim he was "tormented" by the death is on p. 72 of Valenstein's book; "why would it not be feasible to relieve anxiety states by surgical means?" on p. 73; "on the eve of my first attempt . . . ," on p. 103; "where is your house . . . ," on p. 104; "the patient behaved normally . . . ," on p. 104; and "I recognized the method could be harmless," on p. 108. "It's over now, I want to live with my daughters" is from Egas Moniz, "Prefrontal Leucotomy in the Treatment of Mental Disorders," *American Journal of Psychiatry* 5 (1937), pp. 1381–1382. Quotes from Walter Freeman and James Watt's patient are from Valenstein, *Great and Desperate Cures*, p. 142; "judgment and insight are apparently not diminished . . ." on p. 143; "a substratum, a common denomina- tor . . . ," on p. 143; "lobotomy patients make good citizens," on p. 162; and the *New York Times* headline, on p. 156. The *Harper's* article is G. W. Gray, "The Attack on Brainstorms," *Harper's*, September 1941, p. 366. The *Saturday Evening Post* article is Waldemar Kaempffert, "Turning the Mind inside out," *Saturday Evening Post*, May

24, 1941, p. 69. The "Psychosurgery Cured Me" article is cited in *Great and Desperate Cures*, p. 156; "can be of significant therapeutic value in the treatment of certain disorders or the relief of certain symptoms," p. 246; "following a lobotomy, many agitated and anxious patients . . . ," p. 252. Harold Sackheim's quotes are drawn from a personal interview, as are Eric Kandel's. For the reader interested in some of the controversy surrounding the potentially negative side effects of Prozac and related SSRIs, information can be found in Joseph Glenmullen's book, *Prozac Backlash: Overcoming the Dangers of Prozac, Zoloft, Paxil, and Other Antidepressants with Safe, Effective Alternatives* (Simon and Schuster, New York, 2000). The writings in the *Nation* are cited in *Great and Desperate Cures*, p. 261. Charlie and Sasha Newitz's quotes are drawn from interviews with them; their identities are protected by pseudonyms. The description of Charlie's surgery and immediate postoperative state are from interviews as well; I was not allowed into the operating room. Suzanne Corkin of MIT provided me with a personal interview and many written sources, among them, "A Prospective Study of Cingulotomy," which can be found in Valenstein's monograph, *Psychosurgery Debate: Scientific, Legal, and Ethical Perspectives* (W. H. Freeman, San Francisco, 1980), pp. 164–204. F. Veristock's article, "Lobotomy's Back," is in *Discover*, October 1997, p. 67.

CONCLUSION

Dorothy Braginsky's quote is from her article "Psychology, Handmaiden to Society," cited in S. Koch and D. Leary, *A Century of Psychology as Science* (American Psychological Association, Washington, D.C., 1992), p. 880. William James's letters are from his *Selected Letters* (University of Virginia Press, Charlottesville, 1997).

Index